GREAT MEALS
—— in ——
One Dish

Other Books by Family Circle

Recipes America Loves Best
Family Circle *Hints Book*
Great Meals on a Tight Budget
Delicious Desserts
Family Circle *ABZ's of Cooking*
Family Circle *Holiday & Special Occasions Cookbook*
The Best of Family Circle Cookbook
Perfect Poultry

GREAT MEALS

in

One Dish

More Than 250 Recipes and
Dozens of Tips to Save You Time and Money

The Editors of

FamilyCircle

Foreword by Jean Hewitt

𝔗imes
BOOKS

SPECIAL PROJECT STAFF

PROJECT EDITOR • *Jo Ann Brett-Billowitz*
FAMILY CIRCLE FOOD EDITOR • *Jean Hewitt*
FAMILY CIRCLE ASSOCIATE FOOD EDITOR • *David Ricketts*
FAMILY CIRCLE GREAT IDEAS EDITOR • *Marie Walsh*
TYPE SUPERVISOR • *Wendy Hylfelt*
TYPESETTING • *Vickie Almquist*
SPECIAL ASSISTANTS • *Helen Russell and Joanne Hajdu*
COVER PHOTO • *Ron Nicolaysen*
ILLUSTRATION • *Lauren Jarrett*

PROJECT MANAGER • *Annabelle Groh*
PRODUCTION EDITOR • *Margaret Chan-Yip*

Library of Congress Cataloging in Publication Data

Main entry under title:

Great meals in one dish.

Includes index.
1. Cookery   I. Family Circle.
TX652.G7254   1985   641.8′2   85-40275
ISBN 0-8129-1270-5

Designed by Giorgetta Bell McRee/Early Birds

Manufactured in the United States of America

9 8 7 6 5 4 3 2

First Edition

Dedicated to the readers of
Family Circle *Magazine*

CONTENTS

FOREWORD

In the 1980s everyone is busy—busy with careers, children, volunteering, keeping fit, and on and on. But the family still has to eat, and once in a while it's fun to ask friends over for pot luck. But what to serve? Bet you already know the answer: a one-pot dinner! Whether it's an oven casserole, a top-of-the-stove stew or a slow-cooker production, every one of the recipes in this book is highly recommended. What's more, they don't take all day to assemble, they are easy to serve and clean-up is minimal.

Special Editor Jo Ann Billowitz chose the recipes, which she gathered from *Family Circle*'s files, and you'll see that they're varied enough to fit all tastes and occasions. There are chapters on soups and stews, main-dish salads, vegetarian dishes, low-calorie and low-cost one-pot meals, quick last-minute recipes, make-ahead ideas and some with foreign accents. Throughout the book, there are tips and hints on cooking techniques, speedy cooking and clean-up, including pointers on microwave cooking.

Choose a recipe with your family's favorite combination of ingredients and fix a one-dish meal tonight. Happy Cooking!

—Jean Hewitt

GREAT MEALS
MEALS
— in —
One Dish

1

Introducing Casserole Cookery

Each one of us appreciates an enjoyable and nourishing meal that takes a minimum amount of time to prepare as well as to clean up—whether it be a beef stew barely bubbling on top of the range for several hours or a vegetable quiche. There is something in this book for the novice to the most experienced cook. In those recipes where more than one preparation container is necessary to obtain a *complete* meal in one dish, we've attempted to use no more than four containers total.

If you are a forever-on-a-diet or health conscious type, the Chinese cuisine tonight, Italian tomorrow night type, or simply the meat-and-potatoes type, there is a meal-in-one treasure in these pages just perfect for you. There are low-cost meals, hearty vegetarian dishes, crowd-pleasing casseroles, even a collection of plan-aheads for days when the thought of having to come up with something for dinner *again* is more than you can handle. When time or energy pressures leave you with nowhere to turn, you can flip to our Small Appliance Magic or our Quick and Easy chapters.

Over 250 of some of the best, triple-tested, one-dish recipes *Family Circle* has to offer are right between these covers—ranging from new and different combinations to time-honored classics with unique twists. In addition, there are hundreds of invaluable hints and charts. So, if you're looking for ways to make meal preparation easier, more efficient and economical, you're bound to have struck it rich with this cookbook!

A WORD ABOUT EQUIPMENT

Selling your family on convenient, nutritious and economical casseroles and other meals-in-one when you know they thrive on steaks, roasts, chops and hamburgers involves ingenuity and planning. Begin by purchasing dishes that complement the food, considering factors such as color, size, shape and material.

The convenience of being able to prepare meals ahead is even greater when you choose containers that can go from the refrigerator or freezer to the oven or microwave. Not all materials are adaptable to such temperature extremes.

Availability of a variety of sizes ranging from one to thirteen quarts is a real plus when family members eat in shifts. Many casseroles or meals-in-one lend themselves to being frozen in individual portions after the casserole is completed. A slight adjustment in time and temperature will more than likely be necessary, but the convenience is worth the extra attention.

General Guidelines

- Always read the use and care product information before you buy. If none is on display, be sure to ask the sales clerk to get it for you.

- For everyday use, a 2- to 3-quart covered casserole is sufficient.

- For entertaining or quantity cooking, choose a 5- to 6-quart covered casserole.

- Whole poultry or large pieces of meat fit best into an oval casserole.

2

Soups and Stews

When those crisp fall days arrive, nothing is more satisfying than a hearty stew or a delicious homemade soup. Soups and stews are low in cost, high in flavor and nutrition, and an excellent way to make good use of that half cup of leftover peas or corn or even salad greens. Whether you prefer the long simmering kind or the under 30-minute type (such as our Green Potato Soup on page 14), there is bound to be a soup or stew in this chapter that suits your fancy. Another bonus of these meals-in-one is that they can be made in advance, so it's no problem if the family members occasionally eat in shifts.

Chowders are always a proven favorite, especially with New Englanders, who have an abundance of fresh seafood. When served with crackers and a salad, a thick, creamy chowder, chock full of your favorite seafood, is truly a delight.

MANHATTAN CLAM CHOWDER

Makes 6 servings.

36 large chowder clams
(quahogs) OR: 2 cans
(7 to 8 ounces each) minced
clams
¼ cup (½ stick) sweet butter
1 large onion, chopped
(1 cup)
1½ cups diced potatoes
(2 medium size)
1 cup diced celery

¾ cup diced carrots
(2 medium size)
¼ cup diced sweet green
pepper
1 can (35 ounces) Italian-style
plum tomatoes, drained
1½ teaspoons leaf thyme,
crumbled
¼ teaspoon white pepper
⅛ teaspoon curry powder

1. Shuck the fresh clams; reserve the broth; chop the clams coarsely. If using canned clams, drain and reserve the broth. The broth from the clams should measure 2 cups; if not, add water or bottled clam juice.
2. Melt the butter in a large saucepan. Sauté the onions until lightly browned.
3. Add the remaining ingredients and extra water, if needed, to cover the vegetables. Bring to boiling; lower the heat; cover and simmer for 30 minutes, or just until the vegetables are tender.
4. Add the fresh or canned clams; turn off the heat; cover and let stand for 2 minutes, or just until the clams are thoroughly hot. Serve with warm buttered pilot crackers, if you wish.

COD AND CLAM CHOWDER

Makes 4 hearty servings.

1 package (1 pound frozen) cod fillets	1 can (6½ ounces) minced clams
1 large onion, chopped (1 cup)	1 2-inch piece thin orange rind (no white)
1 clove garlic, finely chopped	
2 tablespoons olive or vegetable oil	¼ teaspoon leaf thyme, crumbled
1 can (16 ounces) whole peeled tomatoes	⅛ teaspoon pepper
	Lemon wedges
1 bottle (8 ounces) clam juice	Soda crackers

1. Unwrap the fish and let it stand at room temperature for about 5 minutes.

2. Sauté the onion and garlic in the oil in a 3-quart saucepan until soft but not brown, for about 3 minutes. Add the tomatoes, breaking them up with a wooden spoon, clam juice, clams, orange rind, thyme and pepper; simmer for 5 minutes.

3. Cut the block of frozen fish into 1-inch cubes. Add to the tomato mixture and simmer for 10 minutes longer, or just until the fish is tender and flakes easily with a fork. Serve with lemon wedges and crackers.

HELPFUL HINT

Frozen fish makes an excellent base for soups because you can keep it in the freezer, ready to help with last-minute meals.

SCALLOP CHOWDER

Makes about 6 servings.

1 package (12 ounces) frozen scallops
3 cups boiling water
1 teaspoon salt
2 cups diced potatoes (about 2 medium size)
1 cup diced carrots (3 medium size)
1 cup sliced celery
1 medium-size onion, chopped (½ cup)
1 cup milk
1 cup chicken broth
⅛ teaspoon white pepper
2 tablespoons butter or margarine
Lemon slices

1. Cook the frozen scallops in boiling salted water for 3 minutes, or until tender; remove from the water with a slotted spoon; reserve.
2. Add the potatoes, carrots, celery and onion to the same water; simmer until tender, for about 10 minutes. Stir in the milk, chicken broth, pepper and butter. Purée in a blender with ½ cup of the scallops. Return to the pan with the remaining whole scallops and reheat. Garnish with lemon slices.

SHRIMP AND CLAM SOUP

Makes 8 servings.

½ cup frozen chopped onion
½ cup frozen chopped sweet green pepper
2 cloves garlic, crushed and peeled
1 tablespoon vegetable oil
1 teaspoon salt
½ teaspoon pepper
1 can (35 ounces) Italian-style plum tomatoes
2 bottles (8 ounces each) clam juice
1 cup dry white wine
1 pound frozen shelled and deveined shrimp
1 can (8 ounces) minced clams with juice
1½ teaspoons grated lemon rind
¼ cup finely chopped parsley

1. Sauté the onion, green pepper and garlic in the oil in a large saucepan until soft and tender. Add the salt and pepper.
2. Stir in the tomatoes, clam juice and wine. Bring to boiling; lower the heat; simmer for 5 minutes. Set aside until 10 minutes before serving. Reheat; add the shrimp and simmer until they are tender, for about 5 minutes.

3. Add the clams and their juice, lemon rind and parsley; heat until thoroughly hot. (Do not boil.)

Go-with's: Crunchy rolls, tossed green salad, devil's food cake.

YOGURT SOUP WITH MEATBALLS

An unusual way to use yogurt, this soup is lively and filling.

Makes 8 servings.

2	cans (10½ ounces each) condensed beef broth	¼	cup finely chopped green onion (use some of the green)
2⅔	cups water		
½	pound lean ground round	3	containers (8 ounces each) plain yogurt (3 cups)
¼	cup long-grain white rice		
1	can (19 ounces) chick-peas, drained	¼	cup finely chopped parsley
1	package (10 ounces) frozen chopped spinach, thawed OR: 1 cup chopped fresh spinach	¼	cup finely chopped fresh dill OR: 2 teaspoons dried dillweed

1. Bring the broth and water to boiling in a large saucepan. Lower the heat.

2. Shape beef into 1-inch balls without pressing hard, using a small scoop or tablespoon. Add to the broth; stir in the rice. Cover and simmer for 20 minutes. Add the chick-peas, spinach and green onion; simmer covered, for 10 minutes longer. Remove from the heat.

3. Place the yogurt in a large bowl. Gradually stir in 1 cup of the soup, stirring to blend well. Pour back into the hot soup, stirring constantly.

4. Sprinkle the parsley and dill over the soup. Reheat if necessary and serve immediately. Do not let it boil or it will curdle.

MEATBALL MAGIC

To make uniformly-sized meatballs, spread the mixture in a square on a cutting board, then cut into even cubes, using a long, moistened knife; roll into balls with moistened palms. This method is also good for measuring dough for rolls.

To oven-brown meatballs, place them in a shallow baking dish; bake at 350° for 15 minutes, or until golden. No watching needed, either!

CABBAGE-AND-MEATBALL SOUP

A hearty soup that's quick to make and a complete meal when you add crusty bread and a tossed green salad.

Makes 8 servings.

1	pound lean ground chuck	2	leeks, washed and sliced (2 cups)
1	egg		
½	cup soft bread crumbs (1 slice)	2	carrots, sliced (1 cup)
		2	potatoes, pared and diced (2 cups)
6	tablespoons chopped parsley		
		½	of a 2-pound head of cabbage, shredded (4 cups)
1	teaspoon salt		
3	slices bacon	4	cans (13¾ ounces each) beef broth
1	large onion, diced (1 cup)		
2	cloves garlic, crushed and peeled	1	bay leaf
		½	teaspoon leaf thyme, crumbled

1. Combine the beef, egg, bread crumbs, 2 tablespoons of the parsley and the salt in a medium-size bowl; mix lightly with a fork. Shape into 32 balls, using a rounded teaspoon for each.

2. Cook the bacon until it is crisp in a large Dutch oven or kettle; remove and reserve. Brown the meatballs in the bacon drippings a single layer at a time; remove as they brown.

3. Add the onion, garlic and leeks to the Dutch oven; sauté until soft, for about 5 minutes. Stir in the carrots, potatoes, cabbage, broth, bay leaf and thyme; bring to boiling; lower the heat; cover and simmer for 20 minutes. Add the meatballs; simmer for 10 minutes longer, or until the vegetables are tender. Stir in the remaining parsley and reserved bacon.

SICILIAN SAUSAGE SOUP

Sausage adds a fine, robust flavor to this easy 30-minute soup.

Makes 8 servings.

½	pound bulk pork sausage or sweet Italian sausage	1	teaspoon leaf basil, crumbled
1	large onion, chopped (1 cup)	½	cup orzo (rice-shaped macaroni)
1	can (35 ounces) Italian tomatoes	¼	teaspoon salt
2	cans (13¾ ounces each) chicken broth (about 3½ cups)	⅛	teaspoon pepper

1. Cook the sausage in a large saucepan, breaking up the meat with a wooden spoon until all pink color has disappeared. (If using Italian sausage, remove from the casings before cooking.) Sauté the onions in the pan until soft.

2. Add the tomatoes, broth and basil; bring to boiling; stir in the orzo, salt and pepper. Lower the heat and simmer for 20 minutes, or until the orzo is tender. Taste and add more salt and pepper, if you wish.

MONASTERY LENTIL SOUP

Makes 5 servings.

2	large onions, chopped (2 cups)	3	beef bouillon cubes
1	carrot, coarsely grated	1	cup dry lentils, rinsed
½	teaspoon leaf marjoram, crumbled	1	teaspoon salt
½	teaspoon leaf thyme, crumbled	¼	teaspoon pepper
¼	cup olive or vegetable oil	¼	cup dry sherry or dry white wine
1	can (16 ounces) tomatoes	¼	cup chopped parsley
5	cups water	1	cup shredded Cheddar cheese (4 ounces)

1. Sauté the onions, carrots, marjoram and thyme in the oil in a large kettle or Dutch oven, stirring often, until lightly browned, about 5 minutes.

2. Add the tomatoes, water, bouillon cubes, lentils, salt and pepper, stirring to dissolve the cubes. Bring to boiling; lower the heat; cover; simmer for about 1 hour, or until the lentils are tender.

3. Add the sherry and parsley; simmer for 2 minutes.

4. Serve in soup bowls; garnish with a sprinkling of cheese.

MINESTRA WITH SAUSAGE AND GREENS

Full of flavor and color; a substantial meal with bread and a green salad.

Makes 4 servings.

½ pound Italian sausage, hot or sweet or a combination*

1 medium-size onion, finely chopped (½ cup)

2 cans (13¾ ounces each) chicken broth (about 3½ cups)

½ cup water

1 can (19 ounces) red or white kidney beans

½ pound fresh escarole or spinach

Grated Parmesan cheese

1. Cook the whole sausages in a Dutch oven over moderate heat, turning several times until lightly browned, for about 5 minutes. Add the onion and cook until soft.

2. Add the broth, water and kidney beans; bring to boiling; lower the heat and simmer for 10 minutes.

3. Wash the escarole or spinach; shred it coarsely; add to the soup and simmer for 15 minutes more.

4. Remove the sausages; cut them into ¼-inch-thick slices; return to the soup. Serve with cheese.

*If mild sausage is used, add a clove of minced garlic and ½ teaspoon rosemary to the onions as they cook.

A LITTLE TOUCH OF FLAVOR

Small amounts of the specialty sausage, hot and sweet Italian, chorizo or kielbasa, add zest and sturdy protein to pasta sauces, vegetable soups, casseroles and rice dishes.

VEGETABLE-HAM SOUP

A light, yet satisfying main-dish soup that owes its hearty flavor to a leftover ham bone. Ideal for spring suppers with crusty bread and a fruit-topped cheesecake.

Makes 6 servings.

3	tablespoons butter or margarine	2	envelopes or teaspoons instant chicken broth
1	medium-size onion, chopped (½ cup)	2	cups diced, pared potatoes (about 2 medium size)
1	cup sliced carrots (2 to 3)	1½	cups julienne-cut cooked ham
1	cup chopped celery (2 stalks)	½	bunch watercress, cut up (2 cups)
6	cups water		Salt
1	ham bone		Pepper
6	sprigs parsley		
1	bay leaf		

1. Melt the butter in a kettle or Dutch oven. Sauté the onion, carrots and celery until tender. Add the water, ham bone, parsley, bay leaf and chicken broth. Bring to boiling; lower the heat; cover and simmer for 30 minutes.

2. Add the potatoes and ham and continue to cook until the potatoes are tender, for about 15 minutes. Remove the bay leaf, parsley and ham bone. Skim off any fat.

3. Add the watercress and cook only until the stems are tender. Taste; add salt and pepper, if you wish.

SALISBURY BEEF-VEGETABLE SOUP

Makes 6 servings.

½	pound lean chuck	1½	teaspoons salt
1	large onion, chopped (1 cup)	⅛	teaspoon pepper
2	cans (10½ ounces each) condensed beef broth	½	teaspoon leaf thyme, crumbled
½	cup chopped celery (1 stalk)	1	package (10 ounces) frozen peas and carrots
1	medium-size potato, pared and diced (1 cup)	1	can (8 ounces) whole-kernel corn, undrained
1	can (16 ounces) tomatoes	2	tablespoons chopped parsley
½	cup water		

1. Cook the chuck in a large heavy saucepan until all pink disappears; add the onion and sauté until soft. Add the beef broth, celery, potato, tomatoes, water, salt, pepper and thyme. Cook for 20 minutes, or until the vegetables are tender.

2. Stir in the peas and carrots and corn. Heat for 10 minutes longer; sprinkle with parsley. Serve with Parmesan cheese and French bread, if you wish.

GREEN POTATO SOUP

A creamy and mild soup with the added zest of sausages.
Makes about 12 servings (12 cups).

4	large baking potatoes (about 2 pounds)	1	pound fresh greens, shredded (use spinach, kale, lettuce)
8	cups chicken broth (about five 13¾-ounce cans)	2	teaspoons salt
			Pinch of pepper
1	pound sweet or hot Italian sausage links	½	cup heavy cream

1. Pare the potatoes; cut them into ½-inch cubes; wash and drain. Combine the potatoes and half of the broth in a large kettle or Dutch oven. Bring to boiling; lower the heat; cover and simmer for 20 minutes, or until the potatoes are very tender. Mash the potatoes coarsely with a potato masher or fork.

2. While the potatoes are simmering, cook the sausages in a skillet; drain on paper toweling. Peel off the casings and cut the sausages into ¼-inch slices.

3. Add the remaining broth to the mashed potato soup. Bring to boiling; add the greens and cook until the greens are wilted, for about 5 minutes. Stir in the salt, pepper, cream and sausages. Serve immediately.

CORN AND SHRIMP GUMBO

A variation on the traditional Louisiana favorite.

Makes 8 servings.

1	large onion, chopped (1 cup)	½	pound fresh okra pods, cut into ½-inch slices OR:
1	large sweet green pepper, halved, seeded and chopped		1 package (10 ounces) frozen cut okra
1	celery stalk, chopped (½ cup)	1	pound medium-size shrimp, shelled and deveined
2	tablespoons vegetable oil	1	teaspoon salt
2	cans (35 ounces each) whole tomatoes	⅛	teaspoon pepper
2	cups corn kernels (from 3 large ears)	¼	teaspoon filé powder (optional)

1. Sauté the onion, green pepper and celery in the oil in a large saucepan until tender, for about 3 minutes. Add the tomatoes, breaking them up with a spoon.

2. Add the corn, okra, shrimp, salt and pepper and cook over medium heat for 8 to 10 minutes, or until the shrimp are tender. Stir in the filé powder, if using; heat thoroughly.

SAVORY LAMB RAGOUT

An American version of a traditional Irish stew.

Makes 8 servings.

¼ cup plus 1 tablespoon all-purpose flour

3 pounds lean lamb shoulder, cut into 1½-inch cubes

¼ cup vegetable oil

6 medium-size onions, sliced (about 8 cups)

2 cloves garlic, finely chopped

1 cup canned beef broth

2 teaspoons salt

2 teaspoons leaf thyme, crumbled

½ teaspoon freshly ground pepper

12 small new potatoes, pared (about 3 pounds)

2 pounds carrots, cut into 2-inch pieces

1 can (28 ounces) tomatoes, drained

1. Place ¼ cup of the flour and the meat in a plastic bag; shake to coat thoroughly.

2. Heat the oil in a heavy kettle or Dutch oven; brown the meat, part at a time, removing the pieces to paper toweling as they brown.

3. Sauté the onions and garlic in the same kettle until they are soft, for about 5 minutes. Stir in the broth, salt, thyme and pepper and bring to boiling. Return the lamb to the kettle; cover and simmer for 45 minutes.

4. Add the potatoes and carrots; cover and simmer for 45 minutes longer, or until the vegetables are tender. Stir in the tomatoes. Combine the remaining tablespoon of flour in a small amount of cold water in a cup, stirring until smooth. Bring the stew to boiling and stir in the flour mixture. Continue to cook and stir until the sauce is thickened and bubbly.

SAUSAGE-BURGER STEW

Makes 6 servings.

¼	pound (½ cup) liver sausage	½	teaspoon salt
1	pound lean ground chuck or round	2	envelopes or teaspoons instant beef broth
½	cup packaged bread crumbs	2	cups hot water
1	small onion, finely chopped (¼ cup)	4	cups thinly sliced zucchini
		3	cups seasoned hot mashed potatoes
1	egg, beaten		
3	tablespoons vegetable oil	1	medium-size tomato, cut in thin wedges
2	tablespoons all-purpose flour		Paprika

1. Mash the liver sausage with a fork in a large bowl. Add the beef, crumbs, onion and egg; mix well. Divide the mixture and shape it into 12 balls using about ¼ cup for each. Brown the meatballs in the oil in a large skillet; then remove and keep them warm.

2. Pour off all but 2 tablespoons of the drippings from the skillet. Stir in the flour and salt and cook for 1 minute. Combine the instant broth and water in a 2-cup glass measure and pour into the skillet. Cook, stirring constantly, until the sauce is slightly thickened. Return the meatballs to the skillet. Cover; simmer for 10 minutes. Add the zucchini; cook for 10 minutes longer, stirring gently once or twice.

3. Spoon or pipe the mashed potatoes around the edge of the skillet and arrange the tomato wedges on top. Sprinkle the potatoes with paprika. If the skillet isn't flameproof, wrap the handle with aluminum foil. Place the skillet under the broiler to heat and brown the potatoes lightly, about 5 minutes.

```
┌─────────────────────── TOP IT OFF ───────────────────────┐
```

Change the character of any casserole, stew or fricassee by topping it in a new and different way. The choices are almost endless—make dumplings or main-dish pastry, or use refrigerated rolls and biscuits for a quick and easy finish. They're a great way to serve leftovers, too, because they satisfy even the heartiest of appetites. Whatever you choose to make, remember to have the stew or casserole bubbling hot before adding the topping. Otherwise, the results will be soggy and not properly cooked. And don't be tempted to peek when you make dumplings if you want them to be light and fluffy!

• Trim 4 slices of whole-wheat bread and spread with softened butter or margarine and sprinkle with sesame seeds and seasoned black pepper. Cut into 1-inch pieces with a sharp knife. Arrange on the tray of a toaster oven. Bake in a hot oven (425°) for 8 to 10 minutes, or until the seeds are golden and the bread crisp.

• Toss 2 cups of popcorn with 3 tablespoons of melted butter or margarine, 1 teaspoon garlic salt and 3 tablespoons of grated Parmesan cheese. Spread on the tray of a toaster oven. Bake in a hot oven (425°) for 5 minutes, or until very hot.

• Cut Italian or French bread into very thin slices; beat 1 egg white until stiff in a small bowl; add ¼ cup mayonnaise or salad dressing and ¼ cup shredded Cheddar or Swiss cheese; spread on the bread; arrange on the tray of a toaster oven. Bake in a hot oven (425°) for 5 minutes, or until the topping turns golden.

BEEF STEW

Makes 4 servings.

3 slices bacon, cut into small pieces	1 cup dry red wine
4 tablespoons all-purpose flour	1 bay leaf
1 teaspoon salt	Pinch of leaf thyme, crumbled
¼ teaspoon pepper	2 carrots pared and coarsely chopped (1 cup)
2 pounds boneless beef round, cut into 1-inch cubes	2 celery stalks, coarsely chopped (¾ cup)
1 large onion, chopped (1 cup)	2 potatoes, pared and cut into 4 pieces
1 clove garlic, finely chopped	6 to 8 fresh mushrooms, sliced
1 can (8 ounces) tomato sauce	
½ can condensed beef broth (from a 10½-ounce can)	

1. Cook the bacon until crisp in a heavy kettle or Dutch oven; drain the bacon on paper toweling; reserve.
2. Combine the flour, salt and pepper in a plastic bag; shake the beef in the flour mixture to coat it evenly. Brown the meat in the bacon drippings, turning often. (Add a little vegetable oil if needed.)
3. Add the onion and garlic and cook for 3 minutes, or until golden. Add the tomato sauce, broth, wine, bay leaf and thyme; lower the heat; cover and simmer for 1½ hours.
4. Add the carrots, celery, potatoes and mushrooms and cook until the meat and vegetables are tender. Sprinkle with the reserved bacon.

HEARTY MEATBALL STEW

Serve this hearty one-dish meal directly from the skillet it's cooked in.
Makes 6 servings.

1½ pounds lean ground chuck	½ teaspoon leaf oregano,
¾ cup soft bread crumbs	crumbled
(1½ slices)	½ teaspoon leaf thyme,
⅓ cup milk	crumbled
1 teaspoon salt	1 cup diced potatoes
½ teaspoon pepper	(½ pound)
3 tablespoons vegetable oil	1 cup thinly sliced carrots
1 clove garlic, finely chopped	1 cup thinly sliced celery
1 can (6 ounces) tomato paste	¼ pound fresh mushrooms,
¾ cup dry red wine	quartered
1½ cups water	1 tablespoon chopped parsley
1 bay leaf	

1. Combine the meat, crumbs, milk, salt and pepper in a large bowl and blend well. Shape the mixture into 36 balls.
2. Heat the oil in a large skillet and brown the meatballs, turning frequently. Blend in the garlic, tomato paste, red wine, water, bay leaf, oregano and thyme. Bring to boiling; lower the heat and simmer for 10 minutes.
3. Add the potatoes and carrots; cover and simmer for 30 minutes. Add the celery and mushrooms and simmer for 15 minutes longer, or until the vegetables are tender. Sprinkle with chopped parsley.

RECYCLING FOOD DISCARDS

Canned Vegetable Liquid: Use part of the liquid for soups, sauces, stews and gelatin salads. There are vitamins and minerals in these juices.

Carrot Tops: Chop and add to soups, stews or braising liquid for pot roast. Or plant them for a lovely touch of green in your kitchen window.

Celery Tops: Add them to stews or to the water you use for steaming chickens.

Vegetable Parings: Collect parings from carrots, potatoes, turnips, celery tops, and other vegetables. Keep them in a cheesecloth or muslin bag in the freezer. When you have two cups or so, drop the bag into a pot of simmering water along with salt, pepper and herbs, and cook for a couple of hours. When strained, this makes a good vegetable stock to use in soups, stews or casseroles.

Fat: Save the fat from meats for flavoring and frying (render beef suet and chicken fat first). Or make suet balls for birds outside your home in winter.

Green or Vegetable Salad: Drain dressing off leftover salad and tuck the greens into sandwiches, or whirl in a blender with chicken broth for a nicely seasoned soup, hot or cold.

Meat: Use the carcass of chicken, turkey, duck or roasts to make a hearty stock for soup, or to flavor beans, rice or lentils. Use ham bones in soups.

Parsley: Add to soup or use as a substitute for lettuce in sandwiches (especially ham and liver spreads). Chew as a breath freshener.

Evaporated Milk or Tomato Sauce: Store in non-metal containers to avoid that "tinny" taste. Use them in gravy, stew or soup.

Scrambled Eggs: Add to soups or fried rice.

Wine: Add leftover wine to wine vinegar or beef stew or use to baste a roast. Wine is a delicious sauce for fruits.

OVEN-BAKED BEEF STEW

A delicious and easy recipe that makes a meal-in-one dish.

Bake at 350° for 1 hour and 45 minutes.

Makes 6 servings.

1   can (16 ounces) potatoes, drained

1½ pounds beef for stew or boneless chuck, cut into 1½-inch cubes

1   medium-size onion, sliced (½ cup)

1   teaspoon vegetable oil

1   can (10½ ounces) mushroom gravy

1   envelope onion soup mix (from a 2.75-ounce box)

⅓   cup water

1   package (10 ounces) frozen peas

1. Slice the potatoes and place half in a large baking dish.

2. Brown the meat, part at a time, with the onion in the oil in a large skillet. Remove the meat and onion as they brown to the baking dish. Top with the remaining sliced potatoes.

3. Combine the gravy, onion soup mix and water in a small bowl and pour over the meat and potatoes; cover.

4. Bake in a preheated moderate oven (350°) for 1 hour and 45 minutes. Stir in the frozen peas and continue baking for 15 minutes longer, or until the meat is tender.

SOUP AND STEW SAVERS

To save soups and stews that are too salty, add potato, rice or noodles—they'll absorb some of the excess salt.

To remove excess fat from stews, soups and casseroles, chill and remove the fat that rises to the surface. Or drop ice cubes into the pot and remove any fat that clings to them.

CHUCK STEAK STEW

Boneless chuck steak cooked with an assortment of vegetables makes a tasty dinner.

Makes 4 servings.

1	boneless chuck steak from blade chuck steak (about 1¼ pounds)	1	teaspoon salt
1	tablespoon vegetable oil	½	teaspoon leaf basil, crumbled
2	carrots, pared and cut into ½-inch slices	¼	teaspoon pepper
1	medium-size onion, cut into 8 wedges	1	pound potatoes (about 3 medium size), pared and quartered
1	celery stalk, thickly sliced	½	of a 10-ounce package frozen peas
¼	cup tomato purée (from a 28-ounce can)	1	tablespoon all-purpose flour
1	cup water	2	tablespoons cold water

1. Brown the steak in the oil on both sides in a large kettle or Dutch oven; remove the steak and reserve it. Add the carrots, onion and celery and sauté until lightly browned. Add the tomato purée and the 1 cup of water.

2. Return the steak to the kettle and sprinkle it with salt, basil and pepper. Bring to boiling; lower the heat; cover and simmer for 30 minutes. Add the potatoes; cover and simmer for 30 minutes. Add the peas; cover and simmer for 15 minutes.

3. Combine the flour and the 2 tablespoons of cold water in a cup, stirring until smooth; stir into the kettle. Cook, stirring constantly, until thickened.

3

Main-Dish Salads

For a delightful, easy-to-fix meal, few entrées surpass a salad. Vegetables, fruit, meats and even seafood can be combined to make a mouth-watering self-contained meal.

Salads are an excellent way to combine different tastes and textures. This chapter has a delicious example of just some of the varied textures that go into the art of salad preparation. For instance, Shrimp and Cantaloupe Salad (page 37) combines avocado and cantaloupe with cooked shrimp and adds water chestnuts for a light crunchiness.

And what better way is there to beat the summer heat than by enjoying a cool and refreshing main-dish salad served on a bed of the freshest, crispest greens? Prepare it early in the morning, or even the night before and allow it to chill throughout the day.

TOSSED MIXED GREEN ANTIPASTO SALAD

This is a flavorful salad for an outdoor meal.

Makes 6 servings.

1 can (15 ounces) chick-peas, (garbanzos), drained	4 cups bite-size pieces romaine lettuce, chilled
1 sweet green pepper, halved, seeded and chopped (1 cup)	2 cups bite-size pieces leafy or iceberg lettuce, chilled
4 green onions, sliced, with some tops	½ pound cotto salami
1 can (6 ounces) pitted black olives, drained and halved	1 package (8 ounces) mozzarella cheese, cubed
½ cup bottled Italian dressing	2 tomatoes, cut into six wedges
1 clove garlic, halved	1 can (2 ounces) anchovies

1. Combine the chick-peas, green pepper, onions, olives and dressing in a medium-size bowl. Refrigerate, covered, for 1 hour or longer.

2. To serve, rub the inside of a large shallow wooden salad bowl with cut slices of garlic clove; discard. Add the romaine, lettuce, salami and cheese; toss. Add the chick-pea mixture; toss. Top with the tomato wedges and anchovies.

WEST COAST HEALTH SALAD

Topped with a creamy orange dressing, this fresh, crunchy and satisfying salad is perfect for a luncheon or supper meal.

Makes 8 servings.

1 package (8 ounces) cream cheese, softened	½ pound Monterey jack cheese, cut into julienne strips
1 teaspoon salt	
1 teaspoon dry mustard	2 large navel oranges, peeled and sectioned
1 teaspoon grated orange rind	
½ cup orange juice	1 ripe avocado, halved, pitted, peeled and sliced
2 tablespoons honey	
1 large head romaine or iceberg lettuce	½ cup golden raisins
1 pound mung or soybean sprouts (6 to 7 cups)	¼ cup hulled sunflower seeds

1. For the dressing, combine the cream cheese, salt, mustard, orange rind, orange juice and honey in a large bowl; blend until smooth and creamy.

2. Wash, dry and tear the lettuce into pieces into the same bowl. Arrange the cheese, oranges, avocado and raisins over the lettuce. Sprinkle with the sunflower seeds. Toss lightly until well coated.

PITTING, PARING AND SLICING AN AVOCADO

Step 1. Using a small, sharp paring knife, slice halfway through the avocado around the entire circumference. Using both hands, gently twist and pull each half away from the pit. Coat the inside surfaces liberally with lemon juice.

Step 2. Using the same knife, or a vegetable parer, pare the skin from each half, using a lengthwise cutting motion. Coat all surfaces liberally with lemon juice.

Step 3. Place the flat side down and cut crosswise (or lengthwise) into desired-size pieces. Coat the surfaces liberally with lemon juice.

GREEK MACARONI SALAD

This lively salad is an easy make-ahead.

Makes 4 servings.

1 hard-cooked egg	¼ pound feta cheese
½ cup plain yogurt	1 teaspoon leaf oregano,
½ cup olive or vegetable oil	crumbled
2 tablespoons lemon juice	2 large tomatoes
½ teaspoon leaf oregano,	1 slender cucumber
crumbled	1 sweet green pepper
¼ teaspoon salt	½ cup pitted black olives
⅛ teaspoon pepper	½ cup thinly sliced radishes
½ pound *penne* (pens or	¼ cup canned drained
quills)	chick-peas
2 tablespoons red wine	4 green onions, thinly sliced
vinegar	¼ cup finely chopped parsley

1. Mash the egg yolk with a fork in a large bowl. Beat in the yogurt, oil, lemon juice, oregano, salt and pepper to make a dressing; refrigerate.

2. Cook the *penne* following label directions just until *al dente*; drain. Add with the vinegar to the bowl containing the yogurt mixture.

3. Cut the cheese into ½-inch dice; sprinkle with the oregano, pressing lightly to make the herb adhere. Cut 1 tomato in half crosswise; squeeze out the seeds and discard them; chop the pulp coarsely. Trim the cucumber; cut half into thin slices; cut the remainder into ½-inch dice. Halve and seed the green pepper; cut it into julienne strips.

4. Add the cheese mixture, tomatoes, diced cucumber, green pepper, olives, radishes, chick-peas and green onions to the pasta; toss lightly.

5. Toss the dressing with the salad until well coated. Slice the remaining tomato; dice the egg white. Garnish the salad with tomato, egg white, reserved sliced cucumber and parsley. The salad can be covered and refrigerated (without garnish) for up to 2 days.

PEELING HARD-COOKED EGGS

Drain the eggs and shake in the pan until the shells crack. Cover with cold water until the eggs cool. To peel, roll the eggs between your hands.

MACARONI SALAD DELUXE

The tang of yogurt in a favorite salad.

Makes 12 servings.

1 package (1 pound) small shell macaroni
1 cup mayonnaise or salad dressing
1 container (8 ounces) plain yogurt
¾ cup milk
2 teaspoons grated lemon rind
2 tablespoons lemon juice
1 teaspoon salt
½ teaspoon pepper
1 package (10 ounces) frozen peas, thawed
6 ounces Swiss cheese, cut into small cubes (1½ cups)
1 cup thinly sliced green onions (about 1 large bunch)
Chicory

1. Cook the macaroni following label directions; drain.

2. Mix the mayonnaise, yogurt, milk, lemon rind, lemon juice, salt and pepper in a large bowl until smooth.

3. Add the macaroni, peas, Swiss cheese and green onions to the mayonnaise mixture and toss gently to coat with the dressing. Refrigerate the salad until serving time.

4. To serve, line a salad bowl with chicory and mound the macaroni salad in the center.

CORNUCOPIA SALAD PLATTER

An attractive way to serve potato salad for a special occasion.

Makes 8 servings.

2	pounds potatoes	8	slices cotto salami
¾	cup mayonnaise		Boston lettuce
2	tablespoons lemon juice	4	hard-cooked eggs, sliced
½	teaspoon salt	1	medium-size cucumber,
	Pinch of pepper		sliced
1	small onion, finely chopped	16	cherry tomatoes
	(¼ cup)		Carrot curls (optional)
¼	cup bottled hot dog relish		Green onion brushes
1	jar (4 ounces) pimientos,		(optional)
	drained and chopped		Parsley
8	slices bologna		

1. Cook the potatoes in boiling salted water to cover in a large saucepan until tender, for about 25 minutes. Drain, peel and cut into ½-inch cubes to make 4 cups.

2. Combine the mayonnaise, lemon juice, salt and pepper in a large bowl; add the warm potatoes; toss lightly. Let stand at room temperature for 20 minutes.

3. Stir in the onion, relish and pimientos. Spoon about ¼ cup of the salad onto each slice of bologna and salami. Fold the edges of the meat over to form cornucopias and secure with wooden picks. Refrigerate for at least 1 hour.

4. When ready to serve, arrange on a bed of lettuce; remove the wooden picks. Garnish with the hard-cooked eggs, cucumber, cherry tomatoes, carrot curls, green onion brushes and parsley.

SLICING HARD-COOKED EGGS

Slice eggs after they have been chilled. It also helps to wet the knife before each cut.

CARROT CURLS

Step 1. Wash the carrots; peel with a vegetable parer. Holding the carrot away from you at slight downward angle, pare very thin slices along the entire length of the carrot.

Step 2. Curl each slice around your finger or the handle of a wooden spoon. Pierce together with a wooden pick and place in a bowl of ice water. When ready to use, shake off excess water and remove the pick.

GREEN ONION BRUSHES

Step 1. Cut the green onion from the green end to the desired length (1 to 3 inches). Using the point of a small, sharp paring knife, make slashes in one end, turning after each cut to make as many slashes as possible. If you wish, make slashes in the other end, as well, leaving at least ¼ inch uncut in the middle.

Step 2. Place the green onions in a bowl of ice water to allow the ends to curl.

TANGY HAM-POTATO SALAD MOLD

An attractive salad that can be easily prepared
several hours before serving.

Makes 8 servings.

2	pounds potatoes	1	pound cooked ham, diced
½	cup vegetable oil		(3 cups)
3	tablespoons distilled	1	cup diced celery
	white vinegar	1	small onion, chopped
1	tablespoon prepared		(¼ cup)
	mustard	⅔	cup dairy sour cream
1	teaspoon salt	3	hard-cooked eggs, chopped
¼	teaspoon pepper		Lettuce leaves
1	large sweet green pepper		

1. Cook the potatoes in boiling salted water to cover in a large saucepan until tender, for about 25 minutes. Drain; peel and cut into ½-inch cubes to make 4 cups.

2. Combine the oil, vinegar, mustard, salt and pepper in a large bowl. Add the warm potatoes and toss lightly. Let stand at room temperature for 20 minutes.

3. Cut the pepper in half crosswise and seed. Slice half the pepper into rings for garnish; reserve. Cut the remaining half into ¼-inch dice (½ cup).

4. Add the diced green pepper, ham, celery, onion, sour cream and eggs to the potato mixture; mix well. Press into a 4-quart mold or large round bowl. Cover and refrigerate for 2 hours or overnight.

5. To serve, unmold onto a round platter over lettuce leaves. Garnish with the reserved green pepper rings.

HARD-COOKED EGG SUPPLY

Keep hard-cooked eggs on hand for quick, inexpensive dinners. Slice and add them to a cream sauce or a can of creamed soup served over hot biscuites, toast or mashed potatoes. They're also grand for an instant garnish on a chef's salad or a spinach quiche. Chop them to stretch tuna and chicken salads and sandwich fillings.

PARTY POTATO-SEAFOOD SALAD

Makes 6 servings.

1½ pounds potatoes
1 package (10 ounces) frozen peas
⅓ cup vegetable or olive oil
3 tablespoons wine vinegar
1 clove garlic, crushed and peeled
½ teaspoon dry mustard
1 teaspoon leaf basil or oregano, crumbled
1½ teaspoons salt
¼ teaspoon pepper

3 anchovy fillets, finely chopped
1 can (4½ ounces drained weight) tiny shrimp, drained
1 can (7 ounces) salmon or tuna, drained and flaked
1 large sweet green pepper, seeded and chopped (1 cup)
½ cup chopped green onion (include some green)
Romaine lettuce
1 tomato, cut into wedges

1. Cook the potatoes in boiling salted water to cover in a large saucepan until tender, for about 25 minutes. Drain, peel and cut into ½-inch cubes to make 3 cups.

2. Cook the peas, in the same pan used to cook potatoes, following label directions; drain and cool.

3. Combine the oil, vinegar, garlic, mustard, basil, salt and pepper in a large bowl. Stir in the warm potatoes and toss lightly. Let stand at room temperature for 20 minutes.

4. Stir in the peas, anchovies, shrimp, salmon, green pepper and onion. Mix well. Refrigerate for at least 1 hour.

5. To serve, line a salad bowl with romaine leaves. Spoon the salad in the center. Garnish the top with tomato wedges.

SWISS GYPSY SALAD

Accompany this salad with cooked garbanzo or kidney beans tossed with your favorite French dressing and sprinkled with minced chives and chopped parsley. A loaf of crusty bread would also be good.

Makes 6 servings.

2 pounds potatoes (about 6 medium size)
½ pound hard salami, cut into 1½ x ¼-inch strips
½ pound Swiss cheese, cut into 1½ x ¼-inch strips
1 cup cooked green peas OR: 1 cup canned small sweet peas, drained
½ cup sliced sweet pickle
1 cup bottled French dressing

Red leaf lettuce or other salad greens
1 can (2 ounces) flat anchovy fillets, drained and halved (optional)
4 hard-cooked eggs, sliced (for garnish)
4 medium-size ripe tomatoes, halved and sliced crosswise (for garnish)

1. Cook the potatoes in enough boiling salted water to cover in a kettle or Dutch oven. Drain; pare; cut into 1-inch cubes.
2. Combine the potatoes, salami, cheese, peas, pickle and French dressing in a large bowl; toss just until coated. Cover; refrigerate.
3. Remove from the refrigerator 1 hour before serving.
4. To serve, line a large salad bowl with lettuce. Spoon the salad into the bowl. Garnish with the anchovies, if using, and the egg and tomato slices.

COULIBIAC SALAD

Makes 8 servings.

1½ cups long-grain white rice
1 can (4 ounces) sliced mushrooms, drained
½ cup snipped fresh dill
¾ cup mayonnaise
¼ cup dry white wine
2 teaspoons salt
Pinch of pepper
6 tablespoons vegetable oil

2 tablespoons lemon juice
2 cans (16 ounces each) salmon, drained, boned and broken up
1 cup thinly sliced celery
2 tomatoes, cut into thin wedges
Thin lemon slices, halved

1. Cook the rice following label directions; cool to room temperature. Stir in the mushrooms and dill; chill.

2. Add the mayonnaise, wine, 1 teaspoon of the salt and the pepper to the rice mixture. Mix gently. Press the rice mixture into a 6-cup mold. Cover and refrigerate for about 2 hours, or until thoroughly chilled.

3. Beat the oil with the lemon juice and remaining salt and some pepper in a medium-size bowl. Add the salmon and celery; stir gently to mix. Cover; refrigerate until serving time.

4. Just before serving, unmold the rice ring onto a serving platter; spoon the salmon mixture into the center. Arrange the tomato wedges around rice ring; tuck the lemon slices between the rice and salmon mixture.

RUSSIAN FISH SALAD PLATTER

This is one of the best supper salads.

Makes 4 servings.

1	package (10 ounces) frozen or canned mixed vegetables	2	tablespoons finely chopped onion
½	cup mayonnaise		Salad greens
1	tablespoon Dijon-style or yellow mustard	2	cans (7 ounces each) skinless and boneless sardines, tuna or salmon
1	cup diced celery		
4	hard-cooked eggs, chopped		

1. If frozen vegetables are used, cook following label directions until crisp-tender. Drain and rinse with cold water until the vegetables are cold; drain on paper toweling.

2. Blend the mayonnaise with the mustard in a medium-size bowl. Fold in the vegetables (if canned vegetables are used, simply drain and add), celery, eggs and onion.

3. Line a serving platter with the greens; mound the salad in the center and surround with whole sardines or chunks of tuna or salmon.

Suggested Menu: Chilled beet borscht, pumpernickel and butter or cottage cheese and green onion, stewed prune and fresh orange compote.

CURRIED TUNA-RICE SALAD

Tuna, cooked chicken or turkey, plus curry powder—so good, so simple.

Makes 6 servings.

4 cups *cooked* rice
¼ cup bottled oil and vinegar
salad dressing
1 to 3 teaspoons curry powder
2 cans (7 ounces each) tuna,
drained and flaked OR:
2 cups cooked and cubed
chicken or turkey
1 large sweet green pepper,
halved, seeded and chopped
(1 cup)

1 medium-size onion,
chopped (½ cup)
½ cup sliced pitted black
olives
½ cup mayonnaise or salad
dressing
Salt and pepper
Crisp salad greens

1. Toss the rice with the bottled oil and vinegar salad dressing and curry powder until well blended in a large bowl; let stand at room temperature for 15 minutes to blend the flavors.

2. Add the tuna, chicken or turkey, green pepper, onion, olives and mayonnaise or salad dressing; toss lightly to coat well. Taste and season with salt and pepper; cover with plastic wrap and refrigerate for at least 1 hour.

3. Line a large salad bowl with the salad greens; spoon the tuna-rice mixture on top. Garnish with tomato wedges and cucumber slices, if you wish.

MEDITERRANEAN TUNA SALAD

Tuna prepared with Mediterranean accents makes a
zesty and colorful salad.

Makes 6 servings.

¼ cup tarragon vinegar
2 tablespoons lemon juice
1 clove garlic, finely chopped
2 tablespoons chopped
parsley
½ teaspoon leaf basil,
crumbled
½ teaspoon salt
⅛ teaspoon pepper
½ cup olive oil
1½ pounds new red potatoes

1 cup sliced celery
2 cans (7 ounces each) tuna,
drained and broken into
chunks
1 jar (7 ounces) roasted red
peppers
2 hard-cooked eggs, cut into
wedges
1 can (2 ounces) flat anchovy
fillets
Lettuce

1. Combine the vinegar, lemon juice, garlic, parsley, basil, salt, pepper and oil in a jar with a tight-fitting lid; shake until well combined.

2. Cook the potatoes in enough boiling salted water to cover in a kettle or Dutch oven, for about 20 minutes, or until tender. Drain; cool, then slice. (Peel the potatoes before slicing, if you wish.) Place the potatoes and celery in a shallow bowl; pour over the dressing; toss gently to coat the potatoes well. Refrigerate and allow to marinate for at least 2 hours. Refrigerate the tuna, peppers, eggs and anchovies separately.

3. To serve, line a deep platter or shallow bowl with the lettuce. Lift the potatoes from the dressing and arrange on top of the lettuce; reserve the dressing. Top with the tuna, peppers and eggs. Arrange the anchovies on top; drizzle with the reserved dressing and garnish with lemon slices, if you wish.

MARINATED CHICK-PEAS, TUNA AND ARTICHOKE HEARTS

Makes 4 servings.

1 jar marinated artichoke hearts	¼ teaspoon ground cumin
	¼ teaspoon cracked pepper
1 can (19 ounces) chick-peas, drained	¼ cup chopped red onion
	¼ cup chopped parsley
1 can (7 ounces) tuna, flaked	1 small head romaine lettuce
1 tablespoon lemon juice	2 tomatoes, cut into wedges
½ teaspoon salt	Ripe olives (optional)

1. Drain the artichoke hearts, reserving the oil. Halve the artichoke hearts and put them in a medium-size bowl with the chick-peas and tuna.

2. Combine the lemon juice, salt, cumin and pepper with the reserved oil; pour over the chick-pea-tuna-artichoke mixture. Stir in the red onion and parsley; cover and refrigerate for several hours.

3. Wash the romaine; dry well; break into pieces and place in a salad bowl; cover and refrigerate until serving time.

4. When ready to serve, add the chick-pea mixture to the romaine. Toss lightly to coat with the dressing. Arrange the tomato wedges and olives around the edges.

RIJSTTAFEL SALAD

Inspired by the famous Indonesian rice dish with accompaniments.

Makes 6 servings.

1½ cups long-grain white rice	½ cup sliced green onion
1 to 3 teaspoons curry powder	½ cup toasted diced almonds
½ cup bottled thin French dressing	1 cup sliced celery
	3 hard-cooked eggs, chopped
½ cup mayonnaise or salad dressing	½ cup chopped radishes
	½ cup toasted flaked coconut
2 cans (7 ounces each) tuna, drained	1 avocado, peeled, halved, pitted and diced
1 can (8¼ ounces) pineapple chunks, drained	

1. Cook the rice following label directions; place in a glass bowl. Stir the curry powder into the French dressing in a cup; drizzle over the hot rice; toss lightly to mix. Refrigerate for at least an hour.

2. To serve: Stir in mayonnaise or salad dressing and spoon onto a platter.

3. Separate the tuna into chunks and mound on top of the rice salad in the center of the platter. Pile the pineapple chunks, onions, almonds, celery, eggs, radishes, coconut and avocado, spoke fashion, around the edge. Garnish the tuna with a radish rose and serve with more French dressing, if you wish.

SHRIMP AND CANTALOUPE SALAD

Makes 4 servings.

1	large cantaloupe	2	tablespoons distilled white vinegar
½	medium-size ripe avocado		
3	tablespoons lemon juice	2	tablespoons chopped bottled chutney
¾	pound fresh shrimp, shelled, deveined and cooked OR: ½ pound shrimp, cooked	¼	teaspoon salt
		¼	teaspoon curry powder
			Pinch of pepper
½	cup sliced water chestnuts		Romaine lettuce leaves
½	cup vegetable oil		

1. Quarter the cantaloupe and scoop out the seeds. Loosen the fruit from the rind with a grapefruit knife; cut the loosened fruit into 6 crosswise slices.

2. Halve, pit and peel the avocado; cube into a medium-size bowl. Sprinkle the cubes with 1 tablespoon of the lemon juice. Add the shrimp and water chestnuts and toss lightly; chill.

3. Combine the oil, vinegar, chutney, salt, curry powder, pepper and remaining lemon juice in a small bowl; mix well.

4. To serve, arrange the cantaloupe on the romaine leaves; spoon the shrimp mixture over the cantaloupe; spoon the dressing over the salad.

SHELLING AND DEVEINING SHRIMP

Step 1. Hold the shrimp between both thumbs and forefingers with swimmerettes facing up. Gently loosen the shell on either side of the swimmerettes along the entire length of the shrimp. Gently remove the shrimp and discard the shell.

Step 2. Hold the shrimp in one hand; using thumb and first finger of your other hand, pinch out the meat from the tail.

Step 3. Using the point of a small, sharp paring knife, make a shallow slit along the entire length of the top of the shrimp.

Step 4. Gently pull the shrimp apart just enough to insert the tip of a paring knife into the slit. Pull the vein up with the tip of the knife along the entire length of the shrimp.

SHRIMP RÉMOULADE

A mixture of herbs added to oil and vinegar gives a Creole flavor
to this marinated shrimp.

Makes 6 servings.

¼ cup bottled mustard with horseradish
1 tablespoon paprika
1 teaspoon salt
¼ teaspoon cayenne pepper
½ cup tarragon vinegar
¾ cup vegetable oil
1 bunch green onions including tops, coarsely chopped (1 cup)
2 celery stalks, finely chopped (½ cup)
½ cup coarsely chopped parsley
2 pounds frozen shelled and deveined shrimp
1 medium-size head iceberg lettuce, shredded

1. Combine the mustard-horseradish, paprika, salt and cayenne in a small deep mixing bowl. Beat in the vinegar with a rotary beater until well mixed.

2. Continue beating, pouring in oil in a *slow steady* stream, until the sauce is thick and smooth. Stir in the green onions, celery and parsley. Cover and refrigerate.

3. Cook the shrimp following label directions; drain; cool slightly.

4. Pour the sauce over the shrimp; toss gently to coat the shrimp with the sauce. Cover and refrigerate for several hours or overnight.

5. Spoon the shrimp and sauce over a bed of shredded lettuce.

REUBEN'S CHEF SALAD

Makes 4 servings.

1	can (27 ounces) sauerkraut		Rye Croutons (recipe
1	cup shredded carrots		follows)
½	cup chopped sweet green	½	cup mayonnaise
	pepper (½ medium)	2	tablespoons bottled chili
½	cup chopped parsley		sauce
1	package (8 ounces) sliced	1	tablespoon milk
	corned beef	1	green onion, chopped
1	package (6 ounces) sliced		
	Swiss cheese		

1. Drain the sauerkraut; rinse with cold water and drain again. Combine with the carrots, green pepper and parsley in a medium-size bowl. Cover; refrigerate until well chilled.

2. Cut the corned beef and Swiss cheese into julienne strips.

3. Just before serving, place half of the sauerkraut mixture in a large salad bowl; top with half of the Rye Croutons. Repeat the layers. Arrange the corned beef and Swiss cheese on top. Toss to mix.

4. Combine the mayonnaise, chili sauce, milk and green onion in the same medium-size bowl used to chill the sauerkraut mixture; pour over the salad; toss to mix.

Rye Croutons: Cut 3 slices of rye bread into small cubes; toss with 2 tablespoons of melted butter in a shallow baking pan. Bake in a hot oven (400°) for 10 minutes, stirring once or twice.

SAUERKRAUT SALAD WITH CORNED BEEF

An Old World favorite, sauerkraut takes on a new and delicious role in this make-your-own sandwich-salad.

Makes 6 servings.

1	can (27 ounces) sauerkraut		Mustard
1	medium-size onion, chopped (½ cup)		Romaine leaves or shredded lettuce
¼	cup chopped fresh dill OR: 1 tablespoon dried dillweed	1	can (12 ounces) corned beef, chilled and then sliced
1	tablespoon chopped parsley	1	package (8 ounces) sliced Swiss cheese
½	cup bottled Russian dressing		Pickled red cherry peppers (optional)
1	large sweet green pepper, diced (about 1½ cups)		Fresh dill
6	thin slices pumpernickel bread	½	cup dairy sour cream
		½	cup bottled Russian dressing

1. Drain the sauerkraut; rinse with cold water and drain well. Combine the sauerkraut with the onion, dill, parsley and dressing in a large bowl; toss to mix; chill until serving time.

2. Just before serving, add the green pepper. Spread the bread slices lightly with mustard. Line a shallow salad bowl with romaine lettuce; arrange the sauerkraut salad over half of the lettuce; overlap the slices of bread, corned beef and cheese on other half.

3. Garnish with cherry peppers and dill. Combine the sour cream and Russian dressing in a small bowl, and serve on the side.

MUSHROOM AND HAM SALAD

Chunky cubes of ham, mushroom quarters and a bounty of vegetables make a special summer salad.

Makes 6 servings.

1½ pounds cooked ham, cubed (3 cups)

2 cans (16 ounces each) chick-peas, drained

1 large cucumber, pared, halved, seeded and sliced

2 medium-size zucchini, trimmed and cut into sticks

½ pound peas, shelled (½ cup)

½ cup sliced radishes

¾ cup mayonnaise or salad dressing

2 tablespoons cider vinegar

1 to 3 teaspoons curry powder

1 small head romaine lettuce, washed

½ pound mushrooms, wiped and quartered

Sliced pimiento-stuffed olives

1. Combine the ham, chick-peas, cucumber, zucchini, peas and radishes in a large glass or ceramic bowl.

2. Blend the mayonnaise or salad dressing, vinegar and curry powder in a small bowl. Pour over the ham mixture and toss to coat evenly. Cover with plastic wrap and refrigerate for 2 hours, or until serving time. (This can be done early in the day.)

3. Break the romaine leaves into a large serving bowl. Spoon the ham mixture over the greens and arrange the mushroom quarters and sliced olives on top.

4. Garnish with a whole radish, if you wish.

CLEANING MUSHROOMS

Wipe the mushrooms with a damp cloth unless they are very dirty. If dirty, rinse them quickly under cold water and immediately paper towel-dry them.

ZITI AND HAM SALAD
WITH MUSTARD DRESSING

Makes 8 servings.

1	package (16 ounces) ziti macaroni	1	tablespoon Worcestershire sauce
1	tablespoon vegetable oil	2	to 3 teaspoons dry mustard
1	canned (1 pound) ham OR: 1½ cans (12-ounce size) luncheon meat	1	teaspoon salt
		8	drops liquid red pepper seasoning
1	can (about 4 ounces) sliced mushrooms, drained	1	egg
		⅔	cup peanut oil
2	cups diced sweet green pepper	2	tablespoons chopped fresh parsley
1	large red onion, diced (1 cup)	¼	cup grated Parmesan cheese Salad greens
⅓	cup cider vinegar	2	tomatoes, sliced

1. Cook the ziti in boiling salted water following label directions; drain; rinse; drain well. Place in a large bowl; toss with the vegetable oil to prevent sticking.

2. Cut the ham into strips about 2 x ¼-inches long; add with the mushrooms, pepper and onion to the ziti.

3. *To make the Mustard Dressing:* Combine the vinegar, Worcestershire, mustard, salt, red pepper seasoning and egg in the container of an electric blender; cover; whirl at high speed for 15 seconds. Turn the blender to low; add the oil in a thin stream; continue blending for 1 minute. Add the parsley and cheese; pour over the ziti mixture in the bowl. Toss to mix well and chill for several hours.

4. To serve, line a large salad bowl with crisp greens; spoon the salad into the bowl. Garnish with the tomatoes.

PIZZA SALAD

Makes 4 servings.

1   can (8 ounces) tomato
    sauce
2   tablespoons finely chopped
    onion
1   tablespoon red wine vinegar
1   teaspoon Italian seasoning
    Salt to taste
    Crushed red pepper flakes
    to taste
1   to 2 heads leafy green
    lettuce
3   medium-size ripe tomatoes,
    cored and sliced

4   to 5 ounces thinly sliced
    mozzarella or Provolone,
    cut into wide strips
1   package (3 or 4 ounces)
    thinly sliced Genoa or other
    hard salami
1   cup thinly sliced mushrooms
1   jar (6 ounces) marinated
    artichoke hearts, drained
½   cup pitted black olives,
    sliced
    Sweet green pepper strips
    for garnish

1. Combine the tomato sauce, onion, vinegar, Italian seasoning, salt and red pepper flakes in a small bowl. Chill.

2. Arrange a double layer of lettuce leaves on a 12-inch round flat plate to form the "crust." Arrange a layer of tomato slices, then cheese and salami over the lettuce. Top with the mushrooms, artichoke hearts and olives. Garnish with the pepper strips. Drizzle with some of the tomato dressing. Pass the remainder.

SALAD RECYCLABLES

BROCCOLI AND CAULIFLOWER STALKS: Pare, slice thinly and stir-fry or steam for a quick vegetable. Or purée for a soup, or chill and add to a salad.

CELERY TOPS: Use in making soup, or shred thinly and add to tuna and egg salads. Or use in place of parsley to garnish a roast, salad or cold soup.

FRESH HERBS: Dry, freeze or preserve in vegetable oil or vinegar to flavor salads.

GREEN ONION AND LEEK TOPS: Use in soup or as a garnish on cold salads (chop very fine for potato or coleslaw). Wilt leaves and stems under hot water to make garnish for gelatin salads.

LIMP, BRUISED GREENS: Use them to keep rare meat rare during reheating: Line a baking pan with them, layer leftover meat slices on top; then cover with more greens. Warm for about 10 minutes in a very slow (200°) oven.

UNUSED OLIVES OR PIMIENTOS: Cover with vinegar in a glass jar, screw top on tightly; refrigerate until needed.

SLICED ONION DISCOLORATION: If you use a steel knife when slicing, the acid of the onions (and other fruits and vegetables, too) will react with the metal, causing discoloration. A stainless steel knife will end this problem.

SPROUTED ONIONS: Sprouted onions are fine to use if they are still firm. Otherwise, discard the onion, but use the sprout as you would a green onion.

SWEET PICKLE JUICE: Leftover juices from a jar of sweet pickles or pickle relish goes into potato salad in place of the called-for vinegar. It does a much better job of flavoring, too.

TACO SALAD IN LETTUCE LEAVES

Makes 6 servings.

1 pound lean ground round
1 package (1¼ ounces) taco
seasoning mix
¾ cup water
1 can (15 ounces) pinto
beans, rinsed and drained
12 large lettuce leaves
6 ounces Cheddar cheese,
shredded (1½ cups)

1 cup diced fresh tomato
(2 medium size)
½ cup sliced pitted black
olives
1 jar (8 ounces) taco sauce
Dairy sour cream
1 can (6 ounces) frozen
avocado dip, thawed OR:
1 cup homemade guacamole

1. Brown the meat in a large skillet. Drain and discard all fat. Return the meat to the pan; stir in the taco seasoning mix, water and beans. Cook for 15 minutes, stirring frequently. Remove from the heat and let it cool to lukewarm.

2. Roll up each lettuce leaf and arrange on one half of a large platter. Spoon some meat mixture on the other half and top with the cheese, tomato and olives. Put the taco sauce, sour cream and avocado dip in separate containers.

3. To serve, let everyone put some meat mixture on a leaf of lettuce; top with taco sauce, sour cream or avocado dip. Wrap the meat mixture up in the lettuce and eat up!

SPICY TACO SALAD

This hot ground beef-bean salad is served over raw vegetables and
cheese and topped with corn chips. It is a very good entrée for
an informal evening meal.

Makes 6 servings.

1 pound lean ground chuck	1 sweet green pepper, halved,
1 medium-size onion,	seeded and chopped (1 cup)
chopped (½ cup)	3 green onions, sliced, with
1 tablespoon vegetable oil	some tops
1 tablespoon chili powder	1 large tomato, sliced
1 can (8 ounces) tomato sauce	1 cup shredded sharp
1 package (1¼ ounces) taco	Cheddar cheese (4 ounces)
seasoning mix	½ cup sliced pitted black or
¾ cup water	green olives
1 can (15 ounces) red kidney	1 package (6 ounces) corn
beans, drained	chips
4 cups bite-size pieces iceberg	
lettuce, chilled	

1. Cook the meat in a large skillet until no pink remains. Spoon
off all the fat; remove the meat and reserve. Sauté the onion in the
oil until tender in the skillet. Stir in the chili powder; cook for
several seconds; add the tomato sauce, taco mix and water. Return
the meat to the skillet and mix well. Cook slowly, uncovered, for
20 minutes, stirring occasionally. Add the beans and cook just
until heated through.

2. Meanwhile, combine the lettuce, green pepper, green onions,
tomato, cheese and olives in a large salad bowl; toss well.

3. To serve, spoon the hot meat-bean mixture over the lettuce
mixture; top with some of the corn chips. Pass the remaining corn
chips. Serve at once.

LAMB AND RATATOUILLE SALAD

Serve this salad of quickly sautéed vegetables and marinated lamb strips either warm or cold.

Makes 4 servings.

1½ to 2 cups cooked lamb strips (3 x ¼ inches)
½ cup bottled Italian salad dressing
½ cup olive or vegetable oil
1 medium-size eggplant (about 1 pound), peeled and cut into ¾-inch cubes (about 4 cups)
1 large onion, halved lengthwise and cut into thin slivers (1 cup)
1 medium-size sweet green pepper, halved and cut into ½-inch pieces (1 cup)
1 cup sliced celery
¼ pound mushrooms, quartered (about 1 cup)
2 cloves garlic, finely chopped
1 teaspoon leaf oregano, crumbled
½ teaspoon leaf marjoram, crumbled
1 teaspoon salt
¼ teaspoon pepper
1 pint basket cherry tomatoes, halved
Leaf lettuce, if serving cold
Lemon wedges

1. Combine the lamb strips and salad dressing in a small bowl; toss to coat; set aside.

2. Heat ¼ cup of the oil in a large skillet or Dutch oven over high heat. Add the eggplant; stir-fry for 3 minutes, or just until tender. Remove with a slotted spoon to a large bowl.

3. Heat the remaining ¼ cup of oil in the same skillet; add the onion, green pepper, celery, mushrooms and garlic and stir-fry for 4 to 5 minutes.

4. Return the eggplant to the skillet; sprinkle with the oregano, marjoram, salt and pepper; toss gently to mix. Cover; lower the heat and simmer for 3 minutes, or just until the mixture is heated through. Turn into the same large bowl; add the lamb strips with the dressing; toss gently.

5. To serve warm, add the tomatoes; toss gently. To serve cold, cool slightly; cover with plastic wrap; refrigerate. When ready to serve, add the tomatoes; toss. Line a salad bowl with the lettuce leaves; spoon in the salad. Serve with lemon wedges.

GINGERED ASPARAGUS AND STEAK SALAD

A main dish salad with Oriental elegance.

Makes 6 servings.

2 pounds asparagus
1 clove garlic, halved
1 flank steak (about 1¼ pounds)
1 tablespoon vegetable oil
5 tablespoons soy sauce
3 tablespoons white wine vinegar
2 tablespoons sesame or vegetable oil

1 tablespoon fresh chopped gingerroot
1 tablespoon finely chopped green onion
Watercress
1 teaspoon toasted sesame seeds (optional)

1. Wash and trim the asparagus. Cut into 1½-inch lengths; reserve the tips. Partially cook the stalks in boiling salted water for 3 minutes; add the asparagus tips. Continue cooking for 4 minutes longer, or just until crisp-tender. Drain; rinse with cold water to stop the cooking. Drain again.

2. Rub the garlic on both sides of the steak; coat with the vegetable oil.

3. Broil the steak, 3 inches from the heat, for 3 minutes on each side for rare. Cool to room temperature. Cut into very thin slices, holding the knife blade almost parallel to the cutting board.

4. Combine the soy sauce, vinegar, oil, ginger and onion in a small cup. Let stand for 30 minutes for flavors to blend.

5. Arrange the asparagus and steak slices on a serving platter over a bed of watercress. Spoon the ginger sauce over just before serving. Sprinkle with the sesame seeds, if you wish. Toss and serve at room temperature.

4

Meat Dishes

Despite the trend in recent years toward eating less meat, especially those high in cholesterol, and substituting with fish, poultry and veal, the majority of the population probably still feels that a meal is incomplete without meat. For that group, this meat chapter is a winner. Skillet dishes, baked casseroles, one-dish pies or meat-stuffed vegetables are just a sampling of some of the meal-in-one choices that are waiting to be tried.

Since meat is usually the costliest food item, it becomes practical to consider stretching it in one-dish combinations. Furthermore, many of these recipes use less expensive cuts of meat, which guarantees a double reward: You get the satisfaction of having meat, but you have the comfort of knowing that a sizable portion of your week's food allowance is still available.

Some of these recipes, such as Cabbage and Lamb in Lemon Sauce (page 73) and Green Rice and Bacon Casserole (page 75), are special enough to plan for your next small dinner party, and no one will guess that cost was a consideration.

GROUND MEAT

Ground Beef: The most popular form of ground meat is ground beef. It is usually sold in 1-, 2- and 3-pound packages. Butchers estimate the weight of ground meat as it comes from the grinder and place it in mounds on trays; then the meat is wrapped and accurately measured.

Note: All our recipes call for a measured amount of ground meat, but have been developed with this in mind so that a few ounces over or under won't effect the final dish.

Regular Ground Beef is a mixture of lean meat and fat cut from a whole side of beef. It is the budget grind that is also shaped into patties.

Ground Chuck is made only with meat and fat from the chuck, or forequarter. It is the medium-priced ground beef.

Ground Round is the leanest, coming from the round, or hindquarter, and ground with a minimum amount of fat. It is the lowest in calories.

Ground Sirloin, like the cut of meat from which it comes, is highly flavorful. It is, however the most expensive type of ground beef.

Other Ground Meats

Ground Pork is a mixture of lean meat and fat from a whole hog. Cook it until it's well done (no longer pink inside).

Ground Ham is made from cooked cured ham. If you have leftover ham you would like to use up, grind it in a grinder or food processor.

Ground Lamb comes mostly from the neck and shoulder of lamb and can be cooked rare, medium, or well done.

Ground Veal is the lowest in calories of all ground meat and also the most costly; however it has unmatched flavor.

Ground Meatloaf Mixture is usually made up of ground beef, pork, and veal. You can also find packages combining just ground beef and veal or beef and pork. Some supermarkets offer the above combinations ground together.

Sausage can be found fresh or cooked. It has a rich flavor that adds punch to recipes, even when just a little is added. Just keep in mind that most sausage contains pork and if the pork is fresh, rather than cooked, it must be cooked completely before serving. Sausages, too may be found in the frozen food section of the supermarket. To freeze fresh sausage, divide it into recipe- or serving-size portions; wrap tightly in freezer wrap; label, date, and freeze. Use within one month.

Ground Turkey is often available in rolls of 3 pounds or so. Low in calories and cholesterol, it's an ideal substitute for ground beef.

GROUND MEAT BASICS

Plan to make the stop at the meat counter of your supermarket one of the last before checking out. Then bring the ground meat home as soon as possible and get it into the refrigerator right away. Once any meat is ground, it becomes more perishable and the longer it is away from refrigeration, the greater the chance of the ground meat spoiling.

Buy fresh meat on the day or the day before you plan to use it; otherwise divide ground meat into patties or serving-size portions and freeze (see below for directions).

Don't be upset if the inside of your freshly purchased ground meat is darker than the surface. The change in color or "bloom," as the meatmen call it, has left the meat because much of the air has been closed out of the package. Leave the ground meat unwrapped in the refrigerator for a short time and the meat will "bloom" once more.

To store ground meat overnight, loosen the plastic covering it was packaged in at the supermarket, or remove the plastic wrap and re-cover with wax paper. Store in the meat-storage drawer, or the coldest section of the refrigerator.

Don't handle ground meat too much or it will became heavy and compacted. It will also stay lighter and juicier if you add a tablespoon or two of cold water or red wine to each pound of meat. Wet your hands with cold water when making meatballs or hamburger patties. That way the meat won't stick to your hands.

To freeze ground meat, divide ground meat into patties or serving-size portions as soon as you come from the the supermarket. Wrap in freezer wrap or freezer-weight plastic wrap, being sure to have a double layer between patties that will be frozen in the same package for ease of separating later. Label, date and freeze; plan to use within one month of purchase.

To freeze a large batch of ground meat patties, shape meat into patties and place 1-inch apart on a cookie sheet. Fast freeze in the coldest part of the freezer. Pack into freezer-weight plastic bags or heavy-duty aluminum foil. Label, date and return to freezer.

To cook frozen patties, you can remove the patties from the freezer the night before and thaw in the refrigerator. However, if for some reason your plans change and you don't want to serve the patties the next night, the meat must be cooked, then it can be refrozen.

Frozen patties can be cooked but will take a little longer to pan-grill or broil than refrigerated ground meat, as indicated by the times given in the recipes. To pan-grill, sprinkle a heavy skillet with salt and heat until the pan is very hot; brown frozen patties quickly on both sides; lower the heat and cook, turning several times, until the meat is done as you like it. To broil, place patties on a rack in the broiler pan and place the pan on the lowest broiling position in the broiler; broil for 3 to 5 minutes longer than usual on the first side, or until the surface is browned, then turn and broil until the patties are done as you like them.

EASY PAN AMERICAN SKILLET MEAL

Quick-cooking foods make this skillet meal a snap.

Makes 4 servings.

2	tablespoons butter or margarine	1	pound lean ground round or chuck
1	medium-size onion, chopped (½ cup)	1	teaspoon salt
1	large sweet green pepper, halved, seeded and slivered	1	teaspoon sugar
		½	teaspoon ground coriander
1	large clove garlic, crushed and peeled	¼	teaspoon ground ginger
		1	can (16 ounces) tomatoes
		1	cup packaged instant rice

1. Melt the butter in a large skillet. Add the onion, pepper and garlic; sauté until just tender. Push the vegetables to the side of pan. Add the beef, salt, sugar, coriander and ginger and cook until well browned, stirring to break up the beef.

2. Stir in the tomatoes with their liquid and bring to boiling, stirring to break up the tomatoes. Add the rice. Stir until the grains are moistened. Remove from the heat; cover. Let stand until tender, for about 5 minutes.

BEEF AND VEGETABLE SKILLET MEAL

Makes 6 servings.

6 slices bacon, diced
1½ pounds lean ground round
  or chuck
1 large onion, chopped
  (1 cup)
1 can (10½ ounces)
  condensed beef broth
1 cup water
1½ teaspoons salt
  Pinch of cayenne pepper

1 bay leaf
6 medium-size potatoes,
  pared and quartered
2 tablespoons all-purpose
  flour
¼ cup water
2 sweet green peppers,
  halved, seeded and chopped
1 can (16 ounces) tomatoes
¼ cup sliced black olives

1. Cook the bacon in a skillet until it is crisp; remove with a slotted spoon.

2. Shape the beef into 24 meatballs. Brown, half at a time, in the bacon drippings; then remove meatballs and reserve.

3. Drain off all but 2 tablespoons of the drippings from the skillet; sauté the onion until soft. Stir in the beef broth, the 1 cup water, salt, cayenne and bay leaf. Return the meatballs; cover; lower the heat; simmer for 10 minutes.

4. Add the potatoes and simmer for 20 minutes more, or until just tender. Remove the meatballs and potatoes with a slotted spoon. Remove and discard the bay leaf. Combine the flour and remaining water in a cup; stir into the cooking liquid in the skillet. Cook, stirring until thickened.

5. Return the meatballs and potatoes to the skillet. Add the green pepper, tomatoes and olives. Lower the heat; cover and simmer for 5 minutes, or until piping hot. Sprinkle with the crisp bacon.

BUYING MEAT

• Always buy meat on sale since sale prices on meat are often as low as, or lower than, wholesale.
• Look for the dry package and reject meat sitting in its own liquid. The less liquid in the package, the better the meat's quality. Loss of liquid means loss of flavor, nutrition and tenderness. Flavor deteriorates the longer the meat lays in the liquid.
• Learn to recognize the *color* of a fresh piece of meat. Beef should be bright red, pork should have a grayish-white cast, veal should have a pinkish color, smoked meat should be rosy red.

QUICK MEDITERRANEAN DINNER

Fennel-flavored meatballs, zucchini and chick-peas in a tomato and wine sauce, all topped with feta cheese.

Makes 4 servings.

1	pound lean ground lamb or round	3	tablespoons all-purpose flour
½	cup soft bread crumbs (1 slice)	2	tablespoons vegetable oil
1	small onion, finely chopped (¼ cup)	1	can (16 ounces) whole tomatoes
1	clove garlic, finely chopped	½	cup dry white wine
2	tablespoons chopped parsley	2	medium-size zucchini (about 1 pound), halved and cut into 1-inch diagonal slices
¾	teaspoon crushed fennel seeds	1	can (19 ounces) chick-peas, drained
¾	teaspoon salt	½	cup halved pitted black olives
½	teaspoon pepper	2	tablespoons cold water
1	egg	½	cup crumbled feta cheese

1. Mix the lamb lightly with the bread crumbs, onion, garlic, parsley, fennel, ½ teaspoon of the salt, ¼ teaspoon of the pepper and the egg in a medium-size bowl just until combined. Shape into sixteen 1½-inch meatballs. Dust lightly with flour; set the remaining flour aside.

2. Sauté the meatballs in the oil in a large skillet until lightly browned; remove from the pan. Pour off the pan drippings.

3. Add the tomatoes with their liquid and wine to the skillet, breaking up the tomatoes with a wooden spoon and scraping up the browned bits. Bring to boiling. Add the meatballs; lower the heat; cover and simmer for 20 minutes. Add the zucchini, chick-peas and olives and cook until the zucchini is firm-tender.

4. Combine the reserved flour with the water in a small cup; stir into the skillet. Cook just until slightly thickened, for about 1 minute. Sprinkle with the feta cheese.

SKILLET SWISS STEAK

Makes 4 servings.

3	celery stalks, sliced (2 cups)	1	teaspoon dry mustard
1	large onion, sliced	¼	cup chili sauce
2	tablespoons vegetable oil	¼	teaspoon pepper
¼	cup all-purpose flour	3	medium-size potatoes,
1½	teaspoons salt		pared and quartered
2	pounds lean beef round	3	carrots, quartered
	steak, cut 2 inches thick	2	tablespoons chopped
2	cups hot water		parsley
1	envelope instant beef broth		

1. Sauté the celery and onion in 1 tablespoon of the oil in a large skillet until soft; remove and reserve.

2. Pound a mixture of the flour and 1 teaspoon of the salt into both sides of the meat. Brown the meat on both sides in the remaining tablespoon of oil in the skillet.

3. Stir 1 cup of the hot water into the broth and mustard in a 2-cup glass measure. Add to the skillet with the chili sauce, pepper and reserved celery and onion; cover.

4. Simmer for 1 hour and 15 minutes. Stir in the remaining cup of water to thin the gravy. Add the potatoes and carrots and sprinkle with the remaining ½ teaspoon salt.

5. Continue cooking, covered, for 30 to 45 minutes, or until the meat is fork-tender and the vegetables are done. Sprinkle with the parsley and serve.

BEEF CONTADINA

A quick and colorful dinner-in-a-skillet.

Makes 6 servings.

1½ pounds cube steak, cut into 1½-inch pieces
½ teaspoon salt
¼ teaspoon pepper
¼ cup olive oil
8 small new potatoes (about 1¼ pounds), unpeeled and cut into 1½-inch cubes
2 medium-size cloves garlic, finely chopped
1 large sweet green pepper, halved, cored, seeded and cut into 1-inch pieces
1 large sweet red pepper, halved, cored, seeded and cut into 1-inch pieces
1 large tomato, halved, seeded and cut into 1-inch chunks
Pinch of leaf basil
Pinch of leaf marjoram
Pinch of leaf rosemary
2 tablespoons chopped parsley

1. Season the meat with salt and pepper. Sauté the meat in the oil in a large heavy skillet over high heat, turning often, until brown on all sides; transfer the meat with a slotted spoon to a small bowl.

2. Add the potatoes to the skillet and sauté for 1 minute. Lower the heat to medium-low and sauté, turning frequently, for 7 minutes, or until the potatoes are browned. Stir in the garlic and sauté for 1 minute. Add an additional 1 tablespoon of oil, if necessary.

3. Stir in the green and red peppers and tomato chunks; sauté for 5 minutes longer, or until the peppers are crisp-tender.

4. Return the meat to the pan and sprinkle with the basil, marjoram and rosemary. Toss to heat through; sprinkle with parsley and serve immediately.

BEEF PEPPER STEAK

Makes 6 servings.

1   boneless top round steak (about 1 pound), cut 1 inch thick
⅓ cup cornstarch
1   cup long-grain white rice
½ cup vegetable oil
3   medium-size sweet green peppers, halved, seeded and cut into strips

3   medium-size onions, sliced
2   cloves garlic, crushed and peeled
½ cup soy sauce
1   cup water
   Hot cooked rice

1. Cut the meat into ¼-inch-thick slices. Toss with the cornstarch until well coated.
2. Start the rice cooking following label directions.
3. Sauté the meat, a few slices at a time, in ¼ cup of the oil in a large skillet until browned, for about 3 minutes. Remove to a warm platter.
4. Add the remaining oil to the skillet. Add the peppers, onions and garlic and sauté until tender, for about 3 minutes. Return the meat to the skillet.
5. Stir in the soy sauce and water and continue cooking, scraping up the browned bits in the skillet, until the sauce thickens and bubbles. Serve over hot cooked rice.

SPANISH PORK SHOULDER

Makes 6 to 8 servings.

4   pounds boneless pork shoulder
2   teaspoons salt
½ teaspoon pepper
1   clove garlic, crushed and peeled
½ teaspoon leaf thyme, crumbled
2   tablespoons vegetable oil
2   large onions, sliced

1   can (16 ounces) tomatoes
½ cup dry vermouth
2   cups cubed pared butternut squash (1 pound) or thickly sliced unpeeled zucchini
2   tablespoons cornstarch
2   tablespoons cold water
1   can (19 ounces) chick-peas, drained
1   sweet green pepper, sliced

1. Rub the pork with a mixture of salt, pepper, garlic and thyme. Brown in the oil in a Dutch oven. Spread the onions around and over the top of the pork. Add the tomatoes and vermouth. Bring to boiling; lower the heat; cover and simmer for 2 hours.

2. Stir in the squash; continue cooking for 20 minutes, or until the squash is tender.

3. Remove the meat to a carving board. Skim the fat from the liquid. Combine the cornstarch and water in a 1-cup glass measure. Stir into the liquid to thicken it.

4. Add the chick-peas and pepper slices. Heat for 10 minutes while slicing the meat. Return the pork to the pan and serve.

QUICK TIPS FOR BROWNING MEAT

• Choose a large heavy skillet if you haven't a heavy flameproof casserole and make sure it sits evenly on the burner.

• Wipe the meat on paper toweling before browning. If using seasoned flour, coat just before cooking.

• Heat fat or oil in the pan until it is almost smoking. Add just enough of the meat to cover the bottom of the pan, leaving a little space around each piece.

• Brown one side until beads of blood show around the bone on the upper surface; then turn with tongs; repeat until evenly brown on all sides.

• Remove the meat with tongs to a bowl or the lid of the casserole while browning the remaining pieces; then return the browned meat and any juices to the casserole.

• For an extra meaty flavor, pour off and discard all fat from the pan and add a little water, wine or broth to the pan; heat and stir to loosen the cooked-on juices from the bottom of the pan; add to the liquid in the casserole.

BEEF STUFFING PIE

Bake at 375° for 40 minutes.
Makes 6 servings.

1½ cups water
1 package (8 ounces) herb-seasoned stuffing mix
1 pound lean ground chuck
2 eggs

2 packages (10 ounces each) frozen broccoli with cheese sauce in boilable bag
1 tablespoon instant minced onion
1 large tomato, sliced

1. Preheat the oven to moderate (375°).

2. Bring the water to boiling in a large saucepan. Stir in the stuffing mix and remove from the heat; cool slightly. Stir in the meat lightly with a fork; stir in the eggs.

3. Press the mixture into a greased 9-inch pie plate, keeping the bottom ½ inch thick and the side about 1 inch thick. Cover with aluminum foil.

4. Bake in the preheated moderate oven (375°) for 40 minutes, or until the stuffing is firm.

5. Meanwhile, cook the broccoli following label directions. Cut open the pouches; sprinkle each with some onion; pour into the center of the baked stuffing shell. Arrange the tomato slices on top. Cut into wedges to serve.

COAL MINER'S PIE

Bake at 350° for 20 minutes.
Makes 6 servings.

1   **pound lean ground round**
2   **medium-size onions, chopped (1 cup)**
1   **can (15 ounces) tomato sauce**
2   **medium-size sweet green peppers, coarsely chopped**
1   **cup canned corn, drained OR: 1 cup frozen kernel corn**

1   **to 2 teaspoons salt**
1   **teaspoon pepper**
2   **eggs**
1   **tablespoon vegetable shortening**
½   **cup buttermilk**
¾   **cup yellow cornmeal**
1   **tablespoon all-purpose flour**
1   **teaspoon baking soda**

1. Preheat the oven to moderate (350°).

2. Brown the beef and onions in a Dutch oven or large kettle, breaking up the meat with a wooden spoon, until the meat is not longer pink. Stir in the tomato sauce, green pepper, corn, chili powder, 1 teaspoon of the salt and the pepper. Bring to boiling; lower the heat; cover and simmer for 15 minutes.

3. Pour the meat mixture into an ungreased 10-inch deep-dish pie plate.

4. Beat together the eggs, shortening and buttermilk in a small bowl for 1 minute. Beat in the cornmeal, flour, baking soda and remaining ¼ teaspoon salt just until well blended. Spoon over the top of the meat; spread evenly to cover the entire surface. (Some of the mixture may run into the meat, but it will rise during baking.)

5. Bake in the preheated moderate oven (350°) for 20 minutes, or until a wooden pick inserted in the cornmeal layer comes out clean.

CARAWAY PORK AND SAUERKRAUT PIE

A savory pie with a mashed potato topping.

Bake at 375° for 20 minutes.

Makes 6 servings.

1¼	pounds lean boneless pork, cut into ¾-inch cubes	⅛	teaspoon pepper
2	tablespoons vegetable oil	½	cup dairy sour cream
1	medium-size onion, diced (½ cup)	1	tablespoon all-purpose flour
1	medium-size sweet green pepper, cored, seeded and diced (½ cup)	1	can (1 pound) sauerkraut, rinsed and drained
1	clove garlic, minced	1	teaspoon caraway seeds
1	can (8 ounces) tomato sauce	3	cups hot unseasoned mashed potatoes
1	cup chicken broth	¼	cup (½ stick) butter or margarine
2	teaspoons paprika	2	tablespoons milk
		1	egg, lightly beaten

1. Brown the pork, part at a time, in the oil in a large saucepan. Remove with a slotted spoon to paper toweling. Pour off all but 1 tablespoon of the drippings.

2. Sauté the onion, green pepper and garlic in the drippings in the saucepan until golden, about 5 minutes. Return the pork to the pan. Stir in the tomato sauce, chicken broth, paprika and pepper. Bring slowly to boiling; lower the heat; cover and simmer for 1 hour.

3. Preheat the oven to moderate (375°).

4. Combine the sour cream and flour in a medium-size bowl; gradually stir into the pork mixture. Add the sauerkraut and caraway seeds and stir to mix well. Spoon the mixture into a 2-quart casserole.

5. Combine the mashed potatoes with the butter, milk and egg in the same medium-size bowl. Spoon the potatoes in large mounds over the top of the pork mixture, making sure to spread to the sides to seal the edges. Place on a cookie sheet or aluminum foil.

6. Bake in the preheated moderate oven (375°) for 20 minutes, or until the filling is bubbly hot and the potato topping is lightly browned.

CHEESY HAM AND CORN PIE

Bake at 350° for 1 hour.
Makes 8 servings.

¼ cup chopped green onion
1 small sweet green pepper, cored, seeded and finely chopped (⅓ cup)
1 small sweet red pepper, cored, seeded and finely chopped (⅓ cup)
3 tablespoons butter or margarine
4 eggs
¼ cup milk
1 pound diced cooked ham (about 2⅔ cups)
2 packages (10 ounces each) frozen corn kernels, slightly thawed
½ cup shredded Cheddar cheese (2 ounces)
1 teaspoon Worcestershire sauce
¼ teaspoon pepper
1½ packages piecrust mix

1. Sauté the green onion and green and red peppers in the butter in a large skillet until soft, for 5 minutes. Remove from the heat.

2. Beat the eggs and milk in a large bowl until blended. Add the onion-pepper mixture, ham, corn, cheese, Worcestershire and pepper and combine thoroughly.

3. Preheat the oven to moderate (350°).

4. Prepare the piecrust mix following label directions. Roll out a little more than half the pastry on a lightly floured surface with a lightly floured rolling pin to a 12 x 17-inch rectangle. Fit into a shallow 8-cup (11 x 7 x 1½-inch) baking dish and trim the overhang to ½ inch. Spoon the ham and corn mixture into the pastry-lined dish.

5. Roll out the remaining pastry to 10 x 14-inch rectangle. Fit over the filling. Trim the overhang even with the bottom crust. Pinch to seal the edges. Turn the sealed edge under. Pinch to make a stand-up edge; flute. Cut steam vents in the top. Place on a cookie sheet or aluminum foil.

6. Bake in the preheated moderate oven (350°) for 1 hour, or until the filling is bubbly hot and the pastry is golden. Let stand for 15 minutes. Cut into squares.

BEEF, CARROT AND TURNIP PIE

A beef stew with diced vegetables, all combined in a winy broth and topped with a flaky crust.

Bake at 400° for 35 minutes.
Makes 6 servings.

1	pound boneless round, cut into ¾-inch pieces	¼	teaspoon pepper
2	tablespoons vegetable oil	1	cup beef broth
1	cup diced carrot	1	cup dry red wine
1	cup diced turnip	1	tablespoon cider vinegar
1	large onion, diced (1 cup)	2	teaspoons firmly packed light brown sugar
3	tablespoons all-purpose flour	¼	cup chopped parsley
1	teaspoon salt	½	package piecrust mix

1. Brown the beef, part at a time, in the oil in a large skillet over medium heat. Add the carrot, turnip and onion; lower the heat; cover and simmer for 5 minutes. Uncover; sprinkle with the flour, salt and pepper and toss to coat. Stir in the beef broth, wine, vinegar and sugar. Bring to boiling. Lower the heat; cover and simmer for 30 minutes, or until the meat is tender. Stir in the parsley. Spoon the mixture into a 1½-quart casserole.

2. Preheat the oven to hot (400°).

3. Prepare the pastry following label directions. Roll out the pastry on a lightly floured surface with a lightly floured rolling pin into a piece slightly larger than the top of the casserole. Fit over filling; trim the overhang to ½ inch; fold edge under, flush with sides of baking dish (pastry should be inside dish). Pinch to make a stand-up edge and flute. Cut steam vents in the top. Place on a cookie sheet or aluminum foil.

4. Bake in the preheated hot oven (400°) for 35 minutes, or until the filling is bubbly hot and the pastry is golden.

ITALIANISSIMO MEATBALL POT PIE

A hearty pie filled with chick-peas and miniature meatballs accented with the flavor of lemon and spices and herbs.

Bake at 350° for 50 minutes.
Makes 6 servings.

1 pound lean ground round or chuck	¼ teaspoon ground nutmeg
½ cup soft bread crumbs (1 slice)	2 tablespoons olive or vegetable oil
1 egg, slightly beaten	1 teaspoon leaf oregano, crumbled
1 tablespoon milk	1 can (19 ounces) chick-peas, drained and ½ cup liquid reserved
1 clove garlic, finely chopped	
2 teaspoons finely chopped parsley	1 can (14 or 15 ounces) Italian-style tomatoes
1 teaspoon grated lemon rind	
1 teaspoon salt	1 package piecrust mix
¼ teaspoon pepper	

1. Combine the beef, bread crumbs, egg, milk, garlic, parsley, lemon rind, salt, pepper and nutmeg in a large bowl; mix lightly. Shape into 30 small meatballs (about 1 inch in diameter).

2. Brown the meatballs quickly in the oil in a large heavy skillet. Remove with a slotted spoon to paper toweling to drain. Discard the drippings in the pan.

3. Add the cornstarch and oregano to the skillet. Gradually stir in the ½ cup chick-pea liquid and the tomatoes with their liquid, breaking up the tomatoes. Bring slowly to boiling, stirring constantly, until the mixture thickens. Stir in the drained chick-peas and remove from the heat.

4. Preheat the oven to moderate (350°).

5. Prepare the piecrust pastry following label directions. Roll out half the pastry on a lightly floured surface with a lightly floured rolling pin to an 11-inch round. Fit the dough into the bottom of a 9-inch pie plate; trim the overhang to ½ inch.

6. Place the meatballs in the lined pie plate. Spoon the tomato and chick-pea mixture over.

7. Roll out the remaining half of the pastry to an 11-inch round. Fit over the filling and trim overhang even with the bottom crust. Pinch to seal the edges. Turn the sealed edge under. Pinch to make a stand-up edge and flute. Cut steam vents in the top. Place on a cookie sheet or aluminum foil.

8. Bake in the preheated moderate oven (350°) for 50 minutes, or until the filling is bubbly hot and the pastry is golden.

BEEF AND VEGETABLE PIE

Chunks of browned meat patties look like stew meat in this
vegetable-laced filling.
Bake at 400° for 25 minutes.
Makes 8 servings.

2	pounds lean ground round or chuck	1	tablespoon salt
2	cans (13¾ ounces each) beef broth	1	tablespoon Worcestershire sauce
1	package (1 pound) carrots, sliced (about 3 cups)	1	teaspoon leaf thyme
4	celery stalks, cut into ½-inch-pieces (2 cups)	1	bay leaf
3	small onions, cut into wedges	½	cup all-purpose flour
		½	cup cold water
		½	package piecrust mix
		1	egg yolk, beaten with 1 tablespoon water

1. Shape the beef into 4 large square patties, 1 inch thick. Brown the patties in a large skillet about 5 minutes on each side. Remove to paper toweling to drain. Pour off any fat.

2. Add the broth, carrots, celery, onions, salt, Worcestershire, thyme and bay leaf to the skillet; bring to boiling. Cover and cook over low heat until the carrots are tender.

3. Preheat the oven to hot (400°).

4. Combine the flour and water in a cup. Cut the beef patties into 1-inch cubes. Remove the bay leaf from the vegetables; stir in the flour paste until smooth and thickened. Add the beef cubes and spoon the mixture into a shallow 3-quart baking dish.

5. Prepare the piecrust mix following label directions. Roll out to a ⅛-inch thickness. Cut into ¾-inch strips with a pastry wheel. Arrange over the top of the baking dish, pressing firmly along the rim of the dish. Brush with the yolk mixture.

6. Bake in the preheated hot oven (400°) for 25 minutes, or until the filling is bubbly hot and the pastry is golden brown. Garnish with celery leaves, if you wish.

GREEK MEAT PIE

Pungent herbs and tangy cheese combine with beef and rice under a shattery pastry top.

Bake at 375° for 35 minutes.
Makes 6 servings.

1   large onion, chopped (1 cup)
2   tablespoons olive oil
1½ pounds lean ground chuck
1   cup long-grain white rice
1   can (13¾ ounces) chicken broth plus enough water to make 2 cups
½   teaspoon ground cumin
½   teaspoon dried mint leaves
¼   teaspoon leaf thyme, crumbled
1   teaspoon salt
½   teaspoon pepper
1   cup (5 ounces) feta cheese, finely crumbled
8   ounces ricotta cheese
2   eggs, slightly beaten
½   cup chopped walnuts
½   cup chopped parsley
6   tablespoons olive oil heated with 6 tablespoons butter
½   pound frozen phyllo dough, thawed and cut crosswise to make equal-size rectangles

1. Sauté the onion in the oil in a large skillet over medium heat until soft. Add the ground chuck, breaking up the meat as it browns.

2. Stir in the rice, chicken broth, cumin, mint, thyme, salt and pepper. Cover and simmer for 20 minutes.

3. Remove from the heat. Stir in the feta and ricotta cheeses, eggs, walnuts and parsley. Taste and add additional salt and pepper, if needed.

4. Preheat the oven to moderate (375°).

5. Brush a light coating of the oil and butter mixture on the bottom of an 11¾ x 7½ x 1¾-inch baking dish. Brush 8 sheets of phyllo dough with the oil-butter mixture, 1 at a time, and place on the bottom of dish. Spoon the filling over the phyllo. Brush the remaining sheets with oil and butter; place the sheets over the meat mixture, tucking away any overhanging edges.

6. Bake in the preheated moderate oven (375°) for 35 minutes, or until golden. Garnish with cherry tomato slices and parsley, if you wish.

STUFFED PEPPERS ITALIAN-STYLE

Chick-peas are the stretcher here instead of the usual rice.

Bake at 350° for 20 minutes.
Makes 6 servings.

6	medium-size sweet green peppers	1	egg, beaten
1	pound lean ground round or chuck	1	teaspoon leaf oregano, crumbled
1	large onion, chopped (1 cup)	¼	cup finely chopped parsley
1	teaspoon salt	1	package (8 ounces) mozzarella cheese, diced
½	teaspoon fennel seeds, crushed	1	can (15 ounces) tomato sauce
1	can (19 ounces) chick-peas, drained		

1. Preheat the oven to moderate (350°).

2. Cut a slice from the top of each pepper; scoop out the seeds and membranes. Parboil the peppers in a small amount of boiling water for 10 minutes and drain well. Stand in a greased shallow baking pan that just fits them.

3. Brown the beef with the onion, salt and fennel in a large skillet, stirring often to break up the beef. Spoon off all fat and remove from the heat.

4. Add the chick-peas, egg, oregano, parsley and cheese and toss gently to mix. Spoon into the pepper cups. Cover the pan with aluminum foil.

5. Bake in the preheated moderate oven (350°) for 20 minutes, or until bubbly and hot.

HOW TO KEEP STUFFED GREEN PEPPERS FROM COLLAPSING

Bake stuffed peppers in greased muffin tins. The tins will give them some support as they cook. The same trick can be used when making stuffed onions or tomatoes.

STUFFED EGGPLANT

Leftover cooked pork turns this colorful vegetable into a satisfying main dish.

Bake at 375° for 45 minutes.
Makes 4 servings.

2	eggplants (1 pound each)	1	teaspoon salt
1	large onion, chopped (1 cup)	1	can (8 ounces) whole tomatoes
½	cup chopped sweet green pepper	1	cup *cooked* rice
3	tablespoons vegetable oil	2	cups finely diced or chopped cooked pork (leftover)
¼	cup chopped parsley		
½	teaspoon dried mint leaves OR: 1 teaspoon chopped fresh mint leaves	½	cup soft bread crumbs (1 slice)
½	teaspoon leaf oregano, crumbled	¼	cup grated Parmesan cheese

1. Preheat the oven to moderate (375°).

2. Wash the eggplants and cut them in half lengthwise. Scoop out the pulp from the eggplant halves, leaving a ¼-inch-thick shell; dice the pulp.

3. Sauté the onion and pepper in the oil in a large skillet for about 5 minutes. Stir in the parsley, mint, oregano, salt, tomatoes and diced eggplant; heat to boiling. Remove from the heat; add the rice and pork.

4. Spoon the mixture into the eggplant shells. Place in a greased shallow baking pan. Combine the bread crumbs and Parmesan cheese in a small bowl and sprinkle over the stuffed eggplants.

5. Bake, uncovered, in the moderate oven (375°) for 45 minutes, or until the filling is bubbly and the eggplant is tender.

HOW TO BUY AN EGGPLANT WITH FEWER SEEDS

The fewer seeds in an eggplant, the less bitter it tastes. There is a way to tell before you cut into it and this depends on the eggplant's sex! Check the bottom—the end opposite the stem. There you will find a grayish "scar" or indentation about the size of a dime. If the "scar" is oval or oblong, the eggplant is female and will be loaded with seeds. A round "scar" is a male and it will have far fewer seeds.

LAMB-STUFFED ACORN SQUASH

Bake at 375° for 1 hour.
Makes 4 servings.

2	small acorn squash (2 pounds total weight), halved and seeded	¼	teaspoon pepper
1	pound lean ground lamb	2	tablespoons chopped parsley
1	medium-size onion, chopped (½ cup)	2	tablespoons dried currants
2	tablespoons vegetable oil	2	teaspoons distilled white vinegar
1	teaspoon dried mint leaves, crumbled	1	cup frozen mixed vegetables
¼	teaspoon ground cinnamon	1	can (8 ounces) tomato sauce
¾	teaspoon salt	2	tablespoons pine nuts (optional)

1. Preheat the oven to moderate (375°).

2. Place the squash, cut sides down, in a shallow baking pan; add ½ inch of water.

3. Bake in the preheated moderate oven (375°) for 30 minutes; turn cut side up and bake for 10 more minutes.

4. Prepare the filling while the squash bakes. Sauté the lamb and onion in the oil in a large skillet; stir in the cinnamon, salt, pepper, parsley, currants, vinegar, mixed vegetables, tomato sauce and pine nuts. Cook over low heat for 5 minutes to blend the flavors.

5. Mound ½ cup of the filling in each squash half. (Any extra filling may be wrapped in an aluminum foil packet and baked along with the squash or frozen.)

6. Bake the squash for 20 minutes longer.

STUFFED VEGETABLES

Stuffing vegetables is an excellent way to use leftovers. Mix together leftover chopped meat, rice or bread crumbs, chopped cooked vegetables and, if you wish, tomato sauce; if the mixture seems too dry, stir in a beaten egg. You can stuff any vegetable that still holds its shape after you scoop out the center. Some vegetables, such as artichokes, eggplants, green peppers, onions and turnips, are best if parboiled for a few minutes, then stuffed. After stuffing, place in a shallow pan, pour in a thin layer of water, wine or broth, and bake at 350° for 20 to 25 minutes. Others, such as tomatoes, mushrooms and cucumbers, are best stuffed raw and served, or baked as above.

BAKED LAYERED CABBAGE

A first cousin to the Greek moussaka, with cabbage leaves
replacing the eggplant.

Bake at 350° for 40 minutes.
Makes 8 servings.

1	head cabbage (about 3 pounds)	1	can (8 ounces) tomato sauce
1½	pounds lean ground chuck		***Cream Sauce Topping***
1	large onion, chopped (1 cup)	2	tablespoons butter or margarine
2	teaspoons salt		
1	teaspoon leaf oregano, crumbled	2	tablespoons all-purpose flour
1	teaspoon leaf basil, crumbled	½	teaspoon salt
		2	cups milk
½	teaspoon pepper	2	eggs
⅛	teaspoon ground cloves	¼	cup grated Parmesan cheese
⅓	cup long-grain white rice		

1. In a large kettle heat to boiling enough water to cover the cabbage. Trim the damaged outer leaves from the cabbage. Stick a large fork deep into the core; lower the cabbage into the boiling water, holding on to the fork. With a small sharp knife, carefully loosen and remove about 16 leaves from the cabbage as they become soft and pliable; drain. Chop the remaining cabbage coarsely (to make 3 to 4 cups).

2. Heat a large heavy skillet or Dutch oven; add the ground chuck and onion; cook slowly, stirring often, until the meat begins to brown, for about 10 minutes. Stir in the chopped cabbage, salt, oregano, basil, pepper, cloves, rice and tomato sauce; cover. Simmer, stirring often, for 20 minutes.

3. Trim a little off the thick rib from each cabbage leaf. Arrange half of the leaves, overlapping, in a 13 x 9 x 2-inch baking dish or pan and spoon the meat mixture evenly over. Top with the remaining leaves, overlapping as before.

4. Preheat the oven to moderate (350°).

5. Melt the butter in a small saucepan, stir in flour and salt. Gradually stir in milk; bring to boiling, stirring constantly, until the sauce thickens and boils for 1 minute. Remove from the heat. Beat the eggs in a small bowl with a wire whisk; gradually beat in the hot cream sauce. Pour over the cabbage in the casserole and sprinkle evenly with Parmesan cheese.

6. Bake in the preheated moderate oven (350°) for 40 minutes, or until the top is set. Place under the broiler to brown the top a bit more, if you wish. Cut into squares to serve.

CABBAGE AND LAMB IN LEMON SAUCE

Lemon and egg sauce is a delightful complement to lamb and cabbage.
Makes 6 servings.

2	tablespoons all-purpose flour	1	cabbage (2½ to 3 pounds), cut into 6 wedges
1½	teaspoons salt	1	pound small new potatoes, pared, or scrubbed and a 1-inch strip removed around the middle
¼	teaspoon pepper		
6	lamb shoulder chops (2 to 2½ pounds total weight)		
2	tablespoons vegetable oil	2	eggs
1	large onion, sliced	¼	cup lemon juice
1	clove garlic, crushed and peeled		Lemon wedges (optional) Parsley (optional)
1	can (13¾ ounces) chicken broth		

1. Mix the flour, salt and pepper on wax paper. Coat the chops evenly with the mixture, shaking off any excess; reserve any remaining mixture.
2. Heat the oil in a large deep skillet; add the chops and brown evenly on both sides; remove as they brown. Add the onion and garlic to the skillet and sauté until soft. Sprinkle any flour mixture left from the chops over the onion. Stir in the broth and bring to boiling. Arrange the chops, cabbage and potatoes in the skillet; lower the heat; cover. Cook, basting occasionally with the sauce, for 45 to 50 minutes, or until the chops and vegetables are tender.
3. Arrange the chops and vegetables in a deep platter; keep warm. Beat the eggs in a small deep bowl until light and foamy; beat in the lemon juice. Gradually add the hot sauce to the eggs while beating; pour back into the skillet. Cook over low to medium heat, stirring constantly, just until slightly thickened. Do not boil. Pour over the chops and vegetables immediately. Garnish with the lemon wedges and parsley, if you wish.

BAKED EGGPLANT ROLLS

Great for brunch or lunch with a salad and crusty bread.

Bake at 350° for 45 minutes.
Makes 4 servings.

1	large eggplant (about 1½ pounds)	1	egg
⅓	to ½ cup olive oil	1½	teaspoons salt
1	pound lean ground chuck or round	2	teaspoons Worcestershire sauce
1	small zucchini, shredded (1½ cups)	1	can (10¾ ounces) condensed cream of celery soup
½	cup dry instant mashed potatoes	¾	cup milk or light cream
		2	tablespoons grated Parmesan cheese

1. Remove the stem end of the eggplant. Cut the eggplant lengthwise into 8 slices, about ¼ inch thick. Brush the cut sides with oil. Broil about 4 inches from the heat, half of the slices at a time, until lightly browned on both sides. Cool until ready to use.

2. Preheat the oven to moderate (350°).

3. Combine the beef, zucchini, potato flakes, egg, salt and Worcestershire in a large bowl. Divide and shape into 8 oval mounds. Place one mound along the short end of an eggplant slice; roll up. Place the roll seam-side down in a shallow baking dish. Repeat with the remaining slices.

4. Combine the soup and milk in the same bowl and pour over the eggplant rolls. Sprinkle the top with cheese.

5. Bake in the preheated moderate oven (350°) for 45 minutes, or until lightly browned.

GREEN RICE AND BACON CASSEROLE

Bake at 350° for 35 minutes.
Makes 6 servings.

1   medium-size onion, chopped (½ cup)
¼   cup (½ stick) butter or margarine
¼   cup all-purpose flour
1   teaspoon salt
⅛   teaspoon pepper
2½ cups milk
2   cups shredded Cheddar cheese (½ pound)

¼   cup chopped pimiento
1   package (10 ounces) frozen chopped spinach, thawed and well drained
3   cups *cooked* rice (¾ to 1 cup uncooked)
6   to 8 ½-inch-thick slices Canadian bacon (about 1¼ pounds)

1. Preheat the oven to moderate (350°).

2. Sauté the onion in the butter in a medium-size saucepan until golden brown. Blend in the flour, salt and pepper. Add the milk and cook over medium heat, stirring constantly, until the sauce thickens and bubbles for 1 minute. Add 1½ cups of the cheese and stir until melted. Stir in the pimiento and spinach.

3. Spoon half of the rice into a greased 2-quart casserole. Top with half of the sauce. Repeat.

4. Overlap the Canadian bacon slices on top, pressing one edge of each into the rice mixture.

5. Bake in the preheated moderate oven (350°) for 30 minutes. Sprinkle the remaining cheese over the top and bake for 5 minutes longer, or until the cheese is melted and the rice mixture is hot and bubbly.

HUNGARIAN PORK CHOP BAKE

Sauerkraut and lima beans bake with pork chops in this oven meal.

Bake at 350° for 1 hour.

Makes 4 servings.

4	loin pork chops, cut ¾ inch thick	1	cup vegetable juice
½	teaspoon salt	½	teaspoon caraway seeds
⅛	teaspoon pepper	¼	teaspoon leaf thyme, crumbled
1	medium-size onion, sliced	1	package (10 ounces) frozen Fordhook lima beans
1	can (14 ounces) sauerkraut, drained and rinsed	½	cup dairy sour cream

1. Trim the pork chops of extra fat and score the fat edges 1 inch apart. Brown the chops in hot fat rendered from the chops or bacon drippings. Remove from the pan and season with salt and pepper.

2. Preheat the oven to moderate (350°).

3. Sauté the onion slices in same pan (they will separate into rings); stir in the sauerkraut, vegetable juice, caraway seeds, thyme and limas. Spread over a shallow 11¾ x 7½ x 1-inch baking pan. Arrange the pork chops on top and cover with aluminum foil.

4. Bake in the preheated moderate oven (350°) for 1 hour, or until tender.

5. Remove from the oven; move the chops to one end of the dish; stir the sour cream into the sauerkraut mixture; rearrange the chops and serve.

MEATLOAF BAKE

Bake at 350° for 1 hour and 30 minutes.
Makes 4 servings.

1½ pounds ground chuck
½ pound ground pork
1 medium-size onion, chopped (½ cup)
1 small sweet green pepper, chopped (½ cup)
2 celery stalks, chopped
¼ cup chopped parsley
4 slices bread, crumbled
2 eggs
½ cup milk
1 teaspoon salt
¼ teaspoon pepper
4 medium-size unpeeled potatoes, scrubbed and halved
2 green peppers, halved and seeded
2 sweet red peppers, halved and seeded
2 medium-size onions, quartered
Catsup Topping (recipe follows)

1. Preheat the oven to moderate (350°).
2. Combine the chuck, pork, onion, green pepper, celery, parsley, bread, eggs, milk, salt and pepper in a large bowl; mix well. Shape into a loaf and place in a large shallow baking pan.
3. Bake in the preheated moderate oven (350°) for 30 minutes.
4. Meanwhile, parboil the potatoes for 10 minutes. Place the potatoes, peppers and onions around the meat loaf; spread the Catsup Topping over the loaf. Return to the oven and bake for 1 hour longer, basting the vegetables several times with the pan liquids.

Catsup Topping: Combine ½ cup catsup, 1 teaspoon prepared mustard and ¼ teaspoon soy sauce in a cup; mix well.

BEEF AND BEANS

This hearty meal-in-one-dish is the modern version of one that sustained many a cattle driver along the old Chisholm Trail.

Bake at 325° for 2 hours.
Makes 8 servings.

½ pound small dry lima beans
½ pound dry pinto or kidney
   beans
6 cups water
3 slices bacon
4 cross cuts beef shank (3½ to
   4 pounds total weight)
2 tablespoons all-purpose
   flour
2 large onions, chopped
   (2 cups)

1 can (2 pounds, 3 ounces)
   Italian tomatoes
3 teaspoons salt
½ teaspoon pepper
¼ teaspoon crushed red
   pepper
1 teaspoon leaf thyme,
   crumbled
1 bay leaf

1. Pick over the beans and rinse them; place them in a large saucepan or kettle and add the water. Let stand overnight to soak.

2. Next day, bring the beans and liquid slowly to boiling; cover and simmer for 30 minutes. Drain the beans, reserving the liquid.

3. Preheat the oven to slow (325°).

4. Meanwhile, sauté the bacon until crisp in a large skillet. Remove the bacon and set it aside. Coat the beef shanks with the flour. Brown on all sides in the bacon drippings; transfer as they brown to a 12-cup baking dish. Add the beans to the baking dish.

5. Add the onions to the skillet; sauté, stirring often, until lightly browned and tender, 10 minutes. Stir in the remaining ingredients, except the bacon; bring to boiling, stirring and crushing the tomatoes. Pour over the beans and beef shanks. Cover.

6. Bake in the slow oven (325°) for 1 hour and 30 minutes to 2 hours, or until tender, stirring once or twice and adding some reserved bean liquid if the mixture becomes dry. Crumble the bacon over the top.

Note: To quick-soak the beans, boil the beans in the water for 2 minutes and let stand for 1 hour before simmering for 30 minutes.

PEPPERONI PASTA

All your favorite pizza flavorings served up as a spicy spaghetti sauce.

Makes 4 servings.

1 pound fettuccine, green noodles or spaghetti
¼ cup olive or vegetable oil
1 large onion, sliced
2 large cloves garlic, finely chopped
½ pound pepperoni sausage, sliced thin
2 medium-size sweet green peppers, halved, seeded and sliced

1 can (15 ounces) whole peeled tomatoes
1 teaspoon leaf oregano, crumbled
½ teaspoon salt
Freshly grated Parmesan cheese

1. Start cooking the pasta in boiling salted water following label directions.

2. Meanwhile, heat the oil in a large skillet over moderate heat. Add the onion, garlic, pepperoni and peppers and cook for 5 minutes, stirring often. Add the tomatoes, oregano and salt; cover and cook for 5 minutes longer, stirring two or three times. Uncover during the last minute to thicken the sauce slightly.

3. Drain the pasta and serve with the sauce, sprinkled with grated cheese.

5

Poultry Dishes

This chapter is devoted to showing how many delicious meals-in-one can be created from poultry, especially chicken. Chicken, one of the most versatile of protein sources, can be combined with fruits and vegetables in one-dish creations ranging from tropical to down-home cooking. As a tempting sample of chicken's versatility, try the Sweet and Pungent Chicken Breasts recipe (page 89), which shows how deliciously chicken can blend with tangy sauces, fruits and vegetables for an exquisite Oriental feast.

Poultry is both economical and low in calories, making it extremely important to today's thrifty and weight-conscious consumer. Poultry leftovers have limitless possibilities in many casseroles, and cooked chicken can be kept on hand in the freezer for preparing casseroles for unexpected guests. Most one-dish meals including chicken can usually be prepared in less than an hour. Another plus for chicken: It can be a substitute for many dishes specifying higher-priced veal.

WHY POULTRY IS NUTRITIOUS

Chicken is well suited to most dietary needs, providing complete protein at a moderate cost. It is a short-fibered meat and is easy to digest.

If you're cooking slim, chicken is the perfect choice. Chicken contains fewer calories than most meats. A 3½-ounce serving of broiled chicken (without the skin) has only about 136 calories. That same 3½-ounce serving, however, provides 31.2 grams of protein or 52 percent of the average adult daily requirements. Plus you get vitamin A, thiamine, riboflavin, niacin, iron and phosphorous.

More heartening news is that chicken also is lower in fats than most red meats. Three ounces of broiled chicken with skin yields about 9 grams of fat; that amount is doubled or tripled in equal portion to other meats. Chicken skin contains only about 17 percent fat, a small amount compared to the flavor it offers. Interestingly, the fat that is present is two-thirds unsaturated. This is good news especially for people watching their cholesterol intake.

For calorie-wise eating, rely on the addition of herbs and spices, such as rosemary, tarragon or dill, to enhance flavor.

Team chicken with low-calorie vegetables—broccoli, tomatoes, zucchini—instead of starchy fillers.

Cook chicken in low-cal ways—poached in broth, sautéed in a non-stick pan—instead of frying.

If you're really counting calories, don't eat the skin.

TYPES OF CHICKEN

Poultry is government graded to ensure quality. This grading system, U.S. Grade A (or No. 1), U.S. Grade B (or No. 2) and U.S. Grade C (or No. 3), is based on such factors as health, pep, fleshing and feathering. Animals that rate below these grades are rejected.

Here are the types of chickens available today:

Broiler-Fryer: A meaty, tender, all-purpose chicken that tastes good cooked by any method. It weighs around 2½ to 3½ pounds and is marketed at about 7 to 8 weeks.

Roaster: A slightly larger and older chicken. It weighs between 4½ to 6 pounds and is best roasted, as its name implies.

Stewing Chicken or Bro-Hen: A plump meaty bird, a year or a little older. It weighs around 4½ to 6 pounds. Because it is older, this chicken is tougher than either the roaster or broiler-fryer and is best stewed and used in soups, salads or casseroles.

Capon: A young male chicken that has been desexed. It's fleshy and tender with a high proportion of white meat. A capon can weigh from 6 to 9 pounds. It can be cooked many ways but is superb roasted.

Rock Cornish Game Hen: A special breed developed by crossing a Cornish game cock with a white Rock hen. It is marketed at 4 to 6 weeks and weighs 1½ pounds or less. It's popular with white meat lovers.

Chicken in Parts: Available in most markets today, making it possible to buy only those parts you prefer—all breasts, drumsticks, wings, thighs or combinations of any of the above. Skinned and boned breasts and chicken for scallopine are also available. If you're watching your budget, you might consider cutting up parts from a whole chicken.

HOW MUCH TO BUY

Chicken for frying: Allow ¾ to 1 pound per serving.

Chicken for roasting: Allow ¾ to 1 pound per serving.

Chicken for broiling or barbecuing: Allow ½ a chicken or 1 pound per serving.

Chicken for stewing: Allow ½ to 1 pound per serving.

Chicken livers: Allow ¼ pound per serving.

Rock Cornish Game Hen: Allow 1 game hen per person if weight is less than 1 pound.

THE THRIFTY CHICKEN

Whole birds are about 6 to 10 cents less per pound than cut-up chicken. It pays to buy a whole bird and cut it up yourself. Deboning your own chicken breast provides tremendous savings.

Buy chicken breast quarters (wings attatched) when available. They are less expensive the breast halves and you can easily remove the wings to freeze until you have enough for a bonus dish. As a main course allow four wings per person.

Save backs, giblets and bones removed during deboning. Add water and seasoning and simmer for stock.

Keep a container in the freezer for chicken livers. This way you can save them up until you have enough for a meal.

Substitute deboned chicken breasts for veal in your favorite Parmesan and scallopine recipes.

Another cents-saving idea, substitute less expensive chicken parts, such as thighs, in recipes calling for chicken breasts.

When buying a turkey, remember the bigger the bird the more meat there will be in proportion to bone. Half of a 20-pound bird, for example, will be meatier than a 10-pound bird—and less expensive per serving.

Chicken is a versatile meat that's compatible with many other foods. A little chicken will go a long way when you combine it with economical extenders like rice, pasta, dried beans, and sauce for a hearty hot casserole.

MORE POULTRY POINTS

• If you prefer all white or dark meat, you can substitute 2 pounds thighs or breasts for each cut-up chicken.

• Be on the lookout for oval casseroles that could just hold a chicken with an assortment of vegetables. They make such a special way to serve chicken!

• Chicken fillets are sometimes labeled as boneless breast of chicken.

• For smoke-free sautéing or frying of poultry, use equal parts butter or margarine and vegetable oil or olive oil. The addition of the oil increases the smoking temperature of the butter, giving you a more golden skin plus the flavor of the butter.

• You can substitute slices of raw turkey fillet for the boneless chicken in any recipe for stir-fried chicken.

• A few drops of lemon juice are often all that a chicken requires for a special taste. To obtain just a few drops, insert a wooden pick into a lemon; remove the pick and squeeze just the amount you need. Then return the pick to the hole to keep the rest of the juices in.

COUNTRY CHICKEN FRICASSEE

Reminds you of the home-cooked foods you enjoyed when you were a child. Richly browned chicken pieces are bathed in a cream gravy.

Makes 8 servings.

2 broiler-fryers, cut up (2½ pounds each)	1 cup chicken broth
½ cup all-purpose flour	1 cup milk
1 teaspoon seasoned salt	1 cup frozen peas (from a 1-pound bag)
¼ teaspoon seasoned pepper	1 cup frozen whole-kernel corn (from a 1-pound bag)
¼ cup vegetable oil or shortening	

1. Shake the chicken pieces, part at a time, in a mixture of the flour, seasoned salt and pepper in a plastic bag. Reserve the remaining seasoned flour.

2. Heat the oil or shortening until hot in a large skillet. Brown the chicken pieces, part at a time, in the hot oil; remove with tongs and reserve.

3. When all the chicken is fried, pour off all but ¼ cup of the pan drippings; return the chicken pieces to the pan; lower the heat, cover and simmer for 15 minutes, or until the chicken is tender when pierced with a two-tined fork. Remove the chicken to a heated serving platter and keep warm.

4. Sprinkle the reserved seasoned flour over the pan drippings. Cook, stirring constantly, until the mixture bubbles; stir in the chicken broth and milk. Cook, stirring constantly, until the sauce thickens and bubbles for 2 minutes.

5. Add the frozen peas and corn and cook for 3 minutes, or until the vegetables are tender. Spoon the cream gravy over the chicken on the platter. Serve with your favorite biscuits, if you wish.

POLYNESIAN CHICKEN

Pineapple and soy make delicate chicken exotic and delicious.

Makes 4 servings.

2 whole chicken breasts
(about 12 ounces each)
3 tablespoons teriyaki or soy
sauce
3 tablespoons peanut or
sesame seed oil
1 large onion, sliced (1 cup)
1 clove garlic, finely chopped
2 medium-size yellow squash,
trimmed and sliced

1 package (9 ounces) frozen
cut green beans
2 cups water
2 tablespoons dry sherry or
sake
1 can (8½ ounces) pineapple
chunks in syrup
2 tablespoons cornstarch
1 can (5 ounces) water
chestnuts, sliced

1. Remove the chicken from the bones and slice it into thin strips with a sharp knife.

2. Marinate the chicken in the teriyaki or soy sauce in a bowl for 15 minutes.

3. Heat the oil in a large skillet; remove the chicken from the marinade, reserving the marinade; brown the chicken quickly in the hot oil. Add the onion, garlic, squash and green beans. Sauté, stirring gently, for 3 minutes, or just until shiny and moist.

4. Add the reserved marinade, water and sherry or sake; cover and lower the heat; steam for 5 minutes.

5. While the vegetables steam, drain the syrup from the pineapple into a small cup; stir in the cornstarch to make a smooth paste.

6. Stir into the bubbling liquid and cook, stirring constantly, for 3 minutes; add the pineapple chunks and water chestnut slices and cook for 2 minutes. Serve over Chinese noodles, if you wish.

ZUCCHINI 'N' CHICKEN

You can blend the flavors of many nations into a quick and easy dish.

Makes 6 servings.

3 whole chicken breasts (about 12 ounces each)	½ pound mushrooms, sliced
⅓ cup olive or vegetable oil	1½ cups dry white wine
1 teaspoon salt	½ cup chicken broth
½ teaspoon pepper	2 tablespoons cornstarch
3 large zucchini, sliced	¼ cup cold water
1 clove garlic, finely chopped	2 tablespoons finely chopped parsley
2 tablespoons chopped chives or green onions	

1. Remove the skin and bones from the chicken and cut the meat into 1-inch pieces.

2. Heat the oil in a large skillet and sauté the chicken until brown; sprinkle with salt and pepper. Add the zucchini and toss to coat with the oil. Mix in the garlic and chives or green onions; then add mushrooms, dry white wine and chicken broth.

3. Bring to boiling; lower the heat and cover the skillet. Cook for 10 minutes, or until the chicken and zucchini are tender.

4. Increase the heat under the pan. Combine the cornstarch and cold water in a cup to make a smooth paste. Stir into the bubbling liquid. Cook, stirring constantly, until the sauce thickens and bubbles for 2 minutes. Sprinkle with the parsley just before serving.

CHICKEN BREASTS WITH APRICOTS

Quickly sautéed chicken breasts, sauced with a spinach cream sauce, are accompanied by small Belgian carrots and apricots.

Makes 6 servings.

6	boneless chicken breast halves (2¼ pounds total weight)	1	can (1 pound, 1 ounce) apricot halves, drained
2	tablespoons vegetable oil	1	can (16 ounces) Belgian carrots, drained
2	teaspoons butter	¼	cup finely chopped fresh spinach
3	tablespoons dry white wine		
¼	cup finely chopped green onion	¼	teaspoon salt
1	cup heavy cream	⅛	teaspoon white pepper

1. Sauté the chicken in the oil and butter in a large skillet, for about 6 minutes on each side, or until tender. Remove to a heated serving platter; keep warm.

2. Add the wine to the skillet, scraping up the browned bits over medium heat. Add the green onion and sauté for 3 minutes, or until tender. Add the cream, apricots, carrots, spinach, salt and pepper. Lower the heat; cook, stirring occasionally, for about 10 minutes, or until the sauce thickens and the apricots and carrots are heated through. Arrange the carrots and apricots around the chicken on the serving platter. Spoon the sauce over the chicken.

MEXICALI CHICKEN

Your whole dinner is mixed in one skillet and ready in minutes.

Makes 6 servings.

6	drumsticks with thighs (about 3 pounds total weight)	2	cans (12 ounces each) Mexican-style corn
6	slices bacon, halved	¾	cup milk
⅓	cup all-purpose flour	1	package (10 ounces) frozen lima beans
1	teaspoon salt		
¼	teaspoon pepper	1	cup thinly sliced celery

1. Cut through the chicken legs at the joints to separate the drumsticks and thighs.

2. Sauté the bacon until crisp in a large heavy skillet; remove with tongs and drain on paper toweling.

3. Brown the chicken pieces, part at a time, in the bacon drippings in the same pan; remove the chicken and pour off all but ⅓ cup of the pan drippings.

4. Stir the flour, salt and pepper into the drippings and cook, stirring constantly, until bubbly. Drain the liquid from the corn and add it with the milk to the flour mixture in the pan. Continue cooking and stirring until the gravy thickens and bubbles for 3 minutes. Return the chicken, arranging the pieces in a single layer; cover.

5. Simmer for 20 minutes; pile the chicken in the center of the pan.

6. Place the lima beans and celery at one side of the chicken in the pan; place the corn at other side; cover. Simmer for 5 minutes. Arrange the bacon over the chicken and continue cooking for 5 minutes, or until the bacon is heated through.

SWEET AND PUNGENT CHICKEN BREASTS

You can fix this chicken dish in a jiffy when you start with frozen chicken breasts.

Makes 4 servings.

1 **package (1 pound, 6 ounces) frozen breaded chicken breasts**	1 **medium-size sweet green pepper, halved, seeded and cut into slivers**
1 **can (8 ounces) pineapple chunks in pineapple juice**	2 **tablespoons vegetable oil**
⅓ **cup distilled white vinegar**	1 **medium-size tomato, cored and cut into wedges**
2 **tablespoons light brown sugar**	2 **tablespoons cornstarch**
1 **teaspoon soy sauce**	2 **tablespoons cold water**
½ **teaspoon crushed red pepper flakes**	**Hot cooked rice**

1. Prepare the chicken breasts following label directions.

2. Drain the juice from the pineapple into a 2-cup glass measure; reserve the pineapple chunks. Add enough water to the pineapple juice to make 1 cup of liquid; add the vinegar, brown sugar, soy sauce and red pepper flakes; stir to dissolve the brown sugar; reserve.

3. Stir-fry the green pepper in the oil in a large skillet until crisp-tender, for about 2 minutes. Add the pineapple juice-vinegar mixture, reserved pineapple chunks and tomato wedges; bring slowly to boiling. Lower the heat. Combine the cornstarch with the water in a small cup; stir into the skillet and cook just until thickened.

4. Arrange the baked chicken pieces on a serving platter; spoon the vegetables and fruit mixture over the chicken. Serve with hot cooked rice.

JAMAICAN LIVERS AND RICE

Pimiento, tomato and sliced olives give a tropical flavor to economical chicken livers.

Makes 4 servings.

1 **pound chicken livers, halved**	1½ **cups tomato juice**
¼ **cup vegetable oil**	1 **can (6 ounces) sliced**
½ **cup frozen chopped onion**	**mushrooms**
1 **small sweet green pepper,**	1 **small can (4 ounces)**
halved, seeded and diced	**pimiento, diced**
1 **clove garlic, finely chopped**	1 **teaspoon salt**
1½ **cups packaged enriched**	**Pinch of pepper**
pre-cooked rice	**Sliced green or black olives**

1. Brown the chicken livers in the oil in a large skillet; remove and keep warm.

2. Sauté the onion, green pepper and garlic in the oil for 5 minutes.

3. Return the chicken livers to the pan; add the rice, tomato juice, mushrooms and liquid, pimiento, salt and a generous grind of a pepper mill.

4. Bring to boiling; turn off the heat; let the rice stand until all liquid is absorbed, for about 5 minutes.

5. Fluff the rice and garnish with the green or black olive slices.

CHICKEN AND YELLOW RICE CUBAN STYLE

The Cubans who came to Florida in the early nineteenth century to start the cigar industry brought with them this dish they call Arroz con Pollo.

Bake at 350° for 30 minutes.
Makes 8 servings.

½	cup all-purpose flour	2	cups long-grain white rice
1	teaspoon salt	1	can (28 ounces) whole
½	teaspoon pepper		tomatoes
2	broiler-fryers (2 pounds	1	bay leaf
	each), cut up	¼	teaspoon liquid hot pepper
½	cup vegetable oil		seasoning
1	teaspoon achiote* (optional)	2½	cups water
1	large onion, chopped	3	envelopes or teaspoons
	(1 cup)		instant chicken broth
1	cup chopped sweet green	1	package (10 ounces) frozen
	pepper		peas
2	cloves garlic, finely chopped		Parsley sprigs

1. Combine the flour, salt and pepper in a paper or plastic bag. Add the chicken and shake to coat evenly. Heat ¼ cup of the oil in a large heavy skillet; add the achiote and brown for 5 minutes; discard the achiote. Add the chicken and brown on all sides. Place in a 6-quart baking dish.

2. Preheat the oven to moderate (350°).

3. Add the remaining oil to the skillet. Sauté the onion, green pepper and garlic until soft. Add the rice and cook, stirring frequently, for 5 minutes. Add the tomatoes, bay leaf, hot pepper seasoning, water and instant chicken broth; bring to boiling. Stir in the peas; pour the mixture over the chicken in the casserole; cover.

4. Bake in the preheated moderate oven (350°) for 30 minutes, or until the rice is tender. Garnish with the parsley sprigs.

*Achiote or annato seeds are found in Puerto Rican or Cuban food sections of some supermarkets.

PAELLA

A classic chicken, seafood and rice dish that's not as complicated as it may seem.

Bake at 350° for 1 hour.
Makes 8 servings.

1	broiler-fryer (2½ to 3 pounds), cut up	4	tomatoes, peeled and sliced
2	tablespoons all-purpose flour	1	bottle (8 ounces) clam juice
¼	cup olive or vegetable oil	1½	cups water
1½	cups long-grain white rice	1	teaspoon or envelope instant chicken broth
1	large onion, chopped (1 cup)	½	teaspoon salt
1	clove garlic, finely chopped	¼	teaspoon pepper
1	small sweet green pepper, chopped		Several saffron threads
1	pimiento, cut into thin strips	2	cans (8 ounces each) minced clams
1	cup frozen peas (from a 1-pound bag)	1	pound fresh or frozen shrimp, shelled and deveined

1. Coat the chicken pieces with the flour; brown the oil in a large skillet and place in a paella pan or 13 x 9 x 2-inch shallow casserole.
2. Preheat the oven to moderate (350°).
3. Sauté the rice, onion, garlic, green pepper and pimiento in the oil in the same pan, stirring often, for 10 minutes, or until the rice is golden. Spoon over and around the chicken in the dish; top with the peas and tomatoes.
4. Combine the clam juice, water, instant chicken broth, salt, pepper and saffron in the skillet and bring to boiling; pour over the mixture in the dish and cover.
5. Bake in the preheated moderate oven (350°) for 30 minutes. Add the clams and liquid and shrimp; cover and bake for 30 minutes longer, or until the chicken and rice are tender.

Note: If fresh steamer clams are available, buy 12 to 18 and use them in place of the canned minced clams. To cook: Scrub shells well; place in a large saucepan with 1 cup of water; cover; bring to boiling; simmer for 3 to 5 minutes, or until the shells open. Lift out with tongs. Strain the broth through cheesecloth to remove any sand. Measure the broth (you should have 1 cup); substitute for bottled clam juice in step 4. Use clams in shells in place of 2 cans of minced clams in step 5.

TURKEY-ICEBERG STIR-FRY

Cooked chicken can be substituted for the turkey in this recipe.

Makes 4 servings.

1	head iceberg lettuce	1	envelope or teaspoon instant chicken broth
1	medium-size onion, sliced (½ cup)	⅔	cup water
1	clove garlic, crushed and peeled	½	teaspoon leaf basil, crumbled
2	tablespoons peanut or vegetable oil	2	tablespoons lemon juice
6	medium-size carrots, pared and thinly sliced	1	teaspoon cornstarch
		2	cups diced cooked turkey

1. Core, rinse and drain the lettuce completely; shred and refrigerate in a plastic bag or plastic crisper.

2. Sauté the onion and garlic in the oil until soft in a wok or large skillet. Add the carrots and sauté until shiny; stir in the instant chicken broth, water and basil; cover the pan and steam for 5 minutes.

3. Combine the lemon juice and cornstarch in a cup, stirring until smooth. Stir into the skillet until the sauce thickens and bubbles for 3 minutes. Add the turkey and shredded lettuce and toss to coat the lettuce evenly. Serve immediately with Chinese fried noodles, if you wish.

POULET EN CASSEROLE

Classically French, yet easy on the cook. It's a meal-in-one-dish.

Bake at 325° for 1 hour and 15 minutes.
Makes 4 servings.

1	broiler-fryer (about 3 pounds)	½	cup boiling water
1½	teaspoons salt	1	teaspoon instant chicken broth
¼	teaspoon pepper	16	small white onions, peeled
12	small red new potatoes	1	teaspoon leaf basil, crumbled
3	tablespoons butter or margarine	1	tablespoon chopped parsley
3	tablespoons vegetable oil		

1. Sprinkle the chicken cavity with ½ teaspoon of the salt and the pepper. Scrub the potatoes and pare a band around the center of each.
2. Preheat the oven to slow (325°).
3. Melt the butter with the vegetable oil in a large heavy flameproof casserole or Dutch oven. Add the chicken and brown on all sides.
4. Combine the boiling water and chicken broth in a 1-cup glass measure, stirring until dissolved; add to the casserole.
5. Place the onions and potatoes around the chicken; sprinkle with the basil and remaining 1 teaspoon salt; cover.
6. Bake in the preheated slow oven (325°), basting once or twice with the juices, for 1 hour and 15 minutes, or until the chicken and vegetables are tender. Sprinkle with parsley.

QUICK MACARONI AND CHEESE DELUXE

A super dinner-in-a-dish that can be made with many
alternate ingredients.

Bake at 375° for 40 minutes.
Makes 4 servings.

1   package (8 ounces) elbow
    macaroni
1   can (10¾ ounces)
    condensed cream of chicken
    soup OR: 1 can (10¾
    ounces) condensed cream of
    mushroom soup
1½ cups shredded Cheddar or
    Swiss cheese
½   cup mayonnaise or salad
    dressing
1   teaspoon dry mustard

1   teaspoon salt
¼   teaspoon cayenne or black
    pepper
1   package (10 ounces) frozen
    chopped spinach, cooked
    and well drained OR: 1
    package (10 ounces) frozen
    chopped broccoli, cooked
    and well drained
1   cup diced cooked chicken or
    turkey

1. Preheat the oven to moderate (375°).
2. Cook the macaroni following label directions; drain and keep hot.
3. Combine the soup, cheese, mayonnaise, dry mustard, salt and
cayenne in a large bowl. Add the macaroni and stir well.
4. Spoon the cooked spinach over the bottom of a lightly buttered,
deep 2-quart casserole. Top with the chicken. Spoon the macaroni
mixture over the top.
5. Bake in the preheated moderate oven (375°) for 40 minutes, or
until bubbly hot. Let stand for 5 minutes before serving.

TURKEY CASSEROLE

You can make good use of leftovers with this handy recipe.

Bake at 375° for 35 minutes.
Makes 4 servings.

2	tablespoons butter or margarine	1	can (2 ounces) sliced mushrooms
2½	tablespoons all-purpose flour	2	cups diced cooked turkey
½	teaspoon salt	¼	cup chopped sweet green pepper
¼	teaspoon prepared mustard	1	package (16 ounces) frozen crinkle-cut French-fried potatoes
¼	teaspoon Worcestershire sauce		
1	cup milk	¼	teaspoon seasoned salt
¾	cup shredded Cheddar cheese		

1. Preheat the oven to moderate (375°).

2. Melt the butter in a large saucepan. Stir in the flour, salt, mustard and Worcestershire; cook for 1 minute. Remove from the heat; stir in the milk until smooth. Cook, stirring constantly, until thickened and bubbly.

3. Add ½ cup of the cheese, stirring until the cheese is melted; stir in the mushrooms, turkey and green pepper. Spoon into a 10 x 6 x 2-inch shallow baking dish; top with the potatoes.

4. Bake in the preheated moderate oven (375°) for 30 minutes, or until bubbly hot. Sprinkle with the remaining cheese and seasoned salt. Bake for 5 minutes longer, or until the cheese is melted.

CAREFREE CASSEROLE

Bake at 350° for 20 minutes.
Makes 6 servings.

1	package (10 ounces) frozen peas and carrots	½	cup milk
1	can (10¾ ounces) condensed cream of mushroom soup	3	cups *cooked* rice
		1½	cups diced cooked chicken
½	cup water	½	cup shredded process American cheese

1. Preheat the oven to moderate (350°).
2. Combine the peas, carrots, soup, water and milk in a medium-size saucepan. Bring to boiling; lower the heat and simmer for 3 minutes. Spoon half the mixture into a 1½-quart baking dish.
3. Spoon the cooked rice over the vegetable mixture. Layer the chicken over the rice; sprinkle with salt and top with the remaining vegetable mixture. Sprinkle the top with cheese.
4. Bake in the preheated moderate oven (350°) for 20 minutes or until bubbly hot.

GARBANZO CASSEROLE

A simplified version of the Basque soup-stew Olla Podrida.
Bake at 325° for 1 hour.
Makes 8 servings.

½	pound pepperoni, sliced	2	cups shredded cabbage
2	whole chicken breasts (about 12 ounces total weight)	2	cans (19 ounces each) chick-peas (garbanzos) drained
1	large leek, chopped OR: 1 large onion, chopped (1 cup)	1	can (16 ounces) tomatoes
		1	tablespoon salt
2	cloves garlic, finely chopped	1	teaspoon leaf thyme, crumbled
4	medium-size carrots, pared and sliced	½	teaspoon pepper

1. Sauté the pepperoni in a 3-quart flameproof casserole or large skillet for 5 minutes; remove with a slotted spoon. Cut the chicken breast into 2-inch pieces with kitchen shears.
2. Preheat the oven to slow (325°).
3. Brown the chicken pieces in the pan drippings and remove them with a slotted spoon. Sauté the leek and garlic in the pan drippings; stir in the carrots and cook for 3 minutes; stir in the cabbage and cook for 2 minutes. Add the chick-peas, tomatoes, salt, thyme and pepper and stir to blend well. Return the pepperoni and chicken to the casserole, or spoon the mixture into a 3-quart casserole; cover.
4. Bake in the preheated slow oven (325°) for 1 hour, or until the chicken is tender.

OVER 386 CASSEROLES

Treat your family to a different casserole every night of the year and never repeat once. That's the beauty of this chart which shows you how to team chicken with a starch, vegetable, and sauce to create your best-ever family meals.

Start with your family's favorite, or use parts on supermarket special.

THE WHOLE CHICKEN Brown 1 cut-up chicken, about 2½ pounds, in 2 tablespoons vegetable oil until golden. Season with salt and pepper.

CHICKEN BREASTS Sauté 2 whole chicken breasts, split, about 1½ pounds, in 2 tablespoons butter or margarine for 5 minutes.

CHICKEN THIGHS Fry 8 thighs, about 1½ pounds, in 2 tablespoons butter-flavored vegetable shortening until golden. Sprinkle with seasoned pepper.

WINGS AND DRUMSTICKS Brown 8 chicken wings or drumsticks, about 1½ pounds, in 2 tablespoons vegetable shortening until tender.

Choose any starch from the selection below and use it to line an 8-cup casserole.

3 cups sliced, cooked potatoes seasoned with sautéed onions

4 servings instant mashed potatoes tossed with sliced green onion

1 cup packaged precooked rice cooked in beef broth and chopped parsley

1 package (7 ounces) chicken-flavored rice mix, cooked

8-ounce package noodles, cooked and tossed with toasted sesame seeds

1 cup raw ziti, cooked and tossed with olive oil and mashed garlic

---

1 pound bag frozen French-fried potatoes, cooked and drained

1 package (5¼ ounces) scalloped potato mix, prepared in saucepan

1 cup brown rice, cooked and tossed with sliced almonds

1 package (6¾ ounces) long grain and wild rice mix, cooked

1 cup raw elbow macaroni, cooked in tomato juice and water

8 ounces thin spaghetti cooked *al dente,* drained and tossed in oil

---

Select any vegetable below and add with the browned chicken to the starch in the casserole.

---

1 pound bag frozen peas, cooked and drained

3 small zucchini, sliced and par-boiled, seasoned with oregano

4 large carrots, pared, sliced and parboiled

1 package (10 ounces) frozen lima beans, seasoned with Italian herbs

---

1 bag frozen mixed vegetables, cooked and drained

2 cucumbers, pared, sliced and parboiled

1 pound green beans, tipped and cut-up and blanched

2 cups sliced celery, sautéed in oil

Top with a sauce and bake in moderate oven (375°) for 30 minutes, or until bubbly.

Dilute 1 can condensed cream of mushroom soup with ½ cup milk; add shredded cheese

Stir leaf basil into a 15-ounce can of tomato sauce

Add ½ cup dry red wine to 1 cup beef broth

Make your favorite 2-cup white sauce and stir in ½ cup grated Parmesan cheese and crumbled rosemary

---

Spoon 1 jar (15½ ounces) chunky garden-style spaghetti sauce over and top with shredded mozzarella cheese

1 jar chicken gravy with ½ cup dry white wine and chopped chives

Thicken 2 cups chicken broth with 2 tablespoons cornstarch; add thyme

Add ½ cup light cream to 1 can condensed cream of chicken soup; add crumbled sage

---

You can substitute 2 cups diced cooked turkey or goose, or 8 slices cooked turkey, or 2 cooked Rock Cornish hens, split, for the chicken in the casseroles above.

CHICKEN CHILI

Substitute chicken thighs for ground beef and the most dedicated chili fan will still be delighted.

Makes 12 servings.

1	bag (2 pounds) dried pinto or red kidney beans	1	can (29 ounces) tomatoes
	Water	1	tablespoon salt
2	pounds chicken thighs	2	teaspoons leaf thyme, crumbled
¼	cup vegetable oil	½	teaspoon pepper
2	large onions, chopped (2 cups)		Shredded lettuce
2	to 4 cloves garlic, finely chopped		Shredded Monterey Jack or Cheddar cheese
1	to 4 tablespoons chili powder		Dairy sour cream

1. Wash and pick over the beans; place in a large kettle or Dutch oven; add water to a depth of 2 inches over the beans; bring to boiling; cook for 1 minute; cover the kettle. Allow to stand for 1 hour.

2. Return the beans to boiling; lower the heat and simmer for 2 hours, or until the bean skins burst when blown on. Drain the beans and reserve the cooking liquid.

3. Remove the skin and bones from the chicken thighs; cut the meat into chunks; brown in the vegetable oil in a large kettle or Dutch oven; remove and reserve.

4. Sauté the onions and garlic in the pan drippings until soft; stir in the chili powder and cook for 2 minutes; stir in the tomatoes, breaking them up with the back of a spoon, and salt, thyme and pepper; bring mixture to boiling.

5. Add the reserved chicken, cooked beans and just enough cooking liquid to cover the beans; stir to blend well. Bring to boiling; lower the heat and simmer for 3 hours, adding more cooking liquid if needed, or until the beans are tender.

6. Spoon into a serving bowl and top with shredded lettuce, shredded cheese and sour cream.

CHICKEN SALAD DELUXE

Makes 6 servings.

½ cup mayonnaise
½ cup plain yogurt
1 tablespoon prepared mustard
Dash of lemon juice
4 cups diced cooked chicken
1 can (15 ounces) pineapple chunks, drained
1 cup chopped celery (2 stalks)
½ cup chopped sweet green pepper

2 tablespoons grated onion
½ cup sliced pitted black olives
1 can (11 ounces) mandarin oranges, drained
½ cup cashew nut pieces
Leaf lettuce
1 can (5-ounces) chow mein noodles
1½ cups alfalfa sprouts
Parsley sprigs

1. Combine the mayonnaise, yogurt, mustard and lemon juice in a large bowl. Mix until smooth.

2. Add the chicken, pineapple, celery, green pepper, onion, olives, mandarin oranges and cashews to the mayonnaise mixture. Toss gently to coat with the dressing. Cover and refrigerate the salad until serving time.

3. To serve, spoon the salad onto a lettuce-lined platter and top with the chow mein noodles, alfalfa sprouts and parsley.

6

Seafood Dishes

When preparation time is a consideration, seafood should be your first choice. Most seafood can be prepared in minutes, and its versatility is a marvel. Seafood works wonderfully in combination with cream or wine sauces, vegetables, rice or pasta in oven-baked casseroles or top-of-the-range skillet meals. Serve it cold with a multitude of complementary ingredients, or top a favorite pasta with a tuna-flavored tomato sauce, as in Neptune Spaghetti (page 104).

Most types of popular seafoods are available in either canned or frozen form. This is beneficial to cooks in those sections of the country where fresh seafood is not readily available. The convenience, cost savings, adaptability and nutritional content make them a favorite staple in many kitchens. For example, Spicy Shrimp and Cheese on Rice (page 110) is an elegant dinner party selection.

Also included are some "do-ahead" recipes, such as our Hot Tuna Bake (page 105) and Scandinavian Salmon Bake (page 107), which allow the host or hostess the luxury of enjoying guests without having to bustle about with last-minute preparations.

NEPTUNE SPAGHETTI

A can of tuna makes this delightfully different tomato sauce for spaghetti.

Makes 4 servings.

1 medium-size onion, chopped (½ cup)	¼ teaspoon leaf basil, crumbled
¼ cup chopped sweet green pepper	¼ teaspoon leaf oregano, crumbled
1 tablespoon vegetable oil	⅛ teaspoon pepper
2 cups tomato purée (from a 29-ounce can)	1 can (6½ ounces) chunk tuna
1 cup water	1 can (8 ounces) tomato sauce
1 celery stalk, thinly sliced	½ cup chopped parsley
½ teaspoon salt	1 pound spaghetti, cooked

1. Sauté the onion and green pepper in the oil in a large saucepan until tender, about 3 minutes. Add the tomatoes, water, celery, salt, basil, oregano and pepper; bring to boiling. Lower the heat; simmer, uncovered, stirring occasionally, for about 30 minutes, or until slightly thickened.
2. Drain the tuna; flake coarsely. Add to the saucepan with the tomato sauce and parsley; heat just until bubbly. Pour over the spaghetti.

BAKED TUNA BOAT

Bits of cheese melt while the celery stays crisp in this popular sandwich.

Bake at 400° for 20 minutes.
Makes 4 servings.

1 can (6½ ounces) tuna, drained	¼ cup mayonnaise
½ cup diced celery	3 drops liquid red pepper seasoning
¼ cup chopped sweet pickles	½ teaspoon salt
2 tablespoons chopped green onion	1 teaspoon lemon juice
½ cup cubed Muenster cheese	1 loaf French bread
	2 tablespoons melted butter

1. Preheat the oven to hot (400°).
2. Combine the tuna, celery, pickles, onions and cheese in a medium-size bowl.

3. Blend the mayonnaise, red pepper seasoning, salt and lemon juice in a cup. Pour over the tuna mixture; toss lightly.

4. Cut a thin slice from the top of the bread; hollow out, leaving a ½-inch wall. Spoon the filling into the bread. Replace the top; brush all over with the butter. Wrap in aluminum foil and place on a cookie sheet.

5. Bake in the preheated hot oven (400°) for 20 minutes.

HOT TUNA BAKE

A wonderful combination of tuna and mozzarella cheese,
accented with onion and green pepper.

Bake at 375° for 45 minutes.
Makes 4 servings.

8 slices firm whole wheat or white bread, lightly toasted	4 ounces mozzarella cheese, shredded (1 cup)
1 can (6½ ounces) tuna	2 eggs
¼ cup chopped sweet green pepper	2 cups milk
1 small onion, diced (¼ cup)	½ teaspoon leaf oregano, crumbled
¾ teaspoon salt	

1. Place 4 slices of the bread in a buttered 6-cup shallow baking dish.

2. Drain the tuna; combine it with the green pepper, onion and ¼ teaspoon of the salt in medium-size bowl. Stir in half the shredded cheese. Spread over the bread. Top with the remaining 4 slices of bread.

3. Beat eggs in same bowl. Stir in the milk, the remaining ½ teaspoon salt and oregano. Pour the milk mixture over the bread; sprinkle with the remaining cheese. Cover and refrigerate for at least 1 hour or overnight. Press the bread down into milk before baking.

4. Preheat the oven to moderate (375°). Bake in the preheated moderate oven (375°) for 45 minutes, or until puffed and golden. Remove from the oven. Let stand for 10 minutes before serving.

SAVINGS ON SEAFOOD

Canned mackerel is less expensive than tuna and is a flavorful substitute in sandwich fillings and casseroles.

Save the oil from cans of tuna, sardines and anchovies to use in cooking and salad dressings.

CREAMED TUNA SHORTCAKE

A creamy tuna-vegetable mixture served over hot biscuits stretches
a can of tuna to more servings.

Bake at 400° for 15 minutes.
Makes 4 servings.

2	cups *sifted* all-purpose flour	3	tablespoons all-purpose flour
1	teaspoon salt	¼	teaspoon dry mustard
3	teaspoons baking powder	¼	teaspoon salt
¼	cup vegetable shortening	⅛	teaspoon pepper
¾	cup reconstituted dry skim milk	1½	cups reconstituted dry skim milk
1	can (6½ ounces) tuna	⅛	teaspoon dried dillweed
½	cup chopped celery	¼	cup cubed pasteurized process cheese spread
1	small onion, chopped (¼ cup)	1	cup frozen peas (from 10-ounce package)
¼	cup (½ stick) margarine		

1. Preheat the oven to hot (400°).

2. Make the shortcake: Combine the flour, salt, and baking powder in a medium-size bowl. Cut in the shortening with a pastry blender or fork until crumbly.

3. Stir in ¾ cup milk, mixing lightly with a fork just until the pastry is moistened.

4. Place on a lightly floured surface; knead 10 times. Roll or pat the dough to a ½-inch thickness. Place in a greased 8-inch round baking pan.

5. Bake in the preheated hot oven (400°) for 15 minutes, or just until golden.

6. While the shortcake is baking, make the tuna filling: Drain the tuna; place in the bowl used to prepare the pastry; flake. Sauté the celery and onion in 1 tablespoon of the margarine. Remove to the bowl with the tuna. Heat the remaining 3 tablespoons margarine in the same skillet; stir in the flour, mustard, salt and pepper. Cook for 1 minute. Slowly stir in the milk. Cook, stirring constantly, until the sauce thickens. Stir in dillweed, cheese and peas until the cheese melts.

7. To serve, loosen the shortcake around the edge with a knife; remove to a serving platter; split in half. Place the tuna mixture on the bottom; replace the top; cut into quarters and serve.

SCANDINAVIAN SALMON BAKE

Dill adds a distinctive Danish flavor to a biscuit-topped casserole.

Bake at 400° for 20 minutes.
Makes 4 servings.

3 tablespoons butter or margarine
1 medium-size onion, chopped (½ cup)
½ cup frozen chopped sweet green pepper
3 tablespoons all-purpose flour
2 teaspoons dried dillweed
½ teaspoon salt

Pinch of pepper
2 cups milk
1 can (7¾ ounces) pink salmon
2 teaspoons lemon juice
1 package (10 ounces) frozen peas
1 package (8 ounces) refrigerator biscuits, separated

1. Preheat the oven to hot (400°).
2. Melt the butter in a medium-size saucepan; add the onion and green pepper; sauté for 5 minutes.
3. Blend in the flour, dillweed, salt and pepper; cook, stirring constantly, until the mixture bubbles; stir in the milk slowly.
4. Cook, stirring constantly, until the sauce thickens and bubbles for 2 minutes. Flake the salmon with its liquid into the sauce; add the lemon juice and peas; bring to boiling, stirring often.
5. Pour into 6-cup shallow casserole; arrange the biscuits on top.
6. Bake in the preheated hot oven (400°) for 20 minutes, or until the biscuits are golden.

QUICK-CHANGE SOUFFLÉ

For the soufflé, you will need six eggs and some basic seasonings.
There is a choice of other ingredients to make and flavor the dish
according to what you have on hand.

Bake at 325° for 50 minutes.
Makes 6 servings.

4 tablespoons butter or margarine	1 to 1½ cups shredded or finely diced Cheddar, American or Muenster cheese OR: 1 to 1½ cups mixed odds and ends of diced cheeses OR: 1 can (6½ ounces) tuna, drained and flaked
6 tablespoons all-purpose flour	
1½ cups milk	
1 can (10¾ ounces) condensed cream of celery, mushroom or chicken soup	
	1 teaspoon dried dillweed
2 teaspoons parsley flakes	6 eggs, separated
1 teaspoon salt	1 can (7 ounces) whole-kernel corn with sweet peppers OR: 1 cup cooked mixed vegetables
⅛ teaspoon cayenne pepper	

1. Melt the butter in a medium-size saucepan; stir in the flour; cook, stirring constantly, just until bubbly. Stir in the milk, parsley, salt and cayenne. Cook and stir until the sauce thickens and bubbles for 1 minute. Add the cheese or tuna and dillweed. Stir until the cheese is melted. Remove from the heat.

2. Or, if using one of the soups, pour the soup into a medium-size saucepan; add the parsley, salt and cayenne; stir in the cheese or tuna and dillweed. Heat, stirring constantly, until the cheese is melted or the mixture is hot. Remove from the heat; cool slightly.

3. Preheat the oven to slow (325°).

4. Add the egg yolks, one at a time, beating well with a wooden spoon after each addition. Stir in the corn or mixed vegetables.

5. Beat the egg whites in a large bowl with an electric mixer or wire whisk, just until they form *soft* peaks. (Do not overbeat.) Stir one fourth of the egg whites into the yolk mixture; then fold the yolk mixture into the remaining egg whites until no streaks of white remain. Pour into a buttered 10-cup soufflé or straight-sided baking dish. For "top hat" effect, draw a deep groove through the soufflé mixture 1 inch in from the edge with a teaspoon or metal spatula.

6. Bake in the preheated slow oven (325°) for 50 minutes, or until puffy-firm and golden on top. Serve at once.

SHRIMP AND SAUSAGE JAMBALAYA

Makes 8 servings.

1	medium-size onion, chopped (½ cup)	1	can (13¾ ounces) chicken broth
½	cup chopped sweet green pepper	1	teaspoon salt
½	cup chopped celery	½	teaspoon leaf savory, crumbled
¼	pound chaurice (chorizo) sausage or other hot sausage, sliced ¼ inch thick	½	teaspoon liquid red pepper seasoning
2	tablespoons butter or margarine	1	pound frozen shelled and deveined shrimp
1½	cups long-grain white rice	½	pound cooked ham, diced
2	cups tomato juice	½	cup chopped green onion
			Chopped parsley

1. Sauté the onion, green pepper, celery and sausage in the butter in a large heavy Dutch oven for 5 minutes. Add the rice; cook and stir for 1 minute. Add the tomato juice, chicken broth, salt, savory and red pepper seasoning. Bring to boiling; lower the heat; cover. Simmer, stirring occasionally, for 20 minutes.

2. Stir in the shrimp and ham; continue cooking for 15 minutes longer, or until the rice and shrimp are tender. Stir in the green onion. Serve sprinkled generously with chopped fresh parsley.

SHRIMP WITH FETA CHEESE

Makes 6 servings.

2	cans (16 ounces each) stewed tomatoes	¼	pound feta cheese, crumbled
1	package (1 pound) frozen shelled and deveined shrimp	4	cups hot *cooked* brown rice (1⅓ cups uncooked)
		¼	cup chopped parsley

1. Simmer the tomatoes in a large skillet for 10 to 15 minutes, or until the tomato liquid is reduced by about half.

2. Add the shrimp; simmer just until they begin to turn pink; sprinkle with the cheese. Cover the skillet; simmer for about 5 minutes longer, or until the shrimp are cooked and the cheese is hot.

3. Spoon the rice onto a large serving platter and top with the shrimp mixture. Sprinkle with the parsley.

SPICY SHRIMP AND CHEESE ON RICE

Makes 12 servings.

2 cups chopped celery
2 cups chopped sweet green pepper
1 cup (2 sticks) butter
2 pounds fresh shrimp, shelled and deveined OR: 1½ pounds frozen shelled and deveined shrimp
2 tablespoons all-purpose flour

1 pound pasteurized process cheese spread, shredded
1 pound sharp Cheddar cheese, shredded (4 cups)
2 cans (10 ounces each) tomatoes with chilies
2 cans (6 ounces each) whole mushrooms, drained
6 cups hot cooked rice

1. Sauté the celery and green pepper in the butter in a very large skillet or Dutch oven until tender, for about 5 minutes. Add the shrimp; sauté 5 minutes longer, or until they are pink.
2. Stir in the flour, cheeses, tomatoes with chilies and mushrooms. Cook over low heat until thickened and thoroughly hot. Serve over hot cooked rice.

SHRIMP AND AVOCADO HAITIAN STYLE

Here's a fast skillet dish that could become your favorite "special" for company.

Makes 4 servings.

1 pound frozen shelled and deveined shrimp
1 medium-size onion, finely chopped (½ cup)
¼ cup diced celery
½ cup chopped sweet green pepper
2 tablespoons butter or margarine
1 bay leaf

1 teaspoon finely chopped parsley
⅓ cup tomato paste
1¾ cups water
1 teaspoon salt
Dash of liquid red pepper seasoning
2 medium-size avocados
Hot cooked rice

1. Cook the shrimp following label directions.
2. Sauté the onion, celery and green pepper in the butter in a large

skillet until soft. Stir in the bay leaf, parsley, tomato paste, water, salt and red pepper seasoning.

3. Bring to boiling; lower the heat and simmer, stirring occasionally, for 20 minutes. Remove the bay leaf.

4. Halve, pit and peel the avocados. Cut into slices; add with the shrimp to the skillet. Heat just until thoroughly warmed. Spoon into a serving dish. Garnish with parsley, if you wish. Serve with hot cooked rice.

SEAFOOD LOUISIAN IN AVOCADO

Makes 12 servings.

1	cup mayonnaise	1	teaspoon salt
2	tablespoons French dressing (oil and vinegar type)		Pinch of pepper
½	cup chili sauce		Lobster: cooked meat from 4 lobster tails or 2 whole lobsters
1	tablespoon onion, finely chopped	1	pound shrimp, cooked, peeled and deveined
2	tablespoons drained capers	½	pound deluxe crabmeat
2	teaspoons lemon juice	6	large avocados
2	teaspoons bottled horseradish		Lemon juice
½	teaspoon Worcestershire sauce		

1. Combine the mayonnaise, French dressing, chili sauce, onion, capers, lemon juice, horseradish, Worcestershire, salt and pepper in a large bowl; stir until smooth.

2. Add the lobster, shrimp and crabmeat; toss lightly just until mixed. Chill until ready to serve.

3. To serve, halve the avocados and remove the pits. Brush the cut surfaces with lemon juice to prevent darkening. Spoon the seafood into the avocado cavities.

HOW TO KNOW WHEN SHRIMP ARE COOKED

When shrimp turn pink, they are cooked. To prevent overcooking, don't boil them, just simmer. Also, remove them from the cooking liquid immediately, or they will keep on cooking and toughen.

AVOCADO HALVES WITH TUNA SALAD

Warm cheese biscuits and a frosty fruit sherbet are good go-withs.

Makes 6 servings.

⅓ cup mayonnaise or salad dressing
¼ cup light cream
1 can (9¼ ounces) tuna, drained
1 medium-size onion, finely chopped
1 clove garlic, crushed and peeled
1 cucumber, pared and diced
6 pimiento-stuffed green olives, chopped
1 teaspoon salt
3 large avocados
Lemon juice

1. Combine the mayonnaise and cream in a small bowl; stir until smooth. Flake the tuna into the same bowl. Add the onion, garlic, cucumber, olives and salt; toss lightly until just mixed. Chill until serving time.
2. Halve the avocados and remove the pits. Brush the cut surfaces with lemon juice to prevent darkening. Spoon the tuna mixture into the avocado cavities. Garnish with a sprig of watercress, if you wish.

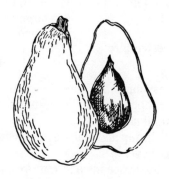

AVOCADO FACTS

• To fast-ripen an avocado, place it overnight in a very slow oven (175° or less).
• To cut an avocado without mashing it, peel it gently, then cut.
• When an avocado is too ripe to slice for a salad, mash it to make guacamole. Grow a handsome avocado plant from the pit.

OYSTER LOAF

A legendary peace offering from errant husbands to their irate wives.

Bake at 350° for 15 minutes.
Makes 4 servings.

1 can (8 ounces) whole oysters, drained	1 loaf French bread (about 15 inches)
¼ cup all-purpose flour	¼ cup (½ stick) butter, melted
⅛ teaspoon cayenne pepper	Vegetable oil
1 egg, beaten	1 cup shredded lettuce
1 teaspoon milk	1 tomato, thinly sliced
¼ teaspoon salt	Chili sauce
½ cup packaged bread crumbs	Lemon wedges

1. Coat the oysters with the flour mixed with the cayenne pepper. Dip in the egg beaten with the milk and salt; coat with the bread crumbs. Refrigerate for about 30 minutes to set the coating on the oysters.

2. Preheat the oven to moderate (350°).

3. Cut a thin slice from the top of the loaf; hollow it out, leaving a ½-inch shell. Brush the loaf and top slice inside and out with melted butter. Place on a cookie sheet.

4. Toast in the preheated moderate oven (350°) for 15 minutes.

5. Meanwhile, pour oil to a 1½-inch depth into a medium-size saucepan; heat to 375°. Fry the oysters, a few at a time for 2 to 3 minutes, or until golden. Drain on paper toweling.

6. Fill the hot toasted loaf with a layer of shredded lettuce, then the tomato slices and finally the hot oysters. Cover with the top of the loaf. Serve with chili sauce and lemon wedges.

SWEET AND SOUR SCALLOP KABOBS

Bake at 400° for 22 minutes.
Makes 6 servings.

1 package (6¼ ounces) fried rice mix with vermicelli and almonds OR: 1 package (7 ounces) instant fried rice mix
1 package (10 ounces) frozen Brussels sprouts, partially thawed and each halved
1 can (16 ounces) whole carrots, drained
1 tablespoon vegetable oil

2 packages (8 ounces each) frozen batter-fried scallops, partially thawed
¾ cup apricot or peach preserves
3 tablespoons sweet and spicy bottled French dressing
2 tablespoons prepared mustard
½ teaspoon ground ginger

1. Cook the rice mix following label directions; keep warm.
2. Preheat the oven to hot (400°).
3. Gently toss the Brussels sprouts and carrots with the oil in a large bowl. Thread the scallops, sprouts and carrots alternately on six 15-inch metal skewers. Place on a foil-lined jelly-roll pan, allowing the skewers to rest on the edge of the pan so that the ingredients do not touch the bottom of the pan.
4. Bake in the preheated hot oven (400°) for 20 minutes.
5. Combine the preserves, French dressing, mustard and ginger in a small saucepan; bring to boiling. Brush some of the sauce over the kabobs; bake for 2 minutes more, or until glazed.
6. Spoon the rice onto a warm platter; arrange the kabobs on top. Pass the remaining sauce.

FISH AND VEGETABLE TEMPURA

Makes 4 servings.

1 small bunch broccoli
3 large carrots
3 medium-size potatoes
2 eggs
1 cup water
¾ cup all-purpose flour

Vegetable oil for frying
1 pound fresh or frozen fish
fillets, cut into 1-inch pieces
(cod, flounder or other
white fish)

1. Cut off the woody stems of the broccoli. Separate the flowerets and cut stems into ¼-inch-thick strips. Peel and halve the carrots; cut into ¼-inch-thick strips. Cook the broccoli and carrots in boiling water for 3 minutes; drain and plunge into cold water. Pare and cut the potatoes into ⅛-inch-thick slices; place in cold water.
2. Beat the eggs and water until frothy; stir in the flour just until smooth; set the bowl in a larger bowl filled with ice to keep the batter cool.
3. Heat a 1-inch depth of oil in a large heavy kettle to 375°. Dip the drained vegetables and fish into the batter; fry a few pieces at a time until the vegetables are crisp-tender and the fish is flaky. Drain on paper toweling.

FRESHENING FISH

To give fish a fresh flavor, soak it in salted warm water for 5 minutes; dry on paper toweling; then add to your recipe.

7

Vegetarian Meals

Vegetables, especially when combined with eggs, dairy products, pasta, rice or legumes, make a much desired choice in today's preferred lighter cuisine. When carefully planned, vegetable dishes provide a nutritionally complete meal that is low in calories, and relatively inexpensive. The variety of hearty ingredients reassure the most devout meat-eaters that even *they* may never miss meat.

A classic example of a hearty vegetarian dish is the Spinach Mold (page 122), which can be made with either frozen chopped spinach or broccoli. This excellent dish combines the green vegetable and eggs with a seasoned stuffing mix to give it texture and substance. Served with steamed squash and mushrooms, it is sure to be a favorite.

Vegetarian combinations will persuade "finicky" eaters to get their daily requirements of certain less desired foods, such as spinach, eggs, milk, yogurt, etc. One such example is Linguini with Broccoli, Green Onion and Ricotta Cheese Sauce (page 129). The slowly simmered ricotta and mozzarella cheese sauce, when combined with broccoli flowerets, would convert even the staunchest broccoli hater.

Another redeeming factor for vegetarian meals-in-one is they put very little strain on the budget. With a little preplanning, nutritionally complete vegetarian meals can be substituted regularly for meals which center around meat. A chart for meatless protein alternatives, as well as one for general tips for vegetarian diets, both included in this chapter, could be a starting point to planning more meatless meals-in-one. We've broadened the definition of 'vegetarian' to include some specific recipes that call for fish. The recipes: Pasta Niçoise, (page 130), Scalloped Vegetables and Fish (page 133), and Tuna Aioli (page 133).

MINESTRONE WITH VEGETABLES

Use uncooked leftover vegetables for this rich, thick soup.

Makes 4 servings.

3 tablespoons olive or vegetable oil
1 medium-size onion, finely chopped (½ cup)
1 celery stalk, finely chopped (⅓ cup)
1 small clove garlic, chopped
½ teaspoon leaf rosemary, crumbled
4 cups chopped vegetables (We used carrots, cauliflower, broccoli, a 1-pound can tomatoes, frozen peas. Other suggestions: turnips, green beans, cabbage, zucchini, escarole.)

3½ cups hot water
3 envelopes instant vegetable broth
¼ cup small pasta (such as spaghetti rings)
2 tablespoons minced parsley
½ cup grated Parmesan cheese

1. Heat the oil in a large saucepan; sauté the onion and celery until soft, for about 10 minutes. Stir in the garlic and rosemary.
2. Stir in the vegetables and cook over medium heat, for 5 minutes to blend the flavors; add the hot water and instant vegetable broth. Bring to boiling; lower the heat and simmer for 20 minutes.
3. Add the pasta and cook for 10 minutes, or until tender.
4. Combine the parsley and cheese in a small bowl; serve with the minestrone.

VEGETABLE QUICHE

Bake at 425° for 15 minutes; then at 350° for 20 minutes.
Makes 6 servings.

½ package piecrust mix
1 pound fresh spinach, cooked and well drained
½ cup chopped green onion
1 clove garlic, finely chopped
2 tablespoons butter or margarine
1½ cups shredded Swiss cheese (6 ounces)
3 eggs, lightly beaten
¾ cup milk

1 teaspoon salt
1 teaspoon leaf basil, crumbled
½ teaspoon celery salt
2 medium-size tomatoes, thinly sliced
1 tablespoon packaged bread crumbs
1 tablespoon grated Parmesan cheese

1. Prepare the piecrust mix following label directions, or make your own single-crust pastry recipe. Roll out to a 12-inch round on a lightly floured surface; fit into a 9-inch pie plate. Trim overhang to ½ inch; turn under and flute to make a stand-up edge.

2. Press excess water out of spinach; chop finely.

3. Preheat the oven to hot (425°).

4. Sauté the green onion and garlic in the butter in a medium-size skillet until golden. Add the spinach and cook over medium heat, stirring constantly, until the excess moisture evaporates.

5. Combine the spinach mixture, Swiss cheese, eggs, milk, salt, basil and celery salt in a large bowl; stir to mix well. Turn into the prepared pastry shell. Arrange the thinly sliced tomatoes around the outer edge of the quiche.

6. Bake in the preheated hot oven (425°) for 15 minutes; lower the oven temperature to moderate (350°) and bake for 10 minutes longer. Combine the bread crumbs and Parmesan cheese in a small bowl and sprinkle over the tomato slices. Bake the quiche for 10 minutes longer, or until the top is puffy and the center moves slightly when the quiche is moved gently. Let stand for 10 minutes before serving.

— SMELL YOUR PRODUCE! —

Smell vegetables and fruits before you buy then. Fragrant produce will be the most flavorful when cooked.

TIPS FOR WHOLESOME AND DELICIOUS
VEGETARIAN EATING

• These are some of the food combinations which produce complete proteins: rice + beans or seeds or dairy products (or all three); legumes + grains, seeds or dairy products (or all three); wheat products + beans or dairy products (or both); corn + beans or milk; potatoes + milk or cheese (or both). Enrich vegetarian dishes with eggs and dairy foods whenever possible.

• Keep the following foods handy—they not only add extra protein, but they'll give dishes interesting tastes and textures: wheat germ, nuts, peanuts (a legume), sunflower and sesame seeds.

• Grow your own bean sprouts so you'll always have some handy. These protein-rich nuggets are also rich in vitamin C. Mung beans are easy to sprout. Here's how: (1) Put beans in a jar. (2) Soak for 4 to 6 hours. (3) Cover top of jar with cheesecloth; secure with rubber band. (4) Drain liquid through cloth. (5) Rinse beans daily to keep from drying out. Keep beans at room temperature; continue rinsing process for several days, or until beans have sprouted. (6) Refrigerate sprouts.

• Save the water from cooked vegetables. It's flavorful and rich in nutrients. Use it for cooking the next batch of vegetables, in soups or to cook grains. You can keep it refrigerated for 1 week.

• Milk or cheese sauces not only dress up a vegetable-based dish, they increase its protein value.

• Steaming vegetables retains more vitamins and minerals than cooking them in large amounts of water.

• Stir-fry vegetables for a crunchy texture. Heat a small amount of oil in a frying pan (you don't need a wok); add vegetables. Stir them constantly—it only takes 3 minutes at the most for them to cook. Try stir-fried vegetables over brown rice, topped with cheese.

• Make use of vegetables which are high in protein as well as vitamins and minerals; peas, corn, broccoli, lima beans, greens, mushrooms, asparagus, cauliflower.

• Give your vegetarian dishes a foreign flair. It's easy! Try spinach lasagne, Oriental stir-fried vegetables over rice, Japanese vegetable sukiyaki, Indian vegetable curry with potatoes, beans and hard-cooked eggs. Add authentic-style condiments and beverages.

• Try adapting some of your favorite meat dishes to vegetarian-style cooking—you'll find it a welcome change from that stretch-the-meat rut: meatless chili, cabbage rolls with nuts, seeds or beans, and rice-stuffed peppers.

ASPARAGUS PIE

A pinwheel of asparagus spears atop a delightful sour cream, double-cheese mixture.

Bake at 350° for 30 minutes.
Makes 6 servings.

1	package (8 ounces) frozen asparagus spears
2	eggs
1	cup cottage cheese
¼	cup (½ stick) butter or margarine, melted
¼	cup all-purpose flour

½	teaspoon baking powder
¼	teaspoon salt
1	cup dairy sour cream
1	tomato, peeled and thinly sliced
¼	cup grated Parmesan cheese

1. Cook the asparagus just until tender; drain. Arrange in a spoke pattern on the bottom of a well-greased 9-inch pie pan. (If the asparagus is more than 3½ inches long, allow the tips to extend up the sides of the pan.)

2. Preheat the oven to moderate (350°).

3. Beat the eggs until frothy in a medium-size bowl. Add the cottage cheese and butter and beat until almost smooth. Mix in the flour, baking powder and salt. Stir in the sour cream.

4. Pour the filling into the asparagus-lined pan. Arrange the tomato slices on top. Sprinkle with the cheese.

5. Bake in the preheated moderate oven (350°) for 30 minutes, or until firm in the center. Let stand in the pan for 10 minutes. Cut into wedges; serve warm.

PEAK SEASONS FOR VEGETABLES

To save the most on vegetables, buy them at the peak of the growing season. Look for produce to be on special:
• Winter—Artichokes, avocados, broccoli, Brussels sprouts, cauliflower, mushrooms, parsnips, potatoes
• Spring—Asparagus, cabbage, carrots, green onions, spinach
• Summer—Green and wax beans, beets, corn, okra, onions, peas, sweet green and red peppers, summer squash, tomatoes, zucchini
• Fall—Broccoli, cauliflower, eggplant, mushrooms, onions, parsnips, potatoes, sweet potatoes, acorn and Hubbard squash.

SPINACH-MUSHROOM SQUARES

Bake at 325° for 1 hour.
Makes 6 servings.

2   medium-size onions, finely chopped (1 cup)
¼   pound mushrooms, thinly sliced
2   tablespoons butter or margarine
4   eggs
2   packages (10 ounces each) frozen chopped spinach, thawed and well drained
¼   cup packaged bread crumbs
1   can (10¾ ounces) condensed cream of mushroom soup
⅓   cup grated Parmesan cheese
½   teaspoon salt
½   teaspoon leaf basil, crumbled
¼   teaspoon ground nutmeg
⅛   teaspoon pepper

1. Preheat the oven to slow (325°).
2. Cook the onions and mushrooms in the butter in a large skillet, stirring occasionally, until soft; cool.
3. Beat the eggs in a large mixing bowl until frothy. Stir in the onions, mushrooms, spinach, bread crumbs, soup, 2 tablespoons of the cheese, the salt, basil, nutmeg and pepper until well combined.
4. Spread the mixture in a buttered 9 x 9 x 2-inch baking dish. Sprinkle evenly with the remaining cheese.
5. Bake, uncovered, in the preheated slow oven (325°) until set, for about 1 hour. Cut into squares to serve.

SPINACH MOLD

Bake at 350° for 20 minutes.
Makes 4 servings.

2   packages (10 ounces each) frozen chopped spinach
2   cups herb-seasoned stuffing mix
¾   cup (1½ sticks) butter or margarine, melted
½   cup grated Parmesan cheese
½   cup chopped celery (1 stalk)
1   medium-size onion, chopped (½ cup)
1   tablespoon garlic salt
½   teaspoon leaf thyme, crumbled OR: 1½ teaspoons chopped fresh thyme
½   teaspoon pepper
    Dash of liquid red pepper seasoning
6   eggs, beaten

1. Preheat the oven to moderate (350°). Grease a 6½-cup ring mold.
2. Cook the spinach following label directions; drain well.
3. Combine the spinach, stuffing mix, butter, Parmesan cheese, celery, onion, garlic, salt, thyme, pepper, red pepper seasoning and eggs in a large bowl. Spoon into the ring mold, spreading evenly.
4. Bake in the preheated moderate oven (350°) for 20 minutes, or until the spinach pulls away from the side of the mold and springs back when lightly touched with a fingertip.
5. Carefully pour off any excess accumulated liquid. Run a knife carefully around the edges. Unmold onto a serving plate. Mound the steamed yellow squash and mushrooms in the center, if you wish.

Note: This also works well with frozen chopped broccoli.

VEGETARIAN HERO

A hero is a native American sandwich called by other names in various parts of the country—hoagie, submarine, torpedo or zep.
It is called "hero" because of the heroic appetite needed to finish this hearty sandwich.

Makes 6 servings.

2	packages (4 ounces each) alfalfa sprouts	1	large round loaf sourdough bread, about 9 inches in diameter
1	cup shredded carrots		
1	cup mayonnaise	1	large ripe avocado
2	teaspoons sugar	1	package (8 ounces) sliced mozzarella cheese
4	teaspoons lemon juice		
1½	teaspoons salt	1	package (8 ounces) sliced Provolone cheese
	Pinch of pepper		

1. Mix the sprouts, carrots, mayonnaise, sugar, 2 teaspoons of the lemon juice, salt and pepper in a large bowl. Cut off the top half of the bread; scoop out the center, leaving a shell about 1 inch thick. (Use the inside for crumbs in another recipe.)
2. Halve, pit and slice the avocado; sprinkle with the remaining 2 teaspoons of lemon juice.
3. Place half of the sprout mixture on the bottom of the bread. Top with half of the avocado slices; cover with layers of the cheeses and then the remaining avocado slices and sprout mixture. Replace the top of the bread. Cut into wedges to serve.

MEATLESS SOURCES OF PROTEIN FOR VEGETARIAN MEALS

The National Research Council's Recommended Daily Allowance (RDA) for protein is 56 grams for adult men, 46 grams for adult women. Pregnant and nursing women need an additional 30 and 20 grams, respectively. Remember: Too much protein—at the expense of necessary carbohydrates and fats—is as harmful as too little protein, so plan accordingly. The chart below will help you include the necessary protein in your diet when you are not serving meat.

FOOD	AMOUNT	APPROXIMATE PROTEIN (grams)
Bread		
white, enriched	2 slices	5.2
whole wheat	2 slices	5.2
Cottage cheese	½ cup	16
Dried beans & peas, cooked	½ cup	8
Dried milk	1 cup, reconstituted	8.5
Egg, poached or hard cooked	1	6.5
Hard cheese	1 ounce	7
Peanut butter	2 tablespoons	8
Process American cheese	1-ounce slice	6.6
Rice		
brown	1 cup, cooked	4.9
white, enriched	1 cup, cooked	4.1
Sunflower seed kernels	2 tablespoons	4.4
Tofu (bean curd)	4 ounces	8.8
Walnuts	½ cup, chopped	8.9
Whole milk	1 cup	8.5
Yogurt	1 cup	8.5

VEGETARIAN CASSEROLES

Lovely looking and delicious casseroles can be made out of almost any vegetable. Vegetable casseroles can serve as side dishes, as main dishes with a small amount of meat added, or as meatless main dishes with protein provided by eggs (hard-cooked or in a sauce), cheese, nuts or grains and beans.

GREEN CHILI-MUSHROOM ENCHILADAS

This hearty, satisfying dish can be made almost entirely in advance—only the tortillas should be fried at the last minute.

Makes 4 servings.

3	large onions, finely chopped (2 cups)	2	teaspoons leaf thyme, crumbled
6	cloves garlic, finely chopped	1½	teaspoons salt
⅓	cup vegetable oil	½	teaspoon pepper
1½	cups tomatoes, coarsely chopped	1	pint (2 cups) dairy sour cream
1	can (4 ounces) green chili peppers, seeded and finely chopped	8	canned or frozen tortillas Vegetable oil for frying
½	pound mushrooms, sliced	1	cup shredded Cheddar cheese (4 ounces)
2	tablespoons leaf basil, crumbled		

1. Sauté 1½ cups of the onions and the garlic in the oil in a large skillet until tender, but not brown. Add ½ cup of the tomatoes and the chili peppers; simmer for 5 minutes. Add the mushrooms; simmer until tender. Stir in the basil, thyme, salt and pepper; simmer for 2 minutes longer. Stir in the sour cream; remove the sauce from the heat.

2. Combine the remaining onion and tomato in a small bowl to use as filling.

3. Preheat the oven to hot (400°).

4. Dip the tortillas, one at a time, in hot oil in a skillet for 5 to 8 seconds on each side, or until softened. Drain on paper toweling.

5. Oil a baking dish large enough to hold 4 tortillas. On each tortilla, spread one quarter of the filling, a generous portion of sauce, another tortilla, the rest of the sauce, and top with cheese.

6. Bake in the preheated hot oven (400°) for about 10 minutes, or until the sauce is bubbling and the enchiladas are heated through.

POPULAR PASTAS

There is an immense variety of pastas suitable for use in casserole cooking. Here are a few:

Pastina—Tiny pasta bits good for use in soups or as baby food.

Spaghetti—The long, round, thin favorite, perfect with many kinds of sauces.

Spaghettini—A thinner version of spaghetti most preferred in Italy.

Ziti—Thick hollow tubes of pasta that can be served in baked dishes.

Elbow Macaroni—Curved hollow tubes most widely used in cold salads, casseroles and macaroni and cheese combinations.

Fettuccine—The Romans call it tagliatelle. Excellent with clam sauce or butter and grated cheese.

Linguine—Long flattened macaroni, served with cheese, clam or pesto sauces and grated Parmesan.

Alphabets—Letters made of pasta used mainly in soups.

Lasagne—Flat, wide ribbons of pasta that come plain, or with a ruffled edge, in white or spinach-flavored green.

Macaroni Wheels—Pasta shaped like tiny wagon wheels, used in soups and casseroles, and a favorite with children.

Ravioli—Pillow-shaped pasta filled with either meat or cheese. They are first boiled, then combined with a tomato or cheese sauce.

Farfalle—Pasta shaped like small bows, used in soups, casseroles, or served alone with sauce.

Shells—This pasta comes in small, medium and large sizes. The small ones can be sauced, the larger ones can be stuffed with meat or cheese and baked.

Manicotti—large pasta tubes, first filled with meat or cheese, then baked in a tomato sauce.

Cannelloni—Fat, ridged tubes of pasta also suitable for stuffing.

Vermicelli—This spaghetti has a fine delicate texture and is best when served with a light sauce.

Rigati—Tubes of pasta more finely ridged than cannelloni, usually stuffed and baked in tomato sauce.

Tortellini—These small pasta rings are filled with meat or cheese and dished up in clear consommé or with a plain tomato or a creamy cheese sauce and topped with Parmesan.

Noodles—Flat strands of pasta rich in eggs and often served as an accompaniment to main-dish casseroles, such as Beef Stroganoff. Available in plain (white) and spinach (green).

PASTA WITH ASPARAGUS

Makes 6 servings.

2	pounds asparagus	6	tablespoons (¾ stick) butter
1	pound very thin spaghetti		or margarine
⅓	cup chopped green onion	½	cup light cream
½	teaspoon pepper	½	cup grated Parmesan cheese

1. Wash and trim the asparagus; cut into 1-inch-diagonal pieces. Partially cook in boiling salted water to cover, in a Dutch oven or large kettle for 3 minutes. Drain.

2. Cook the spaghetti in the same Dutch oven or kettle following label directions; drain and return to the kettle.

3. Sauté the onion and pepper in 2 tablespoons of the butter until soft. Add the asparagus and toss to coat.

4. Add the remaining butter and cream to the spaghetti; toss to coat evenly; add the Parmesan; toss well. Add the asparagus mixture and toss gently to distribute evenly. Serve with additional cheese, if you wish.

FETTUCCINE WITH ASPARAGUS AND EGG SAUCE

This innovative pasta dish combines fresh asparagus and fettuccine.

Makes 4 servings.

1	package (12 ounces) fettuccine noodles	1	cup hot water
1½	pounds fresh asparagus, rinsed and cut into 1-inch lengths	1	envelope instant vegetable broth
¼	cup (½ stick) butter or margarine	4	eggs
		1	teaspoon salt
1	medium-size onion, diced	¼	teaspoon pepper
		1	cup grated Parmesan cheese

1. Cook the pasta in boiling salted water following label directions for a total of 9 minutes. Add the asparagus to the kettle during the last 5 minutes.

2. Meanwhile, melt the butter in a small saucepan over moderate heat. Sauté the onion in the butter until soft. Stir in the hot water and instant vegetable broth and simmer for 2 minutes. Drain the fettuccine and asparagus and return to the kettle. Add the onion mixture and toss. Remove from the heat; add the eggs beaten with the salt and pepper and toss quickly. Add the cheese and toss again. Serve immediately with more cheese, if you wish.

LINGUINE WITH CREAMY ZUCCHINI SAUCE

The sauce of finely grated zucchini and mozzarella clings to and flavors this pale green pasta dish.

Makes 4 servings.

1 pound linguine, fusilli or macaroni	½ cup grated Parmesan cheese
⅓ cup olive or vegetable oil	1 pound zucchini, scrubbed and coarsely grated (about 3 cups)
3 large cloves garlic, finely chopped	½ cup chopped parsley
1 package (8 ounces) whole-milk mozzarella cheese, shredded	½ teaspoon salt
	¼ teaspoon pepper

1. Cook the linguine in boiling salted water following label directions; drain.
2. Heat the oil in a large kettle or Dutch oven over moderate heat. Add the garlic and cook for 30 seconds. Return the pasta to the kettle and toss to coat with the oil and garlic.
3. Add the cheeses and toss again. Add the zucchini, parsley, salt and pepper; continue to toss over moderate heat until the cheese and moisture from the zucchini coat the pasta with a light sauce. Serve immediately with additional cheese, if you wish.

LINGUINI WITH BROCCOLI, GREEN ONION AND RICOTTA CHEESE SAUCE

This is a very rich dish and needs nothing more than a salad, hot crusty French bread and fresh fruit to complete the meal.

Makes 6 servings.

1½ tablespoons butter or margarine	4 ounces mozzarella cheese, diced (1 cup)
1 tablespoon all-purpose flour	1 bunch broccoli, cut into flowerets (about 3 cups)
½ teaspoon salt	⅓ cup sliced green onion
¼ teaspoon leaf basil, crumbled	1 pint cherry tomatoes, halved
¼ teaspoon leaf oregano, crumbled	1 pound linguine, cooked following label directions and drained
1¼ cups milk	
½ pound whole milk ricotta cheese	¼ cup chopped Italian or regular parsley

1. Melt the butter in a medium-size saucepan. Stir in the flour, salt, basil and oregano and cook for 1 minute, stirring constantly. Remove from the heat and stir in the milk. Cook, stirring constantly, until the mixture comes to boiling, for about 3 minutes. Stir in the ricotta and mozzarella cheeses and cook over low heat, stirring frequently, until the cheeses melt and the mixture is no longer stringy. If the sauce is too thick, thin it with milk or cream.

2. Steam the broccoli and green onion over boiling water until crisp-tender, for about 3 minutes.

3. Toss the broccoli mixture with the tomatoes and linguine and spoon onto a warm platter. Pour the hot cheese sauce over and sprinkle with parsley.

VEGETABLE LONGEVITY

To get the most out of the vegetables you buy, take care of them as soon as possible after coming home from the store:
• Wash and dry well all leafy vegetables and salad greens and store in plastic bags in the refrigerator; use within 3 days.
• Store potatoes, carrots and turnips in a dark, cool humid place at 45° to 50°, but not in the refrigerator; use in 2 to 3 weeks.

SPAGHETTI WITH SPINACH "PESTO" SAUCE

Makes 4 servings.

3	cloves garlic, crushed and peeled	1	jar (3 ounces) pignoli nuts,* finely chopped or ground
1	tablespoon vegetable oil	1	tablespoon leaf basil, crumbled
2	packages (9 ounces each) frozen creamed spinach, thawed	½	cup grated Parmesan cheese
		1	pound spaghetti

1. Sauté the garlic in the oil in a large skillet just until tender. Add the spinach, nuts, basil and cheese. Cook just until thoroughly heated, for about 5 minutes.

2. Cook and drain the spaghetti following label directions. Reheat the sauce; toss the spaghetti with the sauce.

*Walnuts may be substituted.

PASTA NIÇOISE

The ingredients and seasonings used are much like those in the popular salade Niçoise.

Makes 6 servings.

⅔	cup olive or vegetable oil	2	cans (6½ ounces each) tuna, drained
⅓	cup red wine vinegar		
2	cloves garlic, finely chopped	⅓	cup Greek or black olives
2	tablespoons drained capers	3	medium-sized tomatoes, diced OR: 1 pint basket cherry tomatoes, halved
1	teaspoon salt		
½	teaspoon pepper		
1½	teaspoons leaf basil, crumbled	2	cups sliced celery
		1	cup thinly sliced red onion
1	package (1 pound) rotelle or medium seashell macaroni	½	cup chopped parsley

1. Combine the oil, vinegar, garlic, capers, salt, pepper and basil in a large salad bowl. Beat the dressing with a fork until well blended.

2. Cook and drain the pasta following label directions; add to the bowl and toss to blend. Add the tuna, olives, tomatoes, celery, onion and parsley; toss again. May be served warm or refrigerated and served cold.

PASTA COOKING TIPS

- To cook pasta properly, at least 6 quarts of water should be used for each pound of pasta.
- Bring water to boiling; then add 2 tablespoons salt.
- Don't break long spaghetti into pieces; lower them slowly into the boiling water, curving them around the pot as they soften.
- Add the pasta gradually—in small amounts—to keep the water boiling. Stir frequently to keep the strands or pieces of pasta separate.
- Boil the pasta, uncovered, stirring occasionally to prevent sticking.
- Fresh pasta will cook much faster than dried pasta, in approximately 1 minute. For proper cooking times for dried pasta check label directions.
- Test for doneness 1 to 2 minutes before the time given in directions. Either taste a piece—it should be firm but tender (*al dente*)—or press a bit against the side of the kettle with a fork. If it breaks easily and smoothly, it's done.
- Don't overcook pasta. Drain well and at once in a colander. Serve immediately or keep warm: Place in a colander over simmering water; cover top with aluminum foil or the pot cover and keep warm for up to 1 hour. To keep for more than 1 hour, cook pasta until *al dente,* drain and toss with vegetable oil to coat. Just before serving, plunge pasta into boiling water for 1 minute, drain and toss with melted butter or other sauce.
- Do not rinse cooked hot pasta in cold water unless it is to be served cold in a pasta salad.
- Unopened, pasta keeps fresh for months in a cool, dry place. Opened, it should be placed in a covered container.

NO-MEAT ENCHILADAS

Bake at 350° for 20 minutes.
Makes 4 servings.

Enchilada Sauce
3 tablespoons vegetable oil
1½ tablespoons chili powder
1½ tablespoons all-purpose
flour
1½ cups water
1 teaspoon distilled
white vinegar
½ teaspoon garlic powder
½ teaspoon onion powder
½ teaspoon salt
¼ teaspoon leaf oregano,
crumbled

Filling
Vegetable oil
8 corn tortillas
¾ cup refried beans (from a
1-pound can)
¼ pound Monterey Jack or
Cheddar cheese, shredded
(1 cup)
½ cup cream-style cottage
cheese
1 medium-size onion, finely
chopped (½ cup)
½ cup chopped black olives
(optional)

1. Heat the oil, chili powder and flour in a small saucepan to make a paste. Add the water gradually to make a smooth sauce; add the vinegar, garlic powder, onion powder, salt and oregano. Bring to boiling; lower the heat and simmer, uncovered, for 3 minutes.
2. Pour vegetable oil to depth of ¼ inch in a small skillet. Quickly dip each tortilla into the hot oil with tongs just long enough to soften, for 3 to 4 seconds. Drain on paper toweling.
3. Preheat the oven to moderate (350°).
4. To assemble, place 1 tablespoon each refried beans, Jack cheese, cottage cheese, onion and olives down the center of each tortilla; roll up; place seam-side down in a shallow baking dish just large enough to hold the enchiladas (13½ x 8½ x 2-inches). Pour the sauce over the enchiladas. Sprinkle with the remaining cheese.
5. Bake in the preheated moderate oven (350°) for 20 minutes, or until bubbly.

SCALLOPED VEGETABLES AND FISH

Bake at 350° for 1 hour and 30 minutes.
Makes 6 servings.

2½ cups crumbled unsalted crackers or packaged bread crumbs
1 teaspoon garted Parmesan cheese
3 eggs
1 can (16 ounces) cream-style corn
1 can (16 ounces) peas and carrots, drained
1 large sweet green pepper, halved, seeded and chopped
1 medium-size onion, chopped (½ cup)
1 cup chopped celery (2 stalks)
1 can (16 ounces) mackerel, drained
1 teaspoon salt
1 teaspoon garlic salt
½ cup milk

1. Preheat the oven to moderate (350°).
2. Combine ½ cup of the crumbs and the Parmesan cheese in a small bowl; reserve. Butter a 2-quart baking dish.
3. Beat the eggs until frothy in a large bowl. Add the remaining crumbs, corn, peas and carrots, green pepper, onion, celery, mackerel, salt, garlic salt and milk; mix well. Spoon into the baking dish. Sprinkle the top with the reserved crumb-cheese mixture.
4. Bake in the preheated moderate oven (350°) for 1 hour and 30 minutes, or until bubbly.

TUNA AÏOLI

The Provençale boiled dinner gets its name from the ultra-garlicky mayonnaise with which it's served. This quick version uses canned, frozen and fresh staples and garlicked commercial mayonnaise.

Makes 4 servings.

1 cup mayonnaise
2 large cloves garlic, finely chopped
1 tablespoon lemon juice
¼ teaspoon dry mustard
1 package (10 ounces) frozen Italian green beans
2 cans (6½ ounces) tuna, drained
1 can (19 ounces) chick-peas, drained
1 can (16 ounces) sliced beets, drained
4 carrots, sliced
1 red or white onion, thinly sliced

1. Combine the mayonnaise, garlic, lemon juice and mustard in a small bowl. Cover and refrigerate for at least 30 minutes before serving. Cook the green beans following label directions.

2. Arrange the tuna and vegetables (the vegetables can be heated, chilled or served at room temperature) on a serving platter and serve with garlic (aïoli) sauce.

Suggested Menu: Hairy Marys (spicy tomato juice), sesame breadsticks and butter or herbed cream cheese, frozen bananas in yogurt, drizzled with frozen orange juice concentrate.

TYPES OF RICE

Long-grain white rice—whether Carolina-type, converted, minute-type or quick—is the most widely used. When it's milled, the bran skin under the husk is removed, making it easier to store and quicker to cook.

Both Carolina-type and converted (processed before milling) rices are excellent as side dishes or in entrée pilafs; converted rice in particular has fluffy, separate grains.

Quick (parboiled) and minute-type (or packaged precooked) rices are good choices when you want to save time and ensure uniform results.

Try brown rice when you want to add a nutty flavor to casseroles, soups and side dishes; because only its husk is removed, it takes longer to cook and stays chewier, but also has more protein and natural minerals and vitamins.

Wild rice is actually a water grass, but it often comes packaged with long-grain white rice and is a wonderful accompaniment to poultry dishes.

Toast rice in oil before adding liquid for a richer flavor.

Rice is done when the grains are tender and the liquid is absorbed; then fluff it with a fork.

Prepare about 1 cup of uncooked regular rice or 2 cups of packaged pre-cooked rice for 4 to 6 servings.

Whether plain or mixed with other freezable foods, rice keeps in the freezer 6-8 months. To reheat, add 2 tablespoons of liquid for each cup of rice; simmer for 4 to 5 minutes in a covered saucepan.

Uncooked rice keeps well if stored in a covered container in a dry place.

8

Quick and Easy Meals

In many households today, people don't have the time to prepare elaborate, multi-course meals. When time is a premium, let our Quick and Easy recipes come to the rescue. Most take an hour or less to prepare. We've even included a 30-minute casserole chart (pages 152 and 153), which offers almost unlimited possibilities for meal-in-one creations.

A classic example of a simple yet elegant meal is Spaghetti with Hot and Spicy Clam Sauce (page 149). This dish combines pasta and minced clams with herbs and seasonings that give it a zesty flavor reminiscent of meals prepared at exclusive Italian restaurants.

Another hit with busy families is the Quick-to-Fix Shepherd's Pie (page 143), which can be prepared in record time by utilizing canned goods. With a can of beef stew, canned vegetables and instant mashed potatoes, the primary makings are available to create a hearty dish.

CHICKEN LIVERS WITH BACON AND GREEN BEANS

A tasty way to use economical and nutritious chicken livers.

Makes 4 servings.

1	pound chicken livers	1	package (9 ounces) frozen Italian green beans
4	slices bacon		Hot cooked rice
2	tablespoons all-purpose flour		

1. Trim the livers of any connective tissue or fat. Cook the bacon in a large skillet until crisp; remove to paper toweling; crumble and reserve. Pour the bacon drippings into a cup; measure and return 2 tablespoons to the skillet.

2. Roll the chicken livers in the flour to coat them. Brown on all sides in the drippings, for about 5 to 10 minutes. Stir in ¼ cup water, scraping up the browned bits from the skillet. Add the beans; cover and cook for 10 minutes, or until the beans are tender. The livers should be brown outside and slightly pink inside. Taste; add salt and pepper, if you wish. Sprinkle with the crumbled bacon. Serve with hot cooked rice.

ITALIAN SAUSAGE WITH VEGETABLES

A colorful blend of flavors makes this a peppy main dish.

Makes 4 servings.

1	pound sweet or hot Italian sausages OR: equal amounts of each	2	cans (12 ounces each) vacuum-packed golden whole-kernel corn with sweet peppers
½	cup chopped celery		
1	package (10 ounces) frozen baby lima beans		

1. Cut the sausages into ½-inch-thick slices. Cook in a large skillet until well browned for 15 minutes. Push the sausages to one side; sauté the celery until soft.

2. Stir in the frozen limas and corn. Simmer for 10 minutes, or until heated through.

STUFFED FRANKFURTERS

Bake at 375° for 15 minutes.
Makes 5 servings.

1	pound potatoes (4 medium size), pared	1	can (8 ounces) sauerkraut, drained and rinsed
2	tablespoons butter or margarine	¼	teaspoon caraway seeds
2	tablespoons milk	1	pound frankfurters (about 10)
¼	teaspoon salt	2	tablespoons shredded Cheddar cheese
⅛	teaspoon pepper		

1. Cook the potatoes in boiling salted water in a medium-size saucepan until tender, about 15 minutes. Drain well. Add the butter, milk, salt and pepper; mash well until light and fluffy.
2. Preheat the oven to moderate (375°).
3. Combine the sauerkraut and caraway seeds in a small bowl. Halve the frankfurters lengthwise, cutting almost through to the bottom; spread apart. Place the frankfurters in a shallow baking pan; spoon sauerkraut into the opening. Top with the mashed potatoes. Sprinkle the cheese over the top.
4. Bake in the preheated moderate oven (375°) for 15 minutes.

QUICK MEALS

Finely divide, chop, shred or julienne your meats, poultry fish and vegetables for super-quick cooking.

Make use of variety meats, such as kidneys and liver and fish. They cook in less time than most other meats and poultry.

Stock up your refrigerator with fully cooked meats—like ham steaks, smoked or brown-and-serve sausages. They need only be reheated before serving.

Always keep pasta and the makings for sauces on hand. This kind of meal takes less than 30 minutes to prepare!

When preparing casseroles make two—one for now, the other to freeze for later. Remember: Thawing and reheating is quicker with smaller portions. (Leave out the potatoes when freezing!)

Freeze leftover rice in serving-size portions. To reheat: Defrost at room temperature; then steam, covered, until thoroughly heated.

SALISBURY SKILLET MEAL

Once you make the meat patties, everything else is off the pantry shelf.

Makes 4 servings.

1½ pounds lean ground round or chuck	1 can (16 ounces) whole potatoes
1 small can evaporated milk (⅔ cup)	1 package (10 ounces) frozen peas
1 egg	1 can (4 ounces) sliced mushrooms
1 cup soft bread crumbs (2 slices)	1 envelope dehydrated onion soup mix
½ teaspoon salt	

1. Lightly mix the beef, milk, egg, bread crumbs and salt in a large bowl. Shape into 4 large oval patties 1-inch thick.

2. Drain the potatoes, reserving the liquid in a 1-cup glass measure. Add enough water to make 1 cup if needed. Slice the potatoes.

3. Pan-fry the patties in a large skillet over medium heat until well browned on each side. Push to the side of the pan. Drain off all fat. Add the sliced poatoes, frozen peas, mushrooms with their liquid and soup mix. Stir in the reserved 1 cup of potato liquid. Bring to boiling. Cover and simmer over low heat for 20 minutes, or until the patties are done, stirring once during cooking to blend in the soup mix.

CHINESE FRIED RICE WITH PORK

Makes 4 servings.

3 tablespoons soy sauce	2 cloves garlic, finely chopped
2 tablespoons dry sherry	3 cups cold *cooked* rice
1 teaspoon sugar	1 can (8½ ounces) green peas, drained
½ pound boneless pork loin, cut into ½-inch cubes (1¼ cups)	1 can (4 ounces) whole mushrooms, drained
4 tablespoons vegetable oil	3 eggs
1 large onion, chopped (1 cup)	½ teaspoon salt
	1 tablespoon chopped parsley

1. Combine the soy sauce, sherry and sugar in a medium-size bowl.

Add the pork cubes and allow to marinate in the refrigerator for at least 1 hour. Drain and reserve the marinade.

2. Heat 2 tablespoons of the oil in a large skillet; stir-fry the pork for 3 minutes. Add the onion and garlic and stir-fry for 2 minutes longer. Push the mixture to the side of the skillet.

3. Heat the remaining oil in the center of the skillet. Add the rice and stir-fry for 1 minute. Add the peas, mushrooms and reserved marinade. Mix well.

4. Clear the center of the pan. Beat the eggs lightly with the salt in a small bowl; pour into the center of the skillet. When the eggs begin to set, scramble and mix with the rice mixture. Serve hot, sprinkled with parsley.

CREOLE-STYLE HAM AND RICE

A quick and easy skillet meal of ham and rice flavored with tomatoes and green peppers.

Makes 6 servings.

2 tablespoons bacon drippings or vegetable oil	1 can (16 ounces) peeled whole tomatoes
6 slices cooked ham (about 3 x 4 inches)	1 can (13¾ ounces) chicken broth
1 medium-size onion, chopped (½ cup)	1 bay leaf
1 medium-size sweet green pepper, halved, seeded and cut into strips	½ teaspoon salt
	½ teaspoon leaf thyme, crumbled
1 clove garlic, finely chopped	4 drops liquid hot pepper seasoning
1½ cups long-grain white rice	

1. Heat the drippings or oil in a large skillet. Add the ham and cook until lightly browned. Remove to a plate. Add the onion, green pepper, garlic and rice to the drippings left in the pan. Sauté, stirring often, until the vegetables are just wilted.

2. Stir in the tomatoes with their liquid, broth, bay leaf, salt, thyme and hot pepper seasoning, breaking up the tomatoes with a spoon. Bring to boiling; lower the heat; cover and simmer for 15 minutes. Uncover and arrange the ham on top of the rice. Cover and continue to cook until the rice is tender and the liquid is absorbed.

BRAISED LAMB CHOPS WITH VEGETABLES

A quick, delicious version of lamb stew.

Makes 4 servings.

4   shoulder lamb chops, cut
    ½-inch thick (1¾ pounds
    total weight)
1   can (10¾ ounces) condensed
    cream of celery soup
1   package (24 ounces) frozen
    stew vegetables
½   teaspoon leaf rosemary,
    crumbled

1. Place the lamb chops in a large skillet over low heat. (Do not add fat.) Cook the chops slowly in their own melting fat until brown; turn and brown the other side; remove.

2. Add the soup to the skillet, scraping up the browned bits. Stir in the stew vegetables and rosemary. (Do not add water.) Arrange the lamb chops over the vegetables. Cover and simmer, stirring occasionally, for 30 minutes, or until the lamb chops are tender.

PORK CHOPS WITH RED CABBAGE

A hearty dish for man-size appetites.

Makes 4 servings.

4   loin pork chops, cut 1 inch
    thick (1¾ pounds total weight)
1   large onion, chopped
    (1 cup)
1   jar (15 ounces) sweet/sour
    red cabbage
1   small red apple, quartered,
    cored and sliced

1. Place the pork chops in a large skillet over low heat. (Do not add fat.) Cook the chops slowly in their own fat until brown; turn; brown the other side. Remove.

2. Add the onion to the fat in the skillet and sauté for 5 minutes. Arrange the pork chops over the onions. Lower the heat; cover and cook for 30 minutes, turning once. Remove the cover; cook, turning the chops once or twice, until glazed and most of the liquid has evaporated. Remove the chops and keep them warm.

3. Drain the liquid from the cabbage; stir the cabbage into the skillet with the apple slices; cook until heated thoroughly. Arrange the pork chops over the mixture and serve with hot noodles or spaetzle, if you wish.

SEVEN-LAYER CASSEROLE

When you put this orderly casserole together, all the flavors blend well.

Bake at 350° for 1 hour and 20 minutes.

Makes 4 servings.

1	cup long-grain white rice	½	cup water
1	can (12 ounces) whole-kernel corn	½	cup finely chopped onion
		¾	pound lean ground chuck
1	teaspoon salt	½	teaspoon salt
⅛	teaspoon pepper	⅛	teaspoon pepper
1	can (15 ounces) tomato sauce	¼	cup water
		4	strips bacon, cut in half

1. Preheat the oven to moderate (350°).

2. Layer the ingredients in a 2-quart baking dish in this order: rice, corn and its liquid, the 1 teaspoon salt, ⅛ teaspoon pepper, ½ can of the tomato sauce, the ½ cup water, onion, ground chuck, ½ teaspoon salt, pepper, remaining tomato sauce, and ¼ cup water. Cover meat evenly with bacon. Cover the casserole.

3. Bake in the preheated moderate oven (350°) for 1 hour. Uncover and continue to bake for 20 minutes, or until the bacon is crisp.

TIME AND ENERGY SAVERS

To prevent whole peppercorns from flying all over the kitchen when crushing, use a mortar and pestle, or place the peppercorns in a heavy plastic bag and crush with a meat pounder.

Keep a pastry board or bowl from sliding around on the counter by placing the board or bowl on a wet dishcloth.

If food boils dry while being cooked and burns the pan, boil some baking soda and water in it and let stand overnight for easy cleanup.

Kitchen cleanups will be easier if you prevent grease from spattering while frying. The easiest way is to invert a colander over the skillet or flameproof casserole. It will catch the grease, yet allow the steam to escape.

To remove rust build up on a cast-iron casserole, wash it in sudsy water; scrub with a steel wool pad; then rub with vegetable oil. Place on a cookie sheet in a warm oven, turn off oven and keep in overnight. In the morning, rub off the excess oil. Repeat as needed.

LAMB CASSEROLE

Bake at 375° for 1 hour and 30 minutes.
Makes 4 servings.

4   shoulder lamb chops OR:
    1 pound neck of lamb cut
    into serving pieces
4   medium-size onions, sliced
6   carrots, sliced
4   large potatoes, pared and
    sliced
1   teaspoon garlic powder
    (optional)
1   teaspoon leaf oregano,
    crumbled
¼   cup chopped parsley
2   cups water

1. Preheat the oven to moderate (375°).
2. Layer the lamb, onions, carrots and potatoes in a large casserole (4 to 5 quarts) or Dutch oven. Sprinkle with the garlic powder, oregano and parsley. Pour the water over; cover.
3. Bake in the preheated moderate oven (375°) for 1 hour and 30 minutes, or until the meat and vegetables are tender. Skim off any excess fat before serving.

OLÉ CHILI PIE

Bake at 375° for 18 minutes.
Makes 4 to 6 servings.

1   package (8½ ounces) corn
    muffin mix
1   pound lean ground round or
    chuck
1   package (1⅛ ounces) taco
    seasoning mix
3   ounces natural Colby or
    Cheddar cheese, shredded
    (¾ cup)
1   cup shredded lettuce
1   tomato, seeded and chopped
¼   cup sliced olives

1. Preheat the oven to moderate (375°).
2. Prepare the corn muffin mix following label directions. Spread the batter evenly in the bottom of a greased 9-inch pie plate.
3. Bake in the preheated moderate oven (375°) for 18 minutes, or until golden brown.
4. Meanwhile, prepare the ground meat with taco seasoning mix following label directions; spoon over the hot cornbread. Sprinkle with about half the cheese. Arrange the lettuce, tomato, remaining cheese and the olives on top of the pie.

QUICK-TO-FIX SHEPHERD'S PIE

Bake at 375° for 50 minutes.
Makes 6 servings.

1 can (40 ounces) beef stew	1 can (16 ounces) whole boiled onions, drained
1 can (8 ounces) cut green beans, drained	2½ cups prepared instant mashed potatoes
1 can (8 ounces) sliced carrots, drained	¼ cup grated Parmesan cheese
	1 egg, lightly beaten

1. Preheat the oven to moderate (375°).
2. Combine the beef stew with green beans, carrots and onions in a 9 x 5 x 3-inch loaf pan.
3. Mix the prepared mashed potatoes with the cheese and egg in a small bowl and beat well. Spread all but 1 cup of the potato mixture evenly over the stew mixture in the pan. Put the remaining potatoes in a pastry bag fitted with a large star tube. Pipe rosettes of potatoes all around the border of the pan.
4. Bake in the preheated moderate oven (375°) for 50 minutes, or until the potatoes are golden brown and the stew is bubbly. Remove from the oven and let stand for 10 minutes before serving.

HEARTY BREAKFAST

A tasty dish for lunch or even supper.
Makes 4 servings.

6 slices lean bacon	Salt
1 small sweet green pepper, diced	Pinch of pepper
2 tablespoons finely chopped onion	¼ teaspoon leaf thyme, crumbled
3 large potatoes, cooked, peeled and cut into 1-inch chunks	½ cup shredded Cheddar or Swiss cheese (2 ounces)
	6 eggs

1. Cut the bacon into small strips. Cook the strips in a large skillet until crisp. Remove from the heat and pour off all but 3 tablespoons of the drippings. Add the green pepper, onion and potatoes. Cook over medium heat, stirring frequently with a pancake turner, for about 5 minutes, or until the potatoes are golden.

2. Lower the heat; taste and add salt if needed. Sprinkle the potato mixture with pepper and thyme and top with cheese. Break the eggs into the pan over the potatoes.

3. Cook, stirring constantly, until the eggs coat the potatoes and have set. Serve immediately.

ZUCCHINI AND HAM FRITTATA

A quiche-like dish without a crust that's prepared and served from one pan. Add a mixed green salad and crisp breadsticks for a light meal.

Bake at 350° for 10 minutes.
Makes 6 servings.

3	tablespoons butter or margarine	10	eggs
1	small onion, chopped (¼ cup)	½	cup heavy cream
2	small zucchini, sliced (2 cups)	1¼	teaspoons salt
½	teaspoon Italian seasoning	⅛	teaspoon pepper
		1	cup diced cooked ham
		1	large tomato, peeled and thinly sliced

1. Heat the butter in an ovenproof 10-inch omelet pan or cast-iron skillet. Add the onion, zucchini and Italian seasoning. Sauté over high heat, stirring often, until the zucchini is lightly browned. Remove with a slotted spoon to a bowl, leaving the fat in the pan.

2. Beat the eggs, cream, salt and pepper together in a medium-size bowl until blended. Pour into the pan. Scatter the zucchini and ham over the eggs. Cover and cook over low heat for 20 minutes or until the eggs are partially set.

3. While the eggs are cooking, preheat the oven to moderate (350°). Arrange the tomato slices over the frittata in a single layer.

4. Bake the frittata in the preheated moderate oven (350°) for 10 minutes, or until the center is firm but creamy on top. Loosen the frittata around the side of the pan with a spatula. Cut into wedges to serve.

MACARONI AND CHICK-PEAS
ABRUZZI STYLE

Colorful, easy, good, flavorful.

Makes 6 servings.

1	medium-size onion, sliced	1	teaspoon leaf oregano, crumbled
2	cloves garlic, finely chopped		
¼	cup olive oil	½	teaspoon salt
1	pound hot or sweet Italian sausages, cut into 1-inch pieces	½	teaspoon pepper
		1	can (19 ounces) chick-peas, drained
1	can (32 ounces) Italian tomatoes, broken up	1	pound elbow macaroni
¼	cup finely chopped parsley OR: 2 tablespoons dried parsley flakes	¼	cup grated Parmesan cheese

1. Cook the onion and garlic in the olive oil in a large skillet until tender, but not brown. Remove the onion and garlic with a slotted spoon; reserve.

2. Add the sausage to the oil remaining in the skillet and sauté for 10 minutes, or until no pink remains. Discard any excess oil.

3. Stir in the tomatoes, parsley, oregano, salt and pepper; simmer for 15 minutes.

4. Add the chick-peas and simmer for 5 minutes longer.

5. While the stew is cooking, cook the macaroni following label directions. Drain; spoon into a large bowl and toss with the chick-peas and sausage. Serve additional Parmesan cheese on the side.

HOT FRANKFURTER-MACARONI SALAD

Makes 6 servings.

1 package (8 ounces) elbow macaroni	3 tablespoons drained sweet pickle relish
1 pound frankfurters (about 10)	1 teaspoon salt
½ cup vegetable oil	¼ teaspoon pepper
1 large onion, chopped (1 cup)	1 can (16½ ounces) whole-kernel corn, drained
¼ cup vinegar	1 sweet green pepper, halved, seeded and chopped (1 cup)
1 tablespoon prepared mustard	2 carrots, finely chopped (1 cup)

1. Cook the macaroni following label directions; drain.

2. Cut the frankfurters into 1-inch pieces. Sauté in the oil in a large skillet, turning once or twice, for about 5 minutes; remove with a slotted spoon to paper toweling.

3. Sauté the onion in the oil remaining in the skillet until soft. Add the vinegar, mustard, relish, salt and pepper and mix well. Cook for 1 minute. Add the macaroni, frankfurters and corn and mix well; heat for 5 minutes.

4. Spoon onto a large platter; sprinkle with green pepper and carrots; toss. Serve.

SPAGHETTI WITH SAUSAGE AND ZUCCHINI

This is a delicious alternative to the usual tomato, clam or herb sauces for tossing with spaghetti.

Makes 6 servings.

1½ pound bulk pork sausage	¼ pound mushrooms, sliced
2 cans (10¾ ounces each) condensed cream of chicken soup	¼ cup sliced green onion
	½ teaspoon salt
4 or 5 cups (about 1½ pounds) zucchini, quartered and sliced	¼ teaspoon pepper
	1 pound spaghetti
	Grated Parmesan cheese

1. Cook the sausage in a large skillet until it loses its pink color, breaking it up with a fork as it cooks; stir in the soup.

2. Add the zucchini, mushrooms, green onion, salt and pepper; cook over medium heat for 15 minutes, or until the zucchini is tender.

3. Cook the spaghetti following label directions; drain. Toss the sausage mixture with the cooked spaghetti and Parmesan cheese.

CLAMS IN A SHELL

Makes 6 servings.

1 **package (10 ounces) frozen ready-to-bake pastry shells**	¼ **cup (½ stick) butter or margarine**
1 **can (16 ounces) mixed vegetables**	¼ **cup all-purpose flour**
1 **can (6½ ounces) minced clams**	⅔ **cup nonfat dry milk powder**
½ **cup diced celery**	½ **teaspoon salt**
1 **medium-size onion, diced (½ cup)**	⅛ **teaspoon dried dillweed**
	½ **cup shredded Swiss cheese (optional)**

1. Bake the pastry shells following package directions.

2. Drain the liquid from the mixed vegetables and clams into a 2-cup glass measure; add water to equal 2 cups liquid. Reserve.

3. Sauté the celery and onion in the butter in a medium-size saucepan until tender, for about 5 minutes. Remove from the heat. Add the flour, dry milk powder, salt and dillweed. Gradually stir in the reserved liquid until smooth. Return to the heat and cook, stirring constantly, until thickened. Add the vegetables and clams and cook until thoroughly heated. Add the cheese, if desired; heat just until melted.

4. Serve in the pastry shells.

SPAGHETTI WITH TUNA-TOMATO SAUCE

A colorful and inexpensive entrée for an impromptu meal.

Makes 6 servings.

1	large onion, chopped (1 cup)	½	teaspoon salt
1	clove garlic, finely chopped	¼	teaspoon pepper
2	tablespoons vegetable oil	2	cans (6½ ounces each) tuna, drained and flaked
1	can (28 ounces) Italian tomatoes, coarsely chopped	1	teaspoon anchovy paste
1	can (6 ounces) tomato paste	¼	cup chopped fresh parsley
1	teaspoon leaf oregano, crumbled	1	package (12 to 16 ounces) spaghetti
½	teaspoon leaf basil, crumbled	⅓	cup grated Parmesan cheese

1. Sauté the onion and garlic in the oil in a large saucepan until tender, for about 3 minutes. Add the tomatoes and liquid, tomato paste, oregano, basil, salt and pepper. Cook slowly, uncovered, for 20 minutes.

2. Add the tuna, anchovy paste and parsley. Cook for another 5 minutes.

3. While the tuna-tomato sauce is cooking, cook the spaghetti following label directions; drain.

4. Turn the hot spaghetti into a bowl. Pour the sauce over; sprinkle with the cheese.

FETTUCCINE WITH HAM AND PEAS

Ham, peas and Parmesan cheese enhance the creamy noodles in this dish.

Makes 4 servings.

1	package (1 pound) fettuccine or egg noodles	1	package (10 ounces) frozen green peas or chopped broccoli, partially thawed
6	tablespoons butter or margarine	2	tablespoons all-purpose flour
1	small onion, chopped (¼ cup)	1	cup heavy cream
2	cups julienne-cut cooked ham		Salt
			Pepper
		½	cup grated Parmesan cheese

1. Cook the fettuccine following label directions, just until barely tender.
2. While the pasta is cooking, melt the butter in a large skillet; sauté the onion in the butter until tender. Stir in the ham and vegetables. Stir in the flour; cook for 3 minutes, or until the vegetables are crisp-tender. Stir in the cream gradually. Bring to boiling. Taste and add salt and pepper, if needed.
3. Drain the pasta and return it to the pan. Pour the hot sauce over the fettuccine. Sprinkle with the cheese. Toss and serve immediately.

SPAGHETTI WITH HOT AND SPICY CLAM SAUCE

Fresh hot peppers and a generous gilding of garlic add a delicious touch of spice.

Makes 2 servings.

¼ cup olive oil	½ teaspoon leaf oregano, crumbled
2 cloves garlic, finely chopped	
1 to 2 teaspoons minced hot green or red peppers OR: ¼ teaspoon crushed red pepper flakes	1 package (8 ounces) thin spaghetti
	1 can (6½ ounces) minced clams
½ cup coarsely chopped mushrooms	Salt
	¼ cup chopped parsley
½ cup diced fresh or drained canned tomatoes	2 tablespoons butter, softened
	Grated Parmesan cheese

1. Heat the oil in a large skillet. Add the garlic, peppers, mushrooms, tomatoes and oregano. Sauté, stirring occasionally, until the mushrooms are tender, for about 3 minutes. Remove the skillet from the heat; cover and reserve.
2. Cook the pasta following label directions. Stir the clams into the sauce; bring just to boiling. Taste the sauce; add salt, if needed. Stir in the parsley and butter.
3. Drain the pasta; add to the skillet and toss gently until the pasta absorbs most of the sauce. Divide between two heated plates; serve at once with the grated cheese.

PASTA BELLISSIMA

Pink Canadian bacon, red peppers and emerald peas make this a beautiful and delicious pasta dish.

Makes 6 servings.

¼ cup (½ stick) butter or margarine	1 package (10 ounces) frozen green peas
8 ounces sliced Canadian bacon or ham	1 cup heavy cream
1 jar (7 ounces) roasted sweet red peppers, drained and diced	½ teaspoon salt
	¼ teaspoon pepper
	1 package (1 pound) fettuccine
	1 cup grated Parmesan cheese

1. Melt the butter in a large skillet. Add the bacon; cook and stir for 1 minute. Add the peppers and peas; cook for 1 minute, stirring to coat with the butter.

2. Stir in the cream, salt and pepper. Bring to boiling; lower the heat and simmer, stirring occasionally, until the sauce thickens slightly, for about 3 minutes. Remove the sauce from the heat; reserve while cooking the pasta.

3. Cook the pasta following label directions; drain; return to the kettle. Add the sauce and cheese and toss over low heat until the mixture is well blended and heated through. Serve on heated plates.

BOW TIES WITH SPINACH, BACON AND MUSHROOMS

The pasta version of a spinach and bacon salad.

Makes 4 servings.

½ pound thick-sliced bacon, cut into 1-inch pieces	½ teaspoon pepper
¼ cup (½ stick) butter or margarine	1 package (1 pound) bow ties (*farfalle*)
1 cup thinly sliced green onion	½ pound mushrooms, sliced (2 cups)
½ cup diced sweet red pepper	1 package (10 ounces) fresh spinach, washed and torn in pieces (4 cups)
1 cup chicken broth	1 cup grated Parmesan cheese
2 tablespoons lemon juice Salt	

1. Cook the bacon in a large skillet until crisp. Drain on paper toweling and reserve. Discard all but ¼ cup of the bacon fat in the skillet.

2. Add the butter to the bacon fat; heat. Sauté the onion and red pepper until tender, for about 2 minutes. Stir in the broth and lemon juice. Bring to boiling; lower the heat and simmer for 2 minutes. Taste; add salt, if needed, and the pepper. Remove the sauce from the heat.

3. Cook and drain the pasta following label directions; return to kettle. Add the sauce, mushrooms and spinach. Toss over moderate heat until the sauce is absorbed and the spinach is wilted.

4. Divide among four heated plates; top with the grated cheese and reserved bacon.

THE JERSEY JUMBO

Hero, hoagie, submarine, whatever you call it, this sandwich
(of salami, mortadella, Provolone, lettuce, peppers and caper dressing)
makes a delicious, hearty mouthful.

Makes 6 servings.

2	tablespoons tarragon vinegar	1	package (12 ounces) sliced cotto salami
2	tablespoons olive or vegetable oil	½	pound sliced mortadella
1	tablespoon drained capers	1	package (8 ounces) sliced Provolone cheese, cut in half
¼	teaspoon Italian seasoning, crumbled		
1	large loaf sesame-seeded French or Italian bread (about 15 inches long)	1	small sweet red pepper, halved, seeded and cut into thin strips
1	cup shredded iceberg lettuce	1	small sweet green pepper, halved, seeed and cut into thin strips

1. Combine the vinegar, oil, capers and Italian seasoning in a 1-cup glass measure; stir until blended.

2. Cut a slice from the top of the loaf; reserve. Scoop out the center of the bottom half. (Reserve bread to make crumbs.)

3. Fill the bottom of the loaf with shredded lettuce. Stir the dressing and drizzle half over the lettuce. Fold the salami and mortadella into quarters. Arrange the salami, mortadella and cheese over the lettuce. Top with the pepper strips. Drizzle with the remaining dressing. Cover with the reserved top of the loaf. Cut into serving-size portions.

30-MINUTE CASSEROLES & SKILLET DISHES

PROTEIN	STARCH	VEGETABLE	NICE TO ADD
1 lb. ground beef, browned & crumbled	2 cups cooked bulgur wheat	1 pkg. (10 oz.) frozen peas	Toasted almonds Sliced green onions
1 lb. ground turkey, browned & crumbled	1 pkg. (5 oz.) curried rice mix†	1 pkg. (9 oz.) frozen Italian green beans	Pickled melon rind Chutney
1 lb. meatloaf mixture, cooked	2 cups cooked elbow macaroni	1 pkg. (10 oz.) frozen mixed vegetables	Steak sauce Worcestershire sauce
1½ cups cubed cooked roast beef	1 can (1 lb.) white kidney beans, drained	2 large zucchini, trimmed & diced	Roasted red peppers Pickled mushrooms
8 thin slices cooked baked ham	1 pkg. (7 oz.) rice and vermicelli mix†	2 cups chopped raw celery	Diced apple Dried apricots
2 cups diced cooked turkey or chicken	2 cups cooked brown rice	1 can (1 lb.) whole white onions	Grated carrot Chopped sweet green pepper
1 pkg. (1 lb.) frozen halibut steaks	2 cups sliced cooked potatoes	1 pkg. (10 oz.) frozen succotash	Sliced cucumber Grated onion
1 pkg. (1 lb.) frozen cod fillets	2 cups cooked and drained rigatoni	1 can (16 oz.) tomatoes, broken up	Chopped parsley Sliced black olives
1 pkg. (1 lb.) frozen fish sticks	2 cups frozen French-fried potatoes	1 can (1 lb.) sliced carrots	Chopped peanuts Tartare sauce
1 pkg. (8 oz.) sliced salami, diced	1 can (1 lb.) red kidney beans, drained	1 small eggplant, sliced & diced	
1 pkg. (1 lb.) knackwurst, sliced	1 can (1 lb.) whole white potatoes	1 pkg. (9 oz.) frozen cut green beans	
1 pkg. (1 lb.) frankfurters, scored	1 pkg. (10 oz.) frozen hash-brown potatoes	1 pkg. (10 oz.) frozen baby lima beans	
1 can (7 oz.) tuna fish, drained	1 pkg. (5 oz) Spanish rice mix†	1 pkg. (10 oz.) fresh spinach, washed	
1 can (7¾ oz.) salmon, flaked	2 cups cooked egg noodles	1 pkg. (10 oz.) frozen chopped spinach	
1 can (8 oz.) minced clams	2 cups cooked white rice	1 pkg. (10 oz.) frozen artichoke hearts	
2 cans (4 oz. each) sardines, drained	2 cups cooked kasha	2 large yellow squash, trimmed and sliced	

*For skillet dishes　　**For casseroles　　†Cook following label directions

Choose one ingredient from each of the first 6 columns; bring to bubbling in a large skillet or flameproof casserole; choose a topping from column 7 or 8. Simmer skillet dishes for 15 to 30 minutes, or until the vegetables are tender. Bake casseroles in a hot oven (400°) for 20 to 30 minutes, or until bubbly-hot. Makes 4 servings.

LIQUID	SEASONING	TOPPINGS*	TOPPINGS**
1 can golden mushroom soup	½ tsp. ground coriander	1 cup shredded lettuce	½ cup plain toasted wheat germ
¾ cup chicken broth	2 tbsp. chopped celery leaves	¼ cup toasted coconut	½ cup toasted chopped walnuts
1 can (15 oz.) tomato sauce	1 tsp. leaf oregano, crumbled	1 cup shredded Muenster cheese	4 slices mozzarella cheese, halved
1 jar (15 oz.) Italian cooking sauce	1 tsp. Italian seasoning, crumbled	1 red onion, cut into rings	2 cups prepared mashed potatoes
1 can (10 oz.) chicken gravy	½ tsp. leaf sage, crumbled	1 large pear, halved, cored and sliced	2 cups Chinese noodles
1 pkg, (10 oz.) frozen Italian vegetables	½ teaspoon leaf thyme, crumbled	¼ cup each chopped peanuts and raisins	1 cup cherry tomatoes, halved
2 env. (1 oz. each) white sauce mix†	1 tsp. grated lemon rind	1 large cucumber, scored and sliced	¼ cup each chopped parsley and onion
½ cup dry red wine	1 tsp. leaf marjoram, crumbled	1 jar (1 lb.) pickled sliced beets	½ cup sweet pickle slices
1 can cream of mushroom soup	½ tsp. paprika or seasoned salt	1 large lemon, cut into slices	2 large tomatoes, cut into wedges
1 can (1 lb.) stewed tomatoes	1 tsp leaf basil, crumbled	1 cup herb-flavored croutons	8 thin slices French bread
1 can Cheddar cheese soup	1 tbsp. prepared mustard	1 cup crushed whole wheat flakes cereal	1 cup buttered bread crumbs
1 can (1 lb.) cream-style corn	½ tsp. ground cloves	½ cup diced dill pickle	4 slices process American cheese
1 cup tomato or vegetable juice	1 tbsp. chopped chives	½ cup sliced green onion	1 cup crushed corn chips
2 env. (1 oz. each) hollandaise sauce mix†	1 tsp. leaf tarragon, crumbled	1 cup sautéed mushrooms	1 large orange, cut into thin slices
1 cup dairy sour cream plus ½ cup milk	1 tsp. leaf rosemary crumbled	2 hard-cooked eggs, sliced	1 cup sliced stuffed green olives
1 can cream of celery soup	1 tbsp. lemon juice	1 small sweet red pepper, sliced and seeded	4 slices Swiss cheese, cut into triangles

SAUSAGE AND PEPPER PIZZA

Bake at 450° for 25 minutes.
Makes one 14-inch pizza.

Cornmeal
1 loaf (1 pound) frozen plain bread dough, thawed overnight in refrigerator
½ pound sweet Italian sausages
1 can (15 ounces) tomato sauce with tomato bits

¼ cup grated Parmesan cheese
1 sweet green pepper, halved, seeded and cut into strips
1 sweet red pepper, halved, seeded and cut into strips
2 small onions, sliced
8 ounces shredded mozzarella or pizza cheese (2 cups)

1. Lightly oil one 14-inch round pizza pan; sprinkle lightly with cornmeal. Roll and stretch the bread dough to fit the pan. Let rise for 20 minutes.

2. Preheat the oven to very hot (450°).

3. Remove the sausage from the casings; sauté the meat in a large skillet until no longer pink. Add the tomato sauce; cook, stirring often, until the juices have evaporated and the mixture is almost dry, for about 5 minutes. Remove from the heat and cool slightly. Spread the meat mixture over the dough; sprinkle with Parmesan cheese.

4. Bake in the preheated hot oven (450°) for 10 minutes; remove from the oven. Arrange the peppers and onions over the top; sprinkle with the cheese. Return to the oven. Bake for 15 to 20 minutes longer, or until the crust is golden brown and the cheese is melted and bubbly.

PIZZA SAUCE PERK

To vary flavor of prepared pizza sauces, simmer for 10 minutes with a little sautéed chopped onion and garlic. Add additional seasonings, such as oregano, basil and red pepper flakes.

9

Low-Cost Meals

With most of us feeling the financial squeeze these days, it's no wonder that meal planning becomes difficult. From week to week, it seems that the price of items in our shopping carts escalate. As a result, more thought must go toward creating meals that are not only nutritious but are also economical. But take heart—it is not necessary to spend a fortune on food to serve a delicious, attractive and nutritious meal as this chapter proves. Many low-cost meals actually can taste as if the entire food allowance was spent on that one dish!

A good example of a tasty treat that is extremely economical and nutritious is Piperade (page 161). A half-dozen eggs, some sweet green pepper, a few cherry tomatoes and you have the beginnings of a delicious and colorful meal. Another that is sure to be a hit with children, as well as adults, is the Shortcut Lasagne (page 159). You can get twelve servings at a very low cost per serving.

Complete protein: Nonfat dry milk, skim milk, eggs, American cheese, frozen fish (pollock, turbot, hake, ocean perch, cod), turkey, chicken, pork butt, beef and lamb liver, kidney.

Vegetable protein: Soybeans, lentils, other dried beans, whole-grain breads and cereals, brown rice, enriched white rice, peanuts and peanut butter.

Vitamin A: Collard greens, kale, mustard greens, turnip greens, spinach, broccoli (when well priced), cantaloupe (in season), liver.

Thiamine (Vitamin B-1): Whole-grain or enriched breads and cereals, pork and pork sausage, green peas.

Riboflavin (Vitamin B-2): Nonfat dry milk powder, skim milk, American cheese, whole-grain breads and cereals, liver.

Niacin (Vitamin B-3): Chicken, turkey, tuna canned in oil, liver, peanuts.

Vitamin C: Oranges, orange juice, grapefruit, grapefruit juice, Brussels sprouts, collard greens, broccoli (when well priced), tomatoes, raw cabbage, cauliflower (when well priced); cantaloupe (in season).

Vitamin D: Vitamin D-enriched bread and milk.

Vitamin B: Salad oil and margarine, whole-grain breads and cereals.

Calcium: Nonfat dry milk powder and skim milk, yogurt (preferably homemade), collard greens, turnip greens, kale.

Iron: Liver, beans, whole-grain breads and cereals, hamburger, pot roast.

Note: Iron is an important mineral, but many Americans, especially women, don't get enough in their daily diets, mainly because normal-sized portions of iron-rich foods are insufficient sources. Iron supplements can help; ask your doctor.

Before You Shop

The best way to make the most of your food dollars is to plan before you spend. Set aside time every week to prepare a week's worth of menus:

• Read the weekly food section in your newspaper. Note the plentiful supply list provided by the U.S. Department of Agriculture, as well as advertised specials and coupons. Decide what appeals to you and your family.

• Compare prices of at least two supermarkets. The longer you do this, the easier it will be to spot a good buy. Are there stores in your area that sell certain items—bread, soda, canned goods, dairy products, poultry—for less money? Consider their prices, too; they may still be more reasonable than another store's weekly specials.

• Set a spending limit. It's much easier to decide what to buy if you know much you can afford.

• Plan meals around meat, poultry or fish specials; keep portions of these items small and extend them with more economical beans, potatoes and grains. Remember, a meal needn't always include meat to be nutritious and satisfying.

• Strive for a blend of flavor, texture and color as you plan the rest of the meals, always thinking about the week's specials and things you have in stock. Mix crisp foods with soft ones, tangy dishes with more soothing accompaniments. Include dessert and snacks in your plan, and make them nutritious, too.

• Turn leftovers into "planned overs." Nobody has to know today's "boeuf en casserole" was yesterday's Sunday roast.

Your Shopping List—A Buying Framework

• Write down everything you'll need, making a separate list for each store. Try to limit luxury items and stick to the essentials.

• Calculate how much of each item you'll need. (Keep a record of food you throw out every week, to see how much waste can be reduced.)

• Check your cupboards. What staples are getting low? Are any on special? Buy these and other non-perishables now, when the price is right; you'll build up a food "nest egg" in your own home. Check supplies in your freezer, too.

• Plan ahead for the holidays. If you notice a non-perishable ingredient at a good price, add it to your list.

• Be determined to stick to your list as closely as possible, but be flexible. An advertised special may be disappointing and you might find a still better buy.

When to Shop

When you shop may be as important as where and what you choose to buy. Your mood, as well as the store atmosphere, can have a big effect on your shopping behavior.

• If possible, shop in the mid-morning, when specials have been put out, but aren't sold out.

• As wallets get thin toward the end of the month, stores induce you to buy with extra-special sales. Take advantage of these regular price reductions.

• Avoid shopping when you are tired or hungry—you're much more likely to buy on impulse.

EGGPLANT LASAGNE

Eggplant stretches a pound of meat to make 8 servings.

Bake at 375° for 30 minutes.
Makes 8 servings.

1 pound lean ground chuck
1 tablespoon vegetable oil
1 can (28 ounces) Italian-style tomatoes, broken up
1 teaspoon salt
½ teaspoon leaf basil, crumbled
¼ teaspoon pepper
1 clove garlic, finely chopped
2 eggs

¼ cup milk
½ cup all-purpose flour
1 cup bread crumbs
2 large eggplants (about 1 pound each), cut into ½-inch-thick slices
½ cup vegetable oil
8 ounces mozzarella cheese, shredded (2 cups)
⅓ cup grated Parmesan cheese

1. Brown the beef in the 1 tablespoon oil in a large skillet, breaking it up with wooden spoon. Add the tomatoes, salt, basil, pepper and garlic; bring to boiling. Lower the heat; cover partially and simmer for 30 minutes, stirring occasionally.

2. Beat the eggs with the milk in a pie plate until well mixed. Place the flour on a sheet of wax paper and the bread crumbs on a second sheet of wax paper. Dip the eggplant slices first in the flour and then in the egg mixture; coat with the bread crumbs.

3. Coat a large skillet generously with a little of the ½ cup oil; heat over medium heat. Add enough eggplant slices to cover the bottom. Brown lightly on both sides, adding oil as needed. Drain on paper toweling. Repeat until all the slices are browned.

4. Preheat the oven to moderate (375°).

5. Spread a spoonful of the tomato-meat sauce over the bottom of a 13 x 9 x 2-inch baking dish. Add a layer of eggplant slices and then some of the sauce. Sprinkle with some of the mozzarella and Parmesan. Repeat layering, ending with the cheeses.

6. Bake in the preheated moderate oven (375°) for 30 minutes, or until the sauce is bubbly. Let stand for 10 minutes.

SHORTCUT LASAGNE

You save time when you don't have to cook the noodles first. Just be sure to cover the casserole tightly when baking.

Bake at 350° for 1 hour.
Makes 12 servings.

1 tablespoon vegetable oil	1 package (1 pound) lasagne
1½ pounds lean ground chuck	noodles
1 can (28 ounces) whole	1 carton (12 ounces) cream-
tomatoes	style cottage cheese
1 can (8 ounces) tomato sauce	1 package (8 ounces)
2 envelopes dehydrated	mozzarella cheese,
spaghetti sauce mix	shredded
2 cans (12 ounces each)	¼ cup grated Parmesan cheese
cocktail vegetable juice	Chopped parsley

1. Preheat the oven to moderate (350°).

2. Heat the oil in a large skillet; add the meat and cook, breaking it up with a wooden spoon. Stir in the tomatoes, tomato sauce, sauce mix and vegetable juice. Bring to boiling; lower the heat and simmer for 10 minutes.

3. Cover the bottom of an oiled 13 x 9 x 2-inch baking dish with a thin layer of meat sauce. Then add a layer each of the uncooked noodles, cottage cheese and mozzarella. Repeat the layers until all ingredients are used, ending with the meat sauce.

4. Cover the casserole tightly with heavy-duty aluminum foil. Set on a jelly-roll pan. Bake in the preheated moderate oven (350°) for 1 hour.

5. Remove from the oven and let stand for 15 minutes. Sprinkle with the Parmesan cheese and chopped parsley. Cut into squares to serve.

NO-FUSS BAKED NOODLES

Increase the protein level in this no-fuss dish with leftover diced chicken or turkey.

Bake at 350° for 30 minutes.

Makes 8 servings.

1 package (8 ounces) egg noodles
1 package (10 ounces) frozen cauliflower, partially thawed and cut up
1 package (10 ounces) frozen chopped broccoli, partially thawed
1 can (10¾ ounces) cream of mushroom soup
1 cup dairy sour cream
1 medium-size onion, chopped (½ cup)
1 teaspoon salt
¼ teaspoon pepper
1½ cups shredded Swiss, Muenster or Cheddar cheese (6 ounces)

1. Preheat the oven to moderate (350°).
2. Cook the noodles in a large kettle or Dutch oven following label directions. Drain and return to the kettle. Add the cauliflower, broccoli, soup, sour cream, onion, salt, pepper and cheese. Mix gently and transfer to a 13 x 9 x 2-inch baking dish.
3. Bake in the preheated moderate oven (350°) for 30 minutes.

SPAGHETTI AND MEATBALLS

Mix a small amount of the sauce with the pasta in a serving bowl. Pass the meatballs, extra sauce and extra grated Parmesan separately.

Makes 5 servings.

1 large onion, chopped (1 cup)
1 small sweet green pepper, cored, seeded and chopped
1 clove garlic, finely chopped
2 tablespoons vegetable oil
1 can (28 ounces) Italian-style tomatoes, broken up
1 can (6 ounces) tomato paste
2 cups water
1 teaspoon salt
1 teaspoon leaf basil, crumbled
¼ teaspoon pepper
¼ teaspoon crushed red pepper flakes
Meatballs (recipe follows)
1 pound spaghetti
Grated Parmesan cheese

1. Sauté the onion, green pepper and garlic in the oil in a large saucepan until tender. Add the tomatoes, tomato paste, water, salt, basil, pepper and red pepper flakes; stir to mix well. Bring to boiling; lower the heat; partially cover and simmer for 1 hour, stirring occasionally. Drop meatballs into the sauce and simmer, partially covered, for 30 minutes longer, or until the sauce is thickened.

2. Cook the spaghetti following label directions; drain.

3. To serve, remove the meatballs to a platter and keep them warm. Spoon a little sauce into a serving bowl; place the cooked spaghetti in the bowl; toss, adding more sauce as necessary to coat each strand. Pass the extra sauce and grated Parmesan at the table.

Meatballs: Combine 1 pound ground chuck, 1 cup fresh bread crumbs, 2 eggs, 2 tablespoons chopped parsley, 2 tablespoons grated Parmesan cheese, 1 teaspoon salt, ¼ teaspoon pepper, ¼ teaspoon leaf basil, crumbled, and 1 clove garlic, finely chopped, in a large bowl. Mix lightly until well blended. Shape into balls about 1½ inches in diameter. Makes about 18 meatballs.

PIPERADE

Makes 4 servings.

½	medium-size sweet green pepper, seeded	⅓	cup diced cooked ham
1	small onion, sliced	¼	teaspoon leaf basil, crumbled
1	small clove garlic, crushed and peeled	½	teaspoon salt
			Pinch of pepper
4	tablespoons (½ stick) margarine	6	eggs
		8	cherry tomatoes, halved

1. Slice the green pepper into 1-inch pieces; sauté with the onion and garlic in 2 tablespoons of the margarine in a medium-size skillet until soft, for about 5 minutes.

2. Stir in the ham, basil, salt and pepper and cook until heated through. Remove to a small bowl and cover.

3. Beat the eggs with a rotary beater in a medium-size bowl until foamy. Melt the remaining 2 tablespoons of the margarine in same skillet. Pour in the eggs and stir quickly with a fork until the eggs are almost set. Add the warm vegetables and tomatoes to the top layer of eggs, stirring once or twice. Stop stirring; cook until the edges of the eggs are set. Cut into wedges to serve.

POTATO-EGG PUFF

Almost a meal in itself—just add a crispy vegetable salad.

Makes 4 servings.

1 package (12 ounces) frozen
   shredded hashbrown
   potatoes, thawed
4 eggs, separated
½ cup milk
1 teaspoon salt

⅛ teaspoon pepper
½ cup grated Parmesan cheese
¼ cup chopped parsley
¼ cup (½ stick) butter or
   margarine

1. To quick-thaw potatoes, put them in a sieve and pour very hot water over them. Drain well and pat dry on paper toweling.
2. Beat the egg yolks with the milk, salt and pepper in a large bowl until blended. Stir in the potatoes, Parmesan and parsley.
3. Beat the egg whites until stiff in a small bowl. Fold into the potato mixture.
4. Melt the butter in a large skillet over low heat. Pour in the mixture and spread it evenly. Cover and cook for 10 minutes.
5. Remove from the heat; remove the cover and put the skillet under a preheated broiler, with the top about 6 inches from the heat. Broil for 2 minutes, or until the top is golden brown. Cut into wedges.

HAM AND LIMA BEAN SALAD

Makes 6 servings.

3 tablespoons dairy sour
   cream
1 tablespoon white wine
   vinegar
¼ teaspoon celery seeds
2 packages (10 ounces each)
   frozen Fordhook lima
   beans

1 cup diced cooked ham
   (about 6 ounces ham)
½ cup thinly sliced celery
2 tablespoons finely chopped
   onion
   Salad greens
2 medium-size tomatoes,
   cut into 6 wedges

1. Combine the sour cream, vinegar and celery seeds in a medium-size bowl.

2. Cook the lima beans following label directions; drain and rinse with cold water. Add the beans, ham, celery and onion to the sour cream mixture, stirring gently until well blended. Cover and chill until serving time.

3. Arrange the salad greens on a platter; mound the salad in the center. Arrange the tomato wedges around the edge of the platter.

CALICO BEANS

Bake at 350° for 40 minutes.
Makes 8 servings.

6	slices bacon	1	teaspoon dry mustard
½	pound lean ground chuck	2	teaspoons vinegar
1	medium-size onion, chopped (½ cup)	1	can (16 ounces) pork and beans
½	cup catsup	1	can (15 ounces) kidney beans
1	teaspoon salt	1	can (17 ounces) lima or butter beans
¾	cup firmly packed dark brown sugar		

1. Preheat the oven to moderate (350°).

2. Cook the bacon in a large skillet until crisp; remove to paper toweling to drain; crumble and reserve.

3. Cook the beef in the drippings in the skillet until no pink remains. Add the onion; sauté just until tender.

4. Combine the beef, onion, catsup, salt, brown sugar, mustard and vinegar in a 3-quart baking dish. Partially drain all the beans and add to the baking dish, stirring gently to mix. Sprinkle with the bacon.

5. Bake in the preheated moderate oven (350°) for 40 minutes.

6. Serve with a mixed green salad and cornbread, if you wish.

FRANKFURTER AND MACARONI BAKE

Bake at 350° for 35 minutes.
Makes 8 servings.

2	cups elbow macaroni	2	teaspoons salt
¾	cup diced onion	¼	teaspoon pepper
¾	cup diced carrot	2½	cups milk
¾	cup diced celery	8	ounces mild Cheddar
½	cup (1 stick) butter or		cheese, shredded (2 cups)
	margarine	1	package (1 pound)
6	tablespoons all-purpose		frankfurters (8 to 10),
	flour		sliced ¼ inch thick

1. Preheat the oven to moderate (350°).
2. Cook the macaroni following label directions; drain.
3. While the macaroni cooks, sauté the onion, carrot and celery in the butter until soft in a large saucepan. Stir in the flour, salt and pepper and cook, stirring constantly, just until bubbly.
4. Stir in the milk; continue cooking and stirring until the sauce thickens and bubbles; add the cheese to the sauce, stirring until the cheese is melted.
5. Combine the macaroni, frankfurters and cheese sauce in a large bowl; mix thoroughly. Turn into a 10-cup buttered soufflé or baking dish.
6. Bake in the preheated moderate oven (350°) for 35 minutes, or until the sauce is bubbly hot.

CORNED BEEF HASH

A favorite way to use leftover corned beef.
Makes 4 servings.

1	pound cooked leftover cold corned beef	1	teaspoon pepper
2	medium-size cold boiled potatoes	¼	cup (½ stick) butter or margarine
1	medium-size onion, coarsely chopped (½ cup)	4	eggs
			Parsley sprigs
¼	cup coarsely chopped sweet green pepper		

1. Put the corned beef through a food grinder using the coarse plate. Grind and measure (you should have 3 cups coarsely ground corned beef). Grind the potatoes and measure (you should have 1½ cups coarsely ground potatoes).

2. Combine the corned beef, potatoes, onion, green pepper and black pepper in a large mixing bowl; mix thoroughly.

3. Slowly heat the butter in a heavy 8-inch skillet until foamy.

4. Turn the hash mixture into the skillet, pressing down firmly with a spatula or pancake turner.

5. Cook the hash, uncovered, over medium heat for about 15 minutes, or until a brown crust forms on the bottom. Turn with the spatula so that some of the crust is brought to the top. Cook slowly, turning several times, until the desired crust is formed, adding additional butter if necessary.

6. With the back of a spoon, make 4 shallow indentations on top of the hash. Break an egg into each hollow. Cover; cook for 5 minutes, or to the firmness you desire. (The eggs should be soft enough to make a sauce for the hash.) Garnish with parsley. Serve with catsup or chili sauce, if you wish.

BUDGET STRETCHERS

The bags used to package onions, oranges or what have you at the supermarket make excellent pot scrubbers for casseroles. They can be tied in a bunch with a rubber band and rinsed clean with just a quick swish under the cold water tap.

Buy rice the money-saving way, by the 3-pound bag, and store it in a covered container. Once in a while cook up enough for several meals and keep it in the refrigerator or freezer. Use it in place of other starches, as a pilaf, or for meatloaves, stuffed peppers, salads, rice pudding, or as a base for a casserole with leftover vegetables, meat or cheese.

Save those snack food tag-ends. Crush the last of pretzels, potato chips or crackers and use as a casserole topping.

Don't throw away leftover cheese after a party. Save even the tiniest wedge, grate it, and freeze it in an airtight plastic bag. Add additional scraps as you have them. The grated frozen cheese melts in an instant and is great for chicken, veal parmigiana, omelets, soufflés and the like.

CHILI SKILLET MEAL

A macaroni-luncheon meat dish that's easy to make.

Makes 4 servings.

2 tablespoons butter or margarine	1 can (16 ounces) whole tomatoes
1 large onion, chopped (1 cup)	2 tablespoons sugar (optional)
1 can (12 ounces) luncheon meat, cubed	2 teaspoons chili powder
1 cup elbow macaroni	

1. Melt the butter in a large skillet; add the onion and luncheon meat. Sauté until the onion is soft and the meat is lightly browned.

2. Add the macaroni; cook for 2 minutes, stirring often. Drain off any excess fat. Stir in the tomatoes with their liquid, sugar, if used, and chili powder. Bring to boiling; lower the heat. Cover and simmer until the macaroni is tender, for about 20 minutes, stirring occasionally.

SKILLET MOUSSAKA

All the delicious ingredients of the fabled moussaka are together in this quick-to-fix skillet dish.

Makes 6 servings.

1 medium-size eggplant	⅛ teaspoon pepper
4 tablespoons all-purpose flour	½ teaspoon leaf oregano, crumbled
1 pound lean ground lamb or beef	2 tablespoons butter or margarine
1 medium-size onion, chopped (½ cup)	1 egg yolk, lightly beaten
1 clove garlic, crushed and peeled	1 cup milk
1 can (8 ounces) tomato sauce	4 ounces Monterey Jack cheese, shredded (1 cup)
½ teaspoon salt	Chopped parsley

1. Pare the eggplant and cut it into ½-inch cubes. Coat with 2 tablespoons of the flour.

2. Cook the meat slowly in a large skillet until no pink remains. Add the onion, garlic and cubed eggplant. Cook and stir over moderate heat until the eggplant begins to soften. Stir in the tomato sauce, salt, pepper and oregano and simmer for 5 minutes.

3. Melt the butter in a small saucepan and stir in the remaining 2 tablespoons of flour.
4. Combine the beaten egg yolk with the milk in a small bowl. Add to the butter mixture. Cook and stir over low heat until the sauce is slightly thickened.
5. Stir the hot sauce into the meat mixture; sprinkle with the cheese. Cook over low heat until the cheese melts. Sprinkle with chopped parsley.

LIVER IN TOMATO SAUCE

This delectable casserole features liver slices baked with onions and green peppers in a spicy tomato sauce. Serve with noodles, if you wish.

Bake at 350° for 30 minutes.
Makes 4 servings.

1 pound beef liver	2 tablespoons butter or
5 tablespoons all-purpose	margarine
flour	2 cups tomato juice
1½ teaspoons salt	1 teaspoon Worcestershire
¼ teaspoon pepper	sauce
4 tablespoons vegetable oil	1 teaspoon lemon juice
1 medium-size onion, sliced	1 teaspoon sugar
½ medium-size sweet green	
pepper, chopped (½ cup)	

1. Preheat the oven to moderate (350°).
2. Cut the liver into thin slices, removing any membranes from the edges. Combine 2 tablespoons of the flour, 1 teaspoon of the salt and the pepper and sprinkle over the liver.
3. Brown the liver quickly on both sides in 3 tablespoons of the oil in a medium-size skillet. Remove to a lightly greased 1½-quart casserole.
4. Sauté the onion and green pepper in the remaining 1 tablespoon oil in the same skillet. Spoon over the liver, spreading evenly.
5. Melt the butter in a small saucepan. Add the remaining flour and cook, stirring for 1 minute. Gradually add the tomato juice, stirring constantly. Cook until thickened and bubbly. Add the Worcestershire, lemon juice, sugar and remaining ½ teaspoon salt. Cook for 1 or 2 minutes to blend the flavors. Pour over the liver and vegetables.
6. Bake, covered, in the preheated moderate oven (350°) for 30 minutes.

EMPRESS BEEF

Makes about 4 servings.

3 tablespoons vegetable oil
¼ teaspoon salt
½ pound boneless sirloin steak cut into julienne strips
1 large onion, thinly sliced
3 celery stalks, coarsely chopped (1 cup)
¼ pound fresh or frozen snow peas, each cut in half on the diagonal OR: ¼ pound frozen French cut string beans (about ½ package)
1 can (3 ounces) whole mushrooms, drained and thinly sliced
½ cup coarsely chopped water chestnuts
1 tablespoon cornstarch
½ tablespoon sugar
5 tablespoons soy sauce
½ cup water
Hot cooked rice

1. Heat the oil in a large skillet; add the salt and then the beef; cook, stirring often, over high heat to brown the meat, for about 5 minutes. Add the onion, celery, snow peas, mushrooms and water chestnuts. Continue cooking over high heat, stirring constantly, for 2 to 3 minutes. Cover; lower the heat and simmer for about 3 minutes.
2. Combine the cornstarch, sugar, soy sauce and water in a 1 cup measure; mix well. Add to the skillet and cook, stirring constantly, until the mixture thickens and bubbles for 1 minute. Serve immediately over hot cooked rice.

BEEF-TOM IN ONE

This convenient skillet main dish is made with beef, vegetables
and cheese and may be topped with mashed potatoes, if you wish.
Serve with chili-flavored warm cornbread and fruit salad or sliced
oranges for dessert.

Makes 6 servings.

1	pound lean ground round	1	cup tomatoes from a 16-ounce can, undrained but roughly chopped
1	large onion, chopped (1 cup)		
1	teaspoon salt		
¼	teaspoon pepper	1	can (8 ounces) whole-kernel corn, drained
⅛	teaspoon garlic powder (optional)		
½	teaspoon leaf oregano, crumbled	¼	pound process American cheese, cubed

1. Combine the beef, onion, salt, pepper, garlic powder and oregano
in a large skillet. Cook slowly, stirring often, until the beef is browned
and the onion is tender. Drain off any accumulated fat.

2. Add the tomatoes and corn and mix well. Cover and simmer for 20
minutes, or until the beef is cooked.

3. Remove the skillet from the heat. Stir in the cheese cubes. Let
stand for about 1 minute, or until the cheese melts. Serve
immediately.

Note: Substitute cooked carrots for the tomatoes. Or omit the corn
and top the ingredients with mashed potatoes, if you wish.

TOMATO AND MOZZARELLA SANDWICH LOAF

Makes 6 servings.

1   loaf (12 to 15 inches long) Italian or French bread
¼   cup olive oil
2   ripe tomatoes, cored and sliced
1   package (8 ounces) sliced mozzarella cheese
¾   teaspoon salt
¼   teaspoon pepper

1   medium-size red onion, thinly sliced and separated into rings
1   clove garlic, crushed and peeled
3   tablespoons chopped parsley
½   teaspoon leaf basil, crumbled
1   tablespoon red wine vinegar

1. Cut the loaf in half lengthwise with a serrated knife. Put the bread on a large sheet of aluminum foil. Sprinkle the cut surfaces with 1 tablespoon of the oil.

2. Arrange the tomato and cheese slices alternately and overlapping on the bottom half of the loaf. Sprinkle with salt and pepper. Scatter the onion rings, garlic, parsley and basil evenly over. Drizzle the vinegar and enough of the remaining oil to moisten all ingredients generously. Press the top half of the loaf down on the filling to form a compact shape.

3. Weight the loaf with a platter and let stand at room temperature for at least 30 minutes. Cut into thick portions with a serrated knife.

10

Low-Calorie Dishes

Most health-conscious Americans count calories to stay physically fit, but they sometimes forget that it is extremely important when watching calories not to eliminate essential daily requirements from their diet. As a caring meal planner and preparer, you can ensure that your family's diet is completely balanced with all essential nutrients necessary for maintaining a healthy and fit lifestyle.

In the pages ahead, we have compiled several recipes that are perfect solutions for calorie-conscious eaters. These recipes combine vegetables, starches, and meats in low-calorie combinations. It's hard to believe that a meal tasting so good can be low in calories, but as you can see from the calorie count included with each recipe, it certainly is.

A favorite with dieters will surely be Texas Beef Chili (page 180). The combination of beef, chili powder, garlic and vinegar simmered slowly to blend the flavors is a treat to your tastebuds and your waistline.

GREEN VEGETABLE SOUP (COLD OR HOT)

This basic green soup of fresh vegetables and herbs has many variations.
You can use zucchini in place of, or in addition to, cucumber, add
green beans, green peppers (roast and peel them first or the tough
skins will remain in stringy little slivers), throw in other fresh herbs or
leafy greens, lettuce and watercress. Each combination gives a slightly
different flavor so this is a soup you can experiment with and have
fun with all summer long. Make up batches of the soup stock and freeze,
to bring out for a quick lunch or when unexpected guests drop in.
All that is necessary then is to thaw it, swirl in the yogurt with a blender,
and serve, either hot or chilled.

Makes 8 servings at 60 calories per serving.

2	cups canned chicken broth, skimmed	6	sprigs parsley
3	cucumbers, pared, seeded and sliced	6	sprigs mint
		1	teaspoon salt
6	green onions, peeled and sliced	¼	teaspoon pepper
		½	pound spinach, washed and stems removed
2	cloves garlic, peeled	2	tablespoons lemon juice
1	cup sliced celery	1	to 1½ cups plain yogurt
1	medium-size potato, pared and diced		

1. Combine the chicken broth, cucumbers, green onions, garlic, celery, potato, parsley, mint, salt and pepper in a large saucepan. Bring to boiling; lower the heat; cover and simmer just until the potato is tender but not mushy.

2. Add the spinach and cook just until it wilts down in the hot liquid (at this point you can add and wilt down other leafy greens or add leftover cooked and cubed green vegetables).

3. Purée the mixture through a food mill, or whirl in the container of an electric blender. Stir in the lemon juice and chill. (This basic soup stock can be frozen.)

4. When ready to serve the soup, whirl the mixture in the container of an electric blender with enough of the yogurt to give the soup the consistency you prefer. Add additional salt and pepper to taste. Serve topped with chopped parsley, cucumber, or mint, if you wish.

5. If serving the soup hot, reheat to boiling after puréeing; remove from the heat and whirl in a blender with the yogurt. Heat, but do not allow to boil or the yogurt with curdle.

SEEDING AND SLICING A CUCUMBER

Step 1. Using a vegetable parer or small sharp paring knife, peel the cucumber; slice the cucumber in half lengthwise. Using a spoon or grapefruit knife, run the tip along the inside of the cucumber from about ¼ inch from the edge. Scoop out and discard the seeds.

Step 2. Place flat side down and cut crosswise (or lengthwise) into desired-size pieces.

NEAPOLITAN PEAS AND EGGS

This egg and vegetable combination makes a good brunch dish.

Makes 5 servings at 221 calories per serving.

1	small onion, chopped (¼ cup)	½	cup water
1	tablespoon vegetable oil	1	bag (20 ounces) frozen peas
2	cans (8 ounces each) tomato sauce	⅛	teaspoon pepper
		5	eggs

Sauté the onion in a large skillet until tender. Add the tomato sauce and water; bring to boiling. Add the peas and pepper and cook over high heat until the peas have separated and thawed. Lower the heat. Break the eggs carefully, one at a time, onto the pea mixture, far enough apart so they will cook separately. Cover tightly and simmer for 5 to 10 minutes, or until the eggs are cooked to desired doneness.

SHREDDED CHICKEN AND VEGETABLE CHOW MEIN

Makes 6 servings at 311 calories per serving.

3 cups frozen Oriental-style vegetables with green beans, broccoli, onion and mushrooms (from a 20-ounce poly bag)

2 tablespoons vegetable oil

2 cans (5 ounces each) canned chunk white chicken, rinsed and drained

1 can (16 ounces) mung bean sprouts, drained

1 can (8 ounces) water chestnuts, drained and sliced thin

½ cup bottled teriyaki marinade with wine

1 tablespoon cornstarch

1 can (5 ounces) chow mein noodles

1. Heat a large skillet or wok until hot. Add the frozen vegetables; sprinkle with the oil; toss to mix. Cover and cook for 2 minutes, stirring two or three times.

2. Uncover the skillet and stir the vegetable mixture constantly for about 30 seconds. Add the chicken, bean sprouts and water chestnuts. Stir the teriyaki marinade into the cornstarch in a cup; add the mixture to the skillet, stirring constantly until the marinade mixture thickens and the vegetables and meat are hot.

3. Spoon the skillet mixture over the chow mein noodles. Garnish with orange segments, green onion "brushes" and red pepper, if you wish.

TAKE THE FAT OUT OF EATING WITHOUT SPOILING THE MEAL

• Increase the consumption of vegetables, pasta, legumes and whole grains, and limit your intake of red meats, eggs and whole-milk products.

• Cook with polyunsaturated oils (safflower, soybean, sesame and corn oils) rather than animal fats like lard, bacon drippings or butter.

• Steam, poach or broil fish or poultry instead of frying or stewing. Make use of a steamer, wok or non-stick pan.

• Cut down on the oil in salad dressings by first flavoring the greens with fresh chives, basil, tarragon, sliced onions or green onions, and then make dressing with lowfat yogurt, lemon juice or a good wine vinegar.

TEN-MINUTE SZECHUAN CHICKEN

Makes 4 servings at 221 calories per serving.

2	whole chicken breasts	1½	tablespoons white wine
3	tablespoons cornstarch		vinegar
1	teaspoon monosodium	1	teaspoon sugar
	glutamate (optional)	¼	cup water
1	tablespoon vegetable oil	1	bunch green onions, cut into
3	cloves garlic, finely		1-inch pieces
	chopped	⅛	to ¼ teaspoon cayenne
5	tablespoons soy sauce		pepper

1. Split the chicken breasts in half; skin and bone them. Cut the chicken into 1½-inch cubes. Combine the cornstarch and monosodium glutamate, if using, in a paper bag. Add the chicken pieces and toss lightly to coat.
2. Heat the oil in a large non-stick skillet; add the chicken and garlic. Stir-fry until the chicken is lightly browned.
3. Add the soy sauce, vinegar, sugar and water to the skillet; cover. Cook for 3 minutes, or until the chicken is cooked through.
4. Uncover the skillet and add the green onions and cayenne. Heat for 2 minutes longer.

SPANISH EGGS

Makes 3 servings at 153 calories per serving.

1	small onion, finely chopped	¼	teaspoon garlic salt
	(¼ cup)	⅛	to ¼ teaspoon chili powder
1	cup canned tomatoes,	3	eggs
	chopped	3	slices protein bread, toasted
1	can (4 ounces) mushrooms,		
	drained and chopped		

1. Combine the onion, tomatoes, mushrooms, garlic salt and chili powder in a skillet. Simmer uncovered for 5 minutes, stirring frequently.
2. Break the eggs, one at a time, into a saucer; carefully slip into the simmering sauce so that the yolks remain unbroken. Cover and cook just until the eggs are set—about 3 minutes.
3. Place the toast slices on three plates. Lift the eggs out onto the toast. Spoon the sauce over each serving.

CODFISH CREOLE

Bake at 350° for 40 minutes.
Makes 6 servings at 120 calories per serving.

1½	pounds frozen cod fillets, thawed	⅛	to ¼ teaspoon cayenne pepper
1	sweet green pepper, seeded and chopped	½	teaspoon salt
1	medium-size onion, chopped	¼	cup chopped pimiento-stuffed green olives
½	cup sliced celery	1	can (16 ounces) tomatoes
		1	tablespoon cornstarch

1. Preheat the oven to moderate (350°).

2. Cut the cod fillets into 1½-inch pieces; place in a shallow 2-quart baking dish. Spread the green pepper, onion and celery in a layer over the fish. Sprinkle with the cayenne, salt and chopped olives.

3. Drain the liquid from the tomatoes into a small bowl; reserve. Cut up the tomatoes and arrange over the fish in the baking dish. Combine the cornstarch with the reserved tomato liquid and pour over the contents of the baking dish.

4. Bake in the preheated moderate oven (350°) for 40 minutes, or until the fish flakes easily with a fork.

TUNA-TOPPED EGGPLANT SALAD

Serve this innovative salad for a luncheon entrée or buffet specialty.
Makes 8 servings at 206 calories per serving.

1	medium-size eggplant (about 1¼ pounds), washed	2	tablespoons tomato paste
	Salt	3	tablespoons drained capers
6	green onions (including some tops), sliced	6	pitted black olives, minced
1	cup chopped celery	3	flat anchovy fillets, minced (optional)
½	cup olive oil (approximately)	2	teaspoons sugar
4	canned Italian plum tomatoes, drained and chopped	3	tablespoons wine vinegar
		2	cans (6½ ounces each) tuna, drained and separated into chunks
		¼	cup chopped parsley

1. Cut the unpared eggplant into 1-inch cubes. Put in a colander and sprinkle with salt. Leave to drain for 30 minutes. Rinse in cold water and pat dry with paper toweling.

2. Sauté the green onions and celery in ⅓ cup of the oil in a large skillet for 1 minute. Push aside. Add the eggplant cubes, several at a time, and cook over medium heat, stirring frequently, until soft and golden, adding more oil as needed.

3. Stir in the tomatoes, tomato paste, capers, olives, anchovies, if used, sugar and vinegar. Cook slowly, uncovered, for about 25 minutes.

4. Remove from the heat and cool. Refrigerate for at least 24 hours for the flavors to develop.

5. Spoon the eggplant salad onto a plate. Top with the tuna chunks; sprinkle with parsley.

CUT DOWN ON SUGAR AND NOT EVEN MISS IT

• Read labels to estimate sugar content. Besides sugar, look for the words "dextrose," "maltose," "sucrose," "fructose," "honey," "corn sweetener" and "corn syrup." They all mean sugar. If these appear in the first three ingredients, the product has a high sugar content; also, if several of these different ingredients appear elsewhere in the listing, realize that if you added them all up, "sugar" might well turn out to be the main ingredient.

• Use fruits to sweeten rather than sugar. Pineapple, raisins, bananas, oranges and unsweetened fruit juices can be used in some vegetable and main dishes as well as desserts.

• When making quick breads, cakes and cookies, cut sugar by one-third to one-half. Bring out the sweetness with vanilla extract or a naturally sweet food, such as dates.

• Cut down on soft drinks that contain lots of sugar (6 to 9 teaspoons in 12 ounces). Try calorie-free club soda, seltzer or mineral water, all of which are more thirst-quenching, too.

• Try new combinations of ingredients to get the sweet flavor you like. When cooking, add or increase sweet spices or herbs, such as nutmeg, ginger, mace, cinnamon, cardomom or coriander. Use fresh fruit purées rather than sugar-laden jams and preserves. Put fruit, such as bananas or grapefruit, under the broiler and top with cinnamon for a special sweeter taste.

CALORIE-SAVER'S PAELLA

Even dieters can enjoy this favorite from sunny Valencia when it's made this calorie-saving way.

Broil for 20 minutes. Bake at 350° for 1 hour.
Makes 6 servings at 363 calories per serving.

1	broiler-fryer (about 2 pounds), cut up	1	can (16 ounces) tomatoes
1	large onion, chopped (1 cup)	1½	cups water
1	clove garlic, finely chopped	1	envelope instant chicken broth OR: 1 chicken bouillon cube
1	cup long-grain white rice		
6	small slices hard salami, diced	1	pound fresh shrimp, shelled and deveined OR: 1 package (12 ounces) frozen shelled and deveined raw shrimp
2	teaspoons salt		
¼	teaspoon pepper		
⅛	teaspoon saffron threads, crushed	1	can (4 ounces) pimiento, drained and cut in large pieces

1. Place the chicken, skin-side down, in a single layer on the rack of a broiler pan.

2. Broil, 4 inches from the heat, for 10 minutes; turn; broil for 10 minutes longer, or until lightly browned; reserve. Lower the oven temperature to moderate (350°).

3. Pour 2 tablespoons of the drippings from the broiler pan into a large skillet. Stir in the onion and garlic and sauté until soft; spoon into a 12-cup casserole with the rice, salami, salt, pepper and saffron.

4. Combine the tomatoes with the water and instant chicken broth or bouillon cube in the skillet; bring to boiling, crushing the bouillon cube, if using, with a spoon. Stir into the rice mixture with the shrimp. Arrange the chicken and pimiento on top and cover.

5. Bake in the preheated moderate oven (350°) for 1 hour, or until the liquid is absorbed and the chicken is tender. Garnish with parsley, if desired.

DIETER'S CURRIED LAMB

Lean lamb, green beans and yellow squash make good eating
that's low in calories, too.

Bake at 350° for 1 hour and 30 minutes.
Makes 8 servings at 253 calories per serving.

2	pounds lean boneless lamb shoulder, cubed	1¼	cups water
2	tablespoons vegetable oil	3	large yellow squash, trimmed and sliced
1	large onion, chopped (1 cup)	1	pound green beans, trimmed and cut into 1-inch pieces
2	cloves garlic, finely chopped		
1	tablespoon curry powder		
1	teaspoon salt	2	tablespoons all-purpose flour
¼	teaspoon pepper		
1	can (10½ ounces) condensed chicken broth	¼	cup cold water

1. Preheat the oven to moderate (350°).

2. Brown the lamb, part at a time, in the oil in a 10-cup flameproof casserole or a large kettle; remove and reserve; drain on paper toweling. Pour off all but 1 tablespoon of the pan drippings.

3. Sauté the onion and garlic in the pan drippings. Stir in the curry powder and cook for 2 minutes; return the lamb to the casserole; stir in the salt, pepper, chicken broth and the 1¼ cups water.

4. Bring slowly to boiling; cover. (If using a kettle, spoon lamb mixture into a 10-cup casserole; cover.)

5. Bake in a preheated moderate oven (350°) for 1 hour, or until the meat is almost tender; add the yellow squash and green beans; cover and bake for 30 minutes, or until the meat and vegetables are tender when pierced with a fork.

6. Combine the flour and ¼ cup water in a small saucepan; stir in 1½ cups of the hot cooking liquid from the casserole. (A bulb baster does a quick job.) Cook, stirring constantly, until the sauce thickens and bubbles for 3 minutes. Spoon over the lamb and vegetables. Top with chopped fresh mint, if you wish.

Suggested Variations: Chicken breasts, green onions, broccoli flowerets and sliced mushrooms can be substituted for the lamb and vegetables in this recipe.

TEXAS BEEF CHILI

Makes 6 servings at 181 calories per serving.

1½ pounds lean boneless beef round steak
Vegetable oil
1½ to 2½ tablespoons chili powder
3 tablespoons cornmeal
½ teaspoon instant minced garlic

2 envelopes instant beef broth
3 cups water
1 tablespoon cider vinegar
1 teaspoon salt
⅛ teaspoon pepper

1. Trim all fringe fat from the steak. Cut the steak into ½-inch cubes.
2. Coat a non-stick skillet very lightly with oil. Add the meat cubes and cook over medium heat until browned. Drain the fat from the skillet, if necessary.
3. Stir in the chili powder, cornmeal, garlic, beef broth, water, vinegar, salt and pepper. Cover and simmer for about 1 hour, or until the meat is nearly tender. Uncover; simmer until most of the liquid is evaporated—for about 10 minutes.

CUTTING CASSEROLE CALORIES

- Trim all visible fat from meat before browning or braising.
- Brown meats in a non-stick skillet.
- Substitute cooked shredded cabbage, lettuce or spinach for the bed of pasta or rice in your favorite recipe.
- Use skim milk, skim evaporated milk or chicken or beef broth for cream and whole milk in sauces.
- Substitute lowfat cheese, such as lowfat cottage cheese and lowfat mozzarella, for whole-milk cheese.
- Remove every speck of fat from stews or pot roasts before thickening gravy by refrigerating food or adding a few ice cubes to the liquid. Wait for the fat to harden; then skim it off.

BELL PEPPERS RELLENOS

Makes 4 servings at 226 calories per serving.

8	small well-shaped sweet green peppers	⅛	teaspoon ground cinnamon
¾	pound lean ground round	1	teaspoon garlic salt
1	large onion, finely chopped (1 cup)	2	tablespoons white vinegar
		1	egg
½	to 1½ teaspoons chili powder	1	can (8 ounces) Spanish-style tomato sauce
1	teaspoon leaf oregano, crumbled	½	cup water
¼	teaspoon ground cumin	4	tablespoons shredded extra-sharp Cheddar cheese (1 ounce)

1. Slice off the pepper tops ½ inch down. Cut a circle from each top to remove the stem. Remove the seeds from the pepper cases.

2. Brown the meat without added fat in a non-stick skillet. Drain off any extra fat. Add the onion, chili powder, oregano, cumin, cinnamon and garlic salt. Stir over medium heat until the onion is lightly browned. Remove from the heat and stir in the vinegar and egg.

3. Spoon the meat filling into the pepper cases. Stand the filled peppers in a heavy kettle or Dutch oven. Replace the tops on the pepper cases and pour the tomato sauce and water around the peppers. Cover and simmer for 15 minutes, or until the peppers are just tender and the liquid is reduced to a thick sauce.

4. Sprinkle ½ tablespoon of the grated cheese in the center of each pepper lid. Heat just until the cheese begins to melt. Serve at once.

LOW-CAL BEEF STEW

Try this method for browning onions and beef, without using a drop of fat.

Bake at 325° for 2 hours.
Makes 6 servings at 304 calories per serving.

1 small onion, chopped (¼ cup)	1 teaspoon seasoned salt
½ cup water	¼ teaspoon seasoned pepper
1½ pounds lean boneless beef round, cubed	6 small potatoes, pared
1 can (10½ ounces) condensed beef broth	3 cups sliced celery
1 cup dry red wine or water	3 small zucchini, trimmed and cut into sticks
1 bay leaf	3 cups shredded lettuce
	12 cherry tomatoes

1. Preheat the oven to slow (325°).

2. Simmer the onion in the ½ cup water in a non-stick large skillet for 10 minutes or just until the water evaporates. Continue cooking and stirring constantly over low heat until the onion browns lightly; spoon into a 12-cup casserole.

3. Brown the beef, part at a time, in the same skillet and place in the casserole. Stir the beef broth, wine or water, bay leaf, seasoned salt and pepper into the skillet; bring to boiling, stirring up the browned juices; pour over the beef in the casserole; cover the casserole.

4. Bake in the preheated slow oven (325°) for 1 hour; stir in the potatoes; cover; bake for 30 minutes; stir in the celery and zucchini; cover; bake for 15 minutes; stir in the lettuce and cherry tomatoes; cover; bake for 15 minutes longer, or until the meat and vegetables are tender. Remove the bay leaf. Serve in heated soup bowls.

Suggested Variations: Lean lamb or pork can be substituted for the beef in this recipe. Chicken broth, green beans, carrots, broccoli or cauliflower can also be used in place of the beef broth and listed vegetables.

NO-CRUST LOW-CALORIE QUICHE

Eliminating the pastry and using yogurt in place of cream make this quiche a delicious, de-calorized main dish.

Bake at 375° for 35 minutes.
Makes 6 servings at 204 calories per serving.

1 pound fresh spinach OR: 1 package (10 ounces) frozen spinach
1 bunch watercress
1 tablespoon lemon juice
1 teaspoon butter or margarine
4 eggs
1 cup plain yogurt
½ cup milk
¼ teaspoon ground nutmeg
½ teaspoon salt
¼ teaspoon pepper
¼ cup grated Parmesan cheese
¼ cup finely chopped parsley
1½ cups finely diced cooked ham

1. Preheat the oven to moderate (375°).
2. Wash the fresh spinach and watercress in several changes of water. Pick over and remove any bruised leaves and coarse stems. Press the greens into a large saucepan with just the water that clings to the leaves. Cover and cook just until wilted. (If using frozen spinach cook following label directions.) Drain the spinach and watercress well in a colander, pressing out the excess water with a wooden spoon. Chop very finely with a knife, or purée in the container of an electric blender. Stir in the lemon juice.
3. Grease the bottom and sides of an 8 x 8 x 2-inch baking pan with 1 teaspoon butter.
4. Beat the eggs in a large bowl just until foamy. Beat in the yogurt, milk, nutmeg, salt, pepper, 2 tablespoons of the parsley, the ham and the puréed spinach. Pour into the prepared pan; sprinkle the top with the remaining cheese and parsley. Place the baking pan in a larger pan; then place on a shelf in the oven. Pour boiling water into the outer pan to come halfway up the sides of the baking pan.
5. Bake in the preheated moderate oven (375°) for 35 minutes, or until the custard is set. Test by gently pressing the center with a fingertip (it should be firm to the touch). Remove the pan from the water; let the quiche stand for 10 minutes before serving.

ZUCCHINI BOLOGNESE

Long slender slices of zucchini take the place of lasagne noodles in this calorie-saving version of an Italian classic.

Bake at 350° for 1 hour.
Makes 6 servings at 273 calories per serving.

4 large zucchini (about 2 pounds total weight)	**¾** teaspoons salt
2 medium-size onions, sliced	**1** teaspoon leaf oregano, crumbled
2 sweet or hot Italian sausage links	**½** teaspoon garlic powder
¾ cup water	**½** teaspoon sugar
1 package (8 ounces) lowfat mozzarella cheese, diced	**¼** teaspoon pepper
¼ pound mushrooms, sliced (optional)	**1** can (20 ounces) tomatoes in tomato purée
	½ cup lowfat ricotta cheese (from a 15-ounce container)

1. Trim the zucchini and cut it into very thin lengthwise slices with a very sharp knife.

2. Preheat the oven to moderate (350°).

3. Place the onion slices and Italian sausages in a large skillet with the water; cook over medium heat, stirring often, until the water evaporates; then stir constantly until the onion slices are golden; remove from the heat; chop the sausages.

4. Layer one third of the zucchini slices in a 8-cup shallow casserole; top with part of the cheese and mushroom slices. Combine the salt, oregano, garlic powder, sugar and pepper in a cup; sprinkle part over; layer with one third of the onion-meat mixture and tomatoes in purée. Repeat to make three layers; cover the casserole with aluminum foil.

5. Bake in the preheated moderate oven (350°) for 40 minutes; remove the foil; bake for 20 minutes longer, or until the zucchini is tender and the casserole is bubbly. Spoon the ricotta on top. Let stand for 10 minutes before serving.

Suggested Variations: A cup of diced cooked chicken, ½ pound ground lean beef or ½ pound chicken livers can be substituted for the Italian sausages in this recipe. To save a few more calories, use lowfat cottage cheese rather than the ricotta on top.

KEY WEST PORK

From Florida comes the inspiration for this sweet-sour combination of tropical fruits that go so well with pork.

Bake at 350° for 1 hour and 30 minutes.
Makes 8 servings at 263 calories per serving.

2	pounds lean boneless pork shoulder, cubed	1	acorn squash, cut into ½-inch slices, pared and seeded
2	tablespoons vegetable oil	1	package (9 ounces) frozen artichoke hearts
1	large onion, chopped (1 cup)	1	teaspoon grated lime rind
2	envelopes or teaspoons instant chicken broth	1	tablespoon lime juice
1¼	cups water	1	can (8 ounces) pineapple chunks in pineapple juice
2	teaspoons salt	3	tablespoons cornstarch

1. Preheat the oven to moderate (350°).

2. Brown the pork cubes, part at a time, in the oil in a 10-cup flame-proof casserole or a large kettle; remove to drain on paper toweling; reserve. Pour off all but 1 tablespoon of the pan drippings.

3. Sauté the onion in the pan drippings until soft; return the browned pork to the casserole. Add the chicken broth, water and salt; bring slowly to boiling and cover. (If using a skillet, spoon the pork mixture into a 10-cup casserole; cover.)

4. Bake in the preheated moderate oven (350°) for 1 hour, or until the pork is almost tender; add the acorn squash slices and bake for 15 minutes; add the artichoke hearts and bake for 15 minutes longer, or until the meat and vegetables are tender; stir in the lime rind and juice.

5. Drain the liquid from the pineapple into a small saucepan; blend in the cornstarch; add the pineapple chunks to the kettle.

6. Stir 1½ cups of the hot cooking liquid from the casserole into the saucepan. (A bulb baster does a quick job.) Cook, stirring constantly, until the sauce thickens and bubbles for 1 minute. Taste and sweeten with liquid or granulated sweetener, if you wish. Spoon over the pork and vegetables. Garnish with lime slices, if you wish. Serve a low-calorie fruit gelatin for dessert.

11

International Dishes

The recent surge in popularity of various ethnic cuisines has not been limited to restaurant menus. The trend is also bringing international cooking into the home, as is evident by the ever-increasing supply of ethnic foods found in supermarkets and specialty stores, as well as the availability of various cooking utensils used to prepare those foods.

Experimenting with different foreign cuisines is a great way to bring variety to your everyday menu planning. Simply by using different spices and seasonings, such as a touch of ground ginger, as in Beef and Peppers in Spicy Garlic Sauce (page 201), you add the exotic flare of the Orient. A hint of curry turns a soup or casserole into a Middle Eastern delicacy.

Delight family and friends by creating international meals that will make them feel as if they just embarked on a spur-of-the-moment dining adventure abroad.

MULLIGATAWNY SOUP

From the days of the British in India comes this hearty chicken and vegetable soup. Vary the amount of curry powder you add to suit your own taste.

Makes 6 servings.

6 envelopes or teaspoons instant chicken broth
6 cups boiling water
3 medium-size carrots, pared and sliced
2 celery stalks, sliced
3 cups diced cooked chicken
1 large onion, chopped (1 cup)
¼ cup (½ stick) butter or margarine
1 apple, pared, quartered, cored and chopped
1 to 2 tablespoons curry powder
1 teaspoon salt
¼ cup all-purpose flour
1 tablespoon lemon juice
2 cups hot cooked rice
¼ cup chopped parsley
6 lemon slices

1. Dissolve 1 teaspoon of the instant chicken broth in 1 cup of the boiling water in a medium-size saucepan. Stir in the carrots and celery and cook over medium heat for 20 minutes, or until tender. Add the chicken and heat until hot; keep warm.

2. Sauté the onion until soft in the butter in a Dutch oven; stir in the apple, curry powder to taste and salt; sauté for 5 minutes longer, or until the apple is soft; add the flour. Gradually stir in the remaining instant chicken broth and water; bring to boiling; cover and simmer for 15 minutes.

3. Add the vegetables and chicken with the stock; bring just to boiling. Stir in the lemon juice.

4. Ladle into soup plates or bowls. Pass the hot cooked rice, chopped parsley and lemon slices for garnish, and serve with crusty bread, if you wish.

KABISSUPPE
(Country Cabbage and Rice Soup)

This soup, traditional in the Canton of Schwytz in German Switzerland, is similar to others found all over the country.

Makes 6 servings.

3	tablespoons butter or margarine	1	teaspoon salt
4	to 5 cups shredded cabbage	⅛	teaspoon pepper
1	large onion, thinly sliced (1 cup)	⅛	teaspoon ground nutmeg
4	cans (13¾ ounces each) chicken or beef broth	½	cup long-grain white rice
		1	cup shredded Swiss or Gruyère cheese (4 ounces)

1. Melt the butter in a 4-quart kettle or Dutch oven. Rinse the cabbage in cold water and drain, leaving a little water clinging to it. Add the cabbage and onion to the kettle and cover. Cook over medium heat, stirring often, until the cabbage is golden and almost tender, for about 10 minutes.

2. Add the broth, salt, pepper and nutmeg and simmer, covered for 10 minutes. Add the rice and continue simmering, covered, for 15 to 20 minutes, or until the rice is tender. (Stir frequently to keep the rice separate.) Taste and add more salt and pepper if necessary. Serve in deep soup plates; pass the cheese to sprinkle over.

HUNGARIAN GOULASH

Beer brings a special flavor to this classic stew.

Makes 8 to 10 servings.

4 slices bacon, diced
¼ cup plus 1 tablespoon all-purpose flour
3 pounds lean round beef chuck, cut into 1-inch cubes
2 medium-size onions, coarsely chopped (about 2 cups)
2 cloves garlic, finely chopped
1 tablespoon paprika
1½ teaspoons salt
¼ teaspoon caraway seeds
¼ teaspoon cayenne pepper
1 can (12 ounces) beer
1 cup canned beef broth
1½ pounds potatoes, pared and cubed (about 4 cups)
1 can (16 ounces) Italian-style tomatoes, undrained
½ pound green beans, cut into 2-inch pieces

1. Cook the bacon in a heavy kettle or Dutch oven; drain the bacon on paper toweling; reserve.

2. Place ¼ cup of the flour and the meat in a plastic bag; shake to coat thoroughly. Brown the meat, part at a time, in the bacon drippings (add a small amount of vegetable oil if needed). Remove the meat to a bowl as it browns.

3. Add the onions, garlic, paprika, salt, caraway seeds and cayenne pepper to the remaining fat in the pan. Cook until the onions are tender. Add the beer, beef broth and reserved beef and bacon; bring to boiling; lower the heat. Cover and simmer for 1 hour and 30 minutes.

4. Add the potatoes; cook for 15 minutes. Add the tomatoes and beans and cook for 15 minutes more, or until the beans are tender. Combine the remaining tablespoon of flour with a small amount of cold water in a cup, stirring until smooth. Bring the stew to boiling; stir the flour mixture into the stew. Continue to cook and stir until the sauce is thickened and bubbly. Nice with hot cooked noodles, hot cherry peppers and sour cream.

BALKAN SAUSAGE RAGOUT

A sausage casserole can be made simply with frankfurters or a mixture of frankfurters and knockwurst. Here is a spicy version of the stew typical of all Balkan countries.

Makes 6 servings.

½ pound slab bacon, cut into 1-inch cubes	1 teaspoon leaf marjoram, crumbled
2 tablespoons olive oil	½ teaspoon leaf oregano, crumbled
2 large onions, thinly sliced	1 teaspoon caraway seeds
2 large sweet green peppers, halved, seeded and thinly sliced	1 bay leaf
½ cup water	1½ teaspoons salt
1 can (4 ounces) pimientos, drained and thinly sliced	½ teaspoon pepper
1 can (16 ounces) tomatoes, undrained	6 knockwurst, sliced
1½ teaspoons paprika	2 medium-size potatoes, pared and cubed
½ teaspoon crushed red pepper flakes	2 medium-size zucchini, cubed
	2 tablespoons minced parsley

1. Cover the bacon with water in a Dutch oven. Bring to boiling; lower the heat and simmer for 10 minutes. Drain; rinse and pat dry with paper toweling.

2. Cook the bacon in the oil in the same Dutch oven until almost crisp; remove and reserve.

3. Drain all but 2 tablespoons of fat from the Dutch oven. Sauté the onions and peppers in the oil until tender, for about 5 minutes. Add the water, pimientos, tomatoes, paprika, red pepper flakes, marjoram, oregano, caraway, bay leaf, salt and pepper. Bring to boiling; add the knockwurst, potatoes and bacon. Lower the heat; cover and simmer for 10 minutes.

4. Add the zucchini. Cover and simmer for another 10 minutes, or until the vegetables are tender. Remove the bay leaf.

5. Taste and add additional seasoning, if needed. Sprinkle with parsley. Serve with sour cream, pumpernickel bread and beer, if you wish.

BRESLAU TURKEY

Boneless turkey breast is the perfect choice for a small family.

Makes 6 servings.

1   packaged frozen boneless turkey roast (about 2 pounds), thawed
2   tablespoons vegetable oil
½   teaspoon monosodium glutamate (optional)
½   teaspoon seasoned salt
¼   teaspoon seasoned pepper
1   envelope or teaspoon instant chicken broth
1   medium-size onion, chopped (½ cup)
1   cup water
1   can (16 ounces) cut green beans
2   cups thinly sliced celery
1   cup elbow macaroni

1. Remove the thawed turkey roast from the foil package. Brown slowly in the vegetable oil in a Dutch oven or electric skillet.

2. Stir in the monosodium glutamate, if used, seasoned salt and pepper, instant chicken broth, onion and water. Bring to boiling; cover and lower the heat.

3. Simmer, turning the meat once or twice, for 2 hours, or until tender. Remove to a cutting board and keep warm while cooking the vegetables and pasta.

4. Pour the liquid from the Dutch oven into a 4-cup glass measure; drain the liquid from the green beans into the same cup. Add water, if needed, to make 4 cups. Return to the Dutch oven and bring to boiling.

5. Stir in the celery, macaroni and beans. Cook, stirring several times, for 10 minutes, or until the macaroni and celery are tender and almost all of the liquid has evaporated. Spoon the vegetables onto a heated large deep platter.

6. Carve the turkey into ¼-inch-thick slices; arrange the slices, overlapping, on top of the vegetables on the serving platter. Sprinkle lightly with chopped parsley, if you wish.

HOTCHPOTCH

An added bonus of this dish is the flavorful broth which can be used for soup.

Makes 4 servings.

1 beef brisket (about 2 pounds)	3 medium-size onions
3 medium-size potatoes, pared and cut in half	1 leek, well washed
3 medium-size carrots, pared	4 slices cooked bacon, crumbled

1. Place the brisket in a large kettle or Dutch oven with water to cover. Bring to boiling; lower the heat; cover and simmer for 2½ hours.
2. Add the potatoes, carrots, onions and leek. Simmer, covered, until the vegetables and meat are tender, for about 30 minutes.
3. Remove the vegetables with a slotted spoon to a large bowl. With a potato masher, gently mash the vegetables with just enough stock to moisten them.
4. Mound the vegetables on a serving platter and sprinkle with the crumbled bacon. Slice the brisket and arrange it on top of the vegetables.

DUTCH HERRING SALAD

Makes 4 to 6 servings.

¼ cup red wine vinegar	2 medium-size onions, minced (1 cup)
2 tablespoons sugar	
2 tablespoons water	1 medium-size tart apple, pared, quartered, cored and diced (1 cup)
⅛ teaspoon pepper	
1 jar (8 ounces) herring in wine sauce, drained and cut into ½-inch slices	1 cup diced cooked beets
	¾ cup finely chopped dill pickles
2 medium-size cooked potatoes, peeled and diced (3 cups)	Lettuce leaves
	1 hard-cooked egg, sliced

1. Combine the vinegar, sugar, water and pepper in a large bowl; mix well.
2. Add the herring, potatoes, onion, apple, beets and pickles to the vinegar mixture; toss gently; cover. Refrigerate for at least 4 hours for the flavors to blend, tossing once.
3. To serve, mound the salad on lettuce leaves and garnish with egg slices.

BOEUF NIÇOISE

Black olives, tarragon and a garlicky tomato sauce season beef
to perfection.

Makes 8 servings.

1 eye round beef roast (about 4 pounds)
3 tablespoons olive or vegetable oil
1 large onion, chopped (1 cup)
2 cloves garlic, finely chopped
1 cup chopped celery (2 stalks)
2 large carrots, pared and chopped
1 can (28 ounces) Italian tomatoes
2 teaspoons salt
¼ teaspoon pepper

1 tablespoon chopped fresh tarragon OR: 1 teaspoon leaf tarragon, crumbled
1 bunch leeks, trimmed and washed
1 small yellow turnip, pared and cubed
1 small cauliflower, separated into flowerets
1 pound small white onions, peeled
½ cup pitted black olives, halved
Bottled gravy coloring

1. Brown the beef in the oil in a large oval kettle; remove and reserve. Pour off all but 3 tablespoons of the pan drippings.
2. Sauté the onion, garlic, celery and carrots in the pan drippings until golden. Place the meat over the mixture; add the tomatoes and liquid, salt, pepper and tarragon and cover the kettle.
3. Bring slowly to boiling; lower the heat and simmer for 1 hour and 30 minutes.
4. Arrange the leeks, turnip, cauliflower and onions in piles around the meat. Cover and simmer for 40 minutes, or until the meat and vegetables are tender when pierced with a two-tined fork. Arrange the meat and vegetables in a heated oval casserole and keep warm.

5. Skim the fat from the surface of the liquid in the kettle. Spoon the liquid into container of an electric blender; cover and process on high until smooth; pour into a saucepan. Bring to boiling; taste and season with salt and pepper, if needed. Stir in the olives and gravy coloring and spoon the sauce over the meat.

PORTUGUESE PORK STEW

Juicy pork with shellfish is a splendid combination for a hearty stew.

Makes 8 servings.

2	pounds lean boneless pork shoulder	⅛	teaspoon crushed red pepper flakes
1	tablespoon all-purpose flour	2	large ripe tomatoes OR: 1 8-ounce can whole tomatoes
1½	teaspoons salt		
2	tablespoons olive or vegetable oil	1	cup dry white wine
		1	large sweet red or green pepper, halved, seeded and cut into chunks
2	medium-size onions, sliced		
1	teaspoon paprika	¼	cup chopped parsley
1	teaspoon finely chopped garlic	16	small hard-shell clams (little neck or cherrystone)

1. Trim the excess fat from the pork and cut the meat into 1-inch cubes. Toss with the flour and salt in a large bowl.

2. Heat the oil in a Dutch oven or deep skillet. Brown the pork, removing it as it browns.

3. Add the onions to the skillet and sauté for 5 minutes, or until soft but not brown. Stir in the paprika, garlic and red pepper flakes; cook, stirring often, for 2 to 3 minutes. Stir in the tomatoes and wine and bring to boiling; add the pork and red pepper. Lower the heat; cover and simmer for 1 hour and 15 minutes, or until the meat is just tender. Stir in the parsley.

4. While the pork simmers, scrub the clams under cold running water. Then leave them in cold water, changing the water often.

5. Add the clams to the boiling stew. Cover the skillet tightly and cook over medium heat for 5 minutes, or until the clams open. (Do not overcook; discard any clams that have not opened.) Sprinkle with additional parsley and garnish with lemon wedges, if you wish.

PORTUGUESE SEAFOOD SALAD

Shrimp and sardines are enhanced with flavors borrowed from the Iberian paella.

Makes 6 servings.

½ package (1-pound size) orzo (1¼ cups)
1 can (4½ ounces) shrimp, drained
1 teaspoon finely chopped lemon rind (bright yellow part only)
4 tablespoons lemon juice
2 tablespoons finely chopped onion
¾ teaspoon salt

1 jar (6 ounces) marinated artichoke hearts
¼ teaspoon crumbled saffron threads
1 tablespoon warm water
½ cup cooked green peas
2 cans (about 4 ounces each) sardines
Lettuce leaves
Lemon slices
Watercress

1. Cook the orzo in boiling salted water following label directions; drain; rinse with cold water; drain well.

2. Drain the shrimp; rinse with cold water and place in a large bowl. Stir in the lemon rind, lemon juice, onion, salt and artichokes with their marinade.

3. Soak the saffron in the warm water for 5 minutes and add to the shrimp mixture.

4. Add the orzo and peas; toss well to mix.

5. Refrigerate, stirring once or twice, for at least 2 hours, or until well chilled.

LAMB AND RICE VALENCIA

Skillet-toasted rice adds the special Spanish flavor to this colorful dish.

Bake at 350° for 1 hour.
Makes 6 servings.

1½ cups long-grain white rice
3 tablespoons olive or
   vegetable oil
1 pound small white onions,
   peeled and halved
3 pounds lamb riblets
4 cups chicken broth

2 teaspoons salt
1 teaspoon leaf thyme,
   crumbled
¼ teaspoon pepper
1 package (10 ounces) frozen
   peas

1. Sprinkle the rice over the heated oil in a large skillet; toast, stirring constantly, until the rice turns a rich brown. Remove to a 12-cup shallow casserole with a slotted spoon.

2. Brown the cut edges of the onions in the same pan, adding more oil, if needed; place on the rice in the casserole.

3. Preheat the oven to moderate (350°).

4. Cut the lamb between the ribs into bite-size pieces; brown in the same skillet, part at a time; remove with tongs and place over the rice and onions in the casserole.

5. Stir the chicken broth, salt, thyme and pepper into the pan drippings. Bring to boiling, stirring constantly; pour into the casserole; cover.

6. Bake in the preheated moderate oven (350°) for 45 minutes. Stir the frozen peas into the casserole; cover and bake for 15 minutes longer, or until the liquid is absorbed and the rice is tender.

STIR-FRIED BEEF WITH VEGETABLES

A typical Cantonese stir-fried combination. The Chinese way of thinly slicing meat across the grain allows you to use economical, less tender cuts of beef.

Makes 4 servings.

1	pound lean boneless beef round steak	1	medium-size onion
1	teaspoon sugar	4	tablespoons vegetable oil
1	tablespoon cornstarch	1	can (15 ounces) whole baby corn packed in water OR:
2	tablespoons dry sherry		1 can (8½ ounces) sliced
3	tablespoons soy sauce		bamboo shoots
1	pound fresh green beans	1	teaspoon salt

1. Cut the beef across the grain into ⅛-inch-thick slices. Place the beef in a medium-size bowl; add the sugar, cornstarch, sherry and soy sauce; toss until mixed. Cut the beans into 2-inch diagonal pieces, discarding the ends; slice the onion and put the vegetables in a large bowl.

2. Heat a large deep skillet, Dutch oven or wok over high heat. Add 2 tablespoons of the oil; swirl to coat the bottom and side. Add the beans and onion and stir-fry for 1 minute or until the pieces are coated with oil. Add the corn with its liquid; toss and cover. Cook for about 4 minutes, or until the beans are crisp-tender. Remove the vegetables to the same large bowl; discard the cooking liquid.

3. Reheat the pan. Add the remaining oil; swirl to coat the bottom. Add half of the marinated beef and stir-fry just until browned. Remove to the bowl of vegetables. Stir-fry the remaining beef. Return the vegetables and beef to the pan; add salt and toss to mix. Spoon onto a warm platter and serve with hot fluffy rice, if you wish.

SUCCESSFUL ORIENTAL COOKING

Slice vegetables and meats thinly and to a uniform size and shape. Be sure the knife is razor sharp and vegetables are fresh. Cut mushrooms cross-wise, holding them by stems. Cut carrots and celery in long diagonal slices.

FRESH PORK AND CORNED PORK WITH BAMBOO SHOOTS

A hearty soup. You can substitute 1 cup thinly sliced carrots for the bamboo shoots; add along with the bean curd and celery cabbage.

Makes 4 servings.

2 fresh pork hocks, or 1 hock from the end of the shoulder (about 1½ pounds total weight)	**1 green onion, cut in half**
	½ pound fresh bean curd, cut into thin strips
1 large smoked or corned pork hock (about 10 ounces)	**1 cup sliced Chinese celery cabbage or spinach leaves**
4 cups water	
1 can (8 ounces) bamboo shoots, drained and sliced	

1. Blanch the fresh pork hocks in boiling water to cover for 5 minutes; remove and reserve. If smoked hock is used add to water and blanch for 15 minutes. Rinse hocks under cold water. Put hocks into a kettle or Dutch oven. Add the 4 cups water; bring to boiling and skim. Add the bamboo shoots and green onion; lower the heat and cover. Simmer very slowly for 2 hours and 30 minutes, or until the pork meat begins to fall away from the bone. Remove the hocks from the kettle. Pour the broth into a 4-cup glass measure, leaving the bamboo shoots in the kettle. Let the fat rise to the top and skim. Add water to the broth to make 4 cups of liquid.

2. When the hocks are cool enough to handle, remove and discard the skin and bones; cut the meat into bite-size pieces.

3. Return the meat to the kettle with the 4 cups broth, bean curd and celery cabbage. Bring slowly to boiling; lower the heat and cook for an additional 10 minutes, or until the celery cabbage is crisp-tender. Taste for salt. Serve with hot cooked rice, if you wish.

PREPARING MEAT FOR THIN SLICING

The best way to prepare meat for thin slicing is to place the meat in the freezer for 30 minutes; it will firm up and make slicing easier.

ARGENTINIAN PUCHERO

Makes 8 servings.

2 pounds lean ground meatloaf mixture
½ pound pepperoni
2 tablespoons vegetable oil
1 large onion, chopped (1 cup)
1 clove garlic, finely chopped
½ cup chopped celery (1 stalk)
1 teaspoon salt
¼ teaspoon pepper
2 sprigs parsley
4 cups boiling water
2 tablespoons bottled steak sauce

1 yellow turnip, pared and cut into cubes
3 medium-size carrots, pared and cut into 2-inch pieces
4 sweet potatoes or yams, pared and cut into quarters
2 large white potatoes, pared and cut into quarters
4 medium ears of corn, cut into 2-inch pieces
2 tablespoons all-purpose flour
¼ cup cold water

1. Shape the meatloaf mixture into 1-inch meatballs on wax paper; cut the pepperoni into thin slices.

2. Heat the oil in a kettle or Dutch oven. Brown the meatballs, part at a time; remove with a slotted spoon and drain on paper toweling; pour off all but 2 tablespoons of the fat. Add the pepperoni, onion, garlic, celery, salt and pepper; sauté for 5 minutes, or until the vegetables are almost tender. Return the meatballs to the kettle; add the parsley, boiling water and bottled steak sauce. Bring to boiling; lower the heat; cover and simmer for 30 minutes.

3. Add the turnip, carrots, sweet potatoes and white potatoes and simmer for 50 minutes longer, or until the vegetables are almost tender. Add the corn and simmer for 10 minutes longer.

4. Remove the meatballs and vegetables to a large serving platter. Skim the fat from the liquid in the pan, if necessary. Blend the flour and ¼ cup cold water in a cup. Stir into the boiling liquid in the pan. Cook, stirring constantly, until the sauce thickens and bubbles for 3 minutes. Spoon over the meat and vegetables.

BEEF AND PEPPERS IN SPICY GARLIC SAUCE

Serve this easy stir-fry with rice.

Makes 4 servings.

1 small flank steak or boneless round steak (¾ pound)	2 medium-size sweet red peppers, seeded and cut into thin strips
5 tablespoons soy sauce	¼ pound mushrooms, sliced (¾ cup)
2 tablespoons dry sherry	4 cloves garlic, finely chopped (1 tablespoon)
1 tablespoon cornstarch	
2 tablespoons cold water	
1 tablespoon red wine vinegar	1 tablespoon minced fresh gingerroot OR: ¾ teaspoon ground ginger
4 teaspoons sugar	
2 teaspoons cornstarch	
4 tablespoons vegetable oil	½ teaspoon crushed red pepper flakes
2 medium-size sweet green peppers, seeded and cut into thin strips	⅓ cup canned bamboo shoots, thinly sliced

1. Cut the beef across the grain into thin slices. Combine 2 tablespoons of the soy sauce, 1 tablespoon of the sherry and the 1 tablespoon cornstarch in a medium-size bowl; add the beef slices; mix to coat well.

2. Combine the remaining 3 tablespoons soy sauce, 1 tablespoon sherry, water, vinegar, sugar and the 2 teaspoons cornstarch in a small cup; set aside.

3. Heat 1 tablespoon of the oil in a large skillet until hot; add the red and green pepper strips and mushrooms; stir-fry for 1 minute. Cover and cook for 1 minute. Remove the vegetables with a slotted spoon to a medium-size bowl.

4. Heat the 2 tablespoons of the oil in same skillet; add the meat and stir-fry for 2 to 3 minutes, or until the meat is browned. Remove the meat and add to the vegetables; wipe the skillet clean.

5. Add the remaining tablespoon of oil to the skillet. Add the garlic, gingerroot and red pepper flakes; cook, stirring constantly, for 30 seconds. Return the vegetables, meat and bamboo shoots to the skillet. Restir the cornstarch mixture and add to the skillet. Cook, stirring constantly, until thick and bubbly. Serve immediately with packaged enriched precooked rice made following label directions, if you wish.

SWEET AND PUNGENT PORK

A popular and uniquely Chinese concoction of pork (the most popular
meat in China), pineapple and vegetables. The amber-colored sauce
is achieved by caramelizing the sugar rather than adding catsup,
which many restaurants use.

Makes 4 servings.

1	pound lean boneless pork	2	tablespoons distilled white
½	cup all-purpose flour		vinegar
1¼	teaspoons salt	1	medium-size sweet green
½	teaspoon baking powder		pepper, seeded
½	cup cold water	3	carrots
1	can (20 ounces) pineapple		Vegetable oil for frying
	chunks in pineapple juice	¼	cup sugar
1	tablespoon cornstarch		

1. Cut the pork into 1-inch cubes. Combine the flour, 1 teaspoon of
the salt and the baking powder in a medium-size bowl; add the water,
stirring until smooth. Add the pork cubes; stir until coated.
2. Drain the juice from the pineapple into a 1-cup measure; stir in the
cornstarch, vinegar and remaining salt. Cut the green pepper into
1-inch squares. Cut the carrots into paper-thin diagonal slices.
3. Heat 1 inch of the oil in a 4-quart saucepan or Dutch oven to 370°.
Fry the pork cubes until golden brown, removing the browned pieces
with a slotted spoon to paper toweling to drain. Cut one cube to make
sure the pork is thoroughly cooked.
4. Carefully pour off all the oil from the pan (you can refrigerate the
oil and reuse it in other recipes). Return 1 tablespoon of the oil to the
pan. Add the carrots and stir-fry for 1 minute. Add the green pepper
and stir-fry for 2 minutes; remove to a small bowl. Add the sugar to
the pan. Heat until melted and amber in color, watching carefully so
that it does not burn. Remove the pan from the heat.
5. Restir the cornstarch mixture and pour it over the melted sugar.
It will sizzle, but stir until smooth. Cook over medium heat until
thickened and bubbly. Return the vegetables; cook until the carrots
are tender. Add the pineapple and pork cubes; spoon onto a platter
and serve with hot cooked rice, if you wish.

GLAZED BEEF
(Hua Nui)

A typical Cantonese dish, the beef is poached in water and then stir-fried.

Makes 4 servings.

¾ pound lean boneless round
steak, cut ¾ inch thick
1 egg white
2 tablespoons cornstarch
3½ tablespoons soy sauce
4 cups water
¾ pound small zucchini
(1½-inch diameter)

1 teaspoon cornstarch
½ teaspoon sugar
1 tablespoon cold water
3 tablespoons peanut or corn
oil

1. Cut the beef into ¼-inch-thick slices and then into 1-inch pieces. (This makes about 1½ cups of 1 x ¾ x ¼-inch pieces.)
2. Using a fork, combine the egg white and the 2 tablespoons cornstarch in a medium-size bowl. Add the beef and 2 tablespoons of the soy sauce; mix well, using your hands. Refrigerate for 30 minutes.
3. Bring the water to boiling in a large saucepan. Add the beef and egg white mixture, stirring gently to separate the pieces, for about 1 minute. Drain immediately and cool in a bowl of cold water. Drain; place on paper toweling. (May be done several hours ahead of time.)
4. Cut the zucchini into 1-inch slices; then turn onto the flat side and cut into ¼-inch slices to make about 3 cups of 1½ x 1 x ¼-inch pieces. Reserve.
5. Make the sauce by combining the remaining 1 teaspoon cornstarch, ½ teaspoon sugar, 1 tablespoon cold water and remaining 1½ tablespoons soy sauce in the same bowl used to coat the beef.
6. Heat a wok or skillet until very hot. Add the oil. Place the zucchini in the oil and stir-fry for 1 minute. Raise the heat and add the drained beef. Mix quickly. Stir in the reserved sauce, stirring until the sauce thickens and coats the beef with a clear glaze. Serve with hot cooked rice, if you wish.

STIR-FRIED PORK WITH PEPPERS

Makes 6 servings.

1	pound lean boneless pork cutlets	6	large sweet green peppers, cut into 1-inch pieces (6 cups)
3	teaspoons cornstarch	1½	teaspoons salt
1	teaspoon sugar	2	slices fresh gingerroot, chopped
3	tablespoons soy sauce		
1	tablespoon cold water	1	clove garlic, chopped
5	tablespoons peanut or corn oil	2	tablespoons dry sherry
		2	tablespoons cold water

1. Slice the pork into 2 x ½ x ⅛-inch pieces (there should be about 1½ cups).

2. Combine 1½ teaspoons of the cornstarch, ½ teaspoon of the sugar, the soy sauce and 1 tablespoon water in a medium-size bowl to make the marinade. Add the pork, mixing well by hand; reserve.

3. Heat a large wok or skillet until very hot. Add 2 tablespoons of the oil; add the peppers and stir-fry for 4 to 5 minutes. Add the salt and remaining ½ teaspoon sugar; mix well and transfer to a warm platter.

4. Clean out the wok; then reheat until hot. Add the remaining 3 tablespoons of oil. Mix the pork and marinade again and add to the wok. Add the ginger and garlic; stir-fry over high heat until the pork begins to separate into slices and the color of all the meat has changed. Sprinkle in the sherry; add the peppers; stir and cook to heat through.

5. Mix the remaining 1½ teaspoons of cornstarch with the 2 tablespoons of water in same bowl used to marinate the pork. Slowly pour into wok; stir until the sauce thickens and the clear glaze coats the meat and vegetables. Serve at once.

Note: Cut-up zucchini, celery, asparagus, cauliflower, broccoli, green beans, cabbage or a combination of mushrooms with one of the vegetables can be used instead of the green peppers. If the vegetables needs more cooking after stir-frying, add a tablespoon or two of water, cover and cook over high heat a few minutes longer (do not overcook). Sliced beef or chicken can be substituted for the pork.

TWICE-COOKED PORK
(Hui Kuo Jou)

This method of double cooking (first simmering and then stir-frying)
is in the Western style.

Makes 4 servings.

1¼	pounds loin pork chops, cut 1 inch thick	½	teaspoon cornstarch
½	of a small head cabbage (½ pound)	½	teaspoon sugar
		2	tablespoons cold water
1	clove garlic	3	tablespoons vegetable oil
2	green onions	½	to 1 teaspoon crushed red pepper flakes
2	tablespoons soy sauce		

1. Cut the meat from the bone; place the pork in a large kettle or
Dutch oven. Cover with water to 1 inch above the meat. Cover; bring
to boiling. Lower the heat and simmer for 45 minutes. Remove from
the water and let cool.

2. When the pork is cooled, cut it into 1-inch slices and then into
pieces ⅛ inch thick to make 1 x 1 x ⅛-inch pieces. Place on paper
toweling to dry for 10 minutes.

3. Cut the cabbage into 2 x 1-inch pieces (about 2 cups). Slice the
garlic thinly; set aside on a plate. Split the green onions lengthwise
and cut them into 2-inch long pieces.

4. Combine the soy sauce, cornstarch, sugar and water in a small cup.

5. Heat the wok or skillet until hot. Add the oil and red pepper flakes
and then the sliced pork. Stir-fry for about 3 minutes.

6. Add the garlic and onion and stir-fry for 2 more minutes. Add the
cabbage; cook and stir-fry for 1 more minute.

7. Stir the sauce ingredients until well mixed. Pour into the pork. Stir
and blend over high heat. This dish has no extra sauce, but should
be moist.

KEEPING FRESH GINGER

Cut leftover fresh gingerroot into small pieces and put into a small jar.
Add a little dry sherry, cover the jar and store it in the refrigerator.
Fresh gingerroot can also be sliced, wrapped in aluminum foil and
frozen for up to two weeks.

HONG KONG STIR-FRY

Makes 4 servings.

5 to 6 pork chops (about 1½ pounds total weight)
3 tablespoons vegetable oil
1 Bermuda onion, thinly sliced
1 clove garlic, finely chopped
1 cup sliced mushrooms
1 package (6 ounces) frozen snow peas, thawed

1½ cups chicken broth
1 can (5 ounces) water chestnuts, drained and sliced
1 package (10 ounces) frozen broccoli, cut in pieces, not chopped
¼ cup soy sauce
2 tablespoons cornstarch

1. Trim the fat and bones from the pork chops; cut the meat into thin strips. Cook the pork in the hot oil in a large skillet or wok; push to one side.
2. Add the onion, garlic, mushrooms and snow peas; sauté for a minute or two. Add the chicken broth; cover and steam for 5 minutes. Add the water chestnuts and broccoli; cover and steam for 4 minutes.
3. Mix the soy sauce and cornstarch in a small cup to make a smooth paste; stir into the hot mixture and cook until it thickens and bubbles, for about 3 minutes. Serve with soft Chinese noodles (lo mein), if you wish.

CHILI SHRIMP ON CHINESE CABBAGE

This relatively hot Szechuan dish has been "cooled off" so that you can enjoy the shrimp and peanut flavors. Remove the hot peppers before serving or warn eaters not to eat them.

Makes 4 servings.

1 pound fresh shelled and deveined shrimp OR: 1 pound thawed frozen shrimp	½ teaspoon salt
	½ teaspoon sugar
	1 tablespoon soy sauce
1 small head Chinese celery cabbage	1 clove garlic, finely chopped
	2 tablespoons dry sherry
3 green onions	4 to 6 dried red chili peppers
¼ cup cold water	½ cup unsalted shelled roasted peanuts
1 tablespoon cornstarch	
3 tablespoons vegetable oil	

1. Rinse the shrimp and pat them dry with paper toweling. Cut the cabbage into 1 x 2-inch pieces (you should have about 8 cups). Cut the onions into 1-inch lengths. Mix the water and cornstarch in a 1-cup measure.

2. Heat a large deep skillet, Dutch oven or wok over high heat. Add 1 tablespoon of the oil and swirl to coat the bottom and side. Add the cabbage and stir-fry until coated with oil. Add the salt, sugar and soy sauce. Stir-fry until just crisp-tender. Restir the cornstarch mixture, remove 1 tablespoon and add to the cabbage. Stir until the juices are thickened. Remove the cabbage to a platter; keep warm.

3. Reheat the pan with the remaining 2 tablespoons of oil. Add the shrimp and garlic and stir-fry just until the shrimp turns firm and pink. Add the sherry and chili peppers. Stir-fry to loosen the browned bits in the pan. Restir the cornstarch mixture and pour it over the shrimp. Cook until the sauce is thick and coats the shrimp. Stir in the green onions and peanuts. Taste for salt; add if needed. Spoon the shrimp over the cabbage. Serve with hot fluffy rice, if you wish.

12

Small Appliance Magic

Practically every kitchen today includes at least one time-
and energy-saving appliance to help make cooking easier
and more efficient. The microwave oven is a perfect
example of a much-needed helpmate for today's working person. It
saves hours of cooking time and cooking energy.

Another time-saver is a slow cooker or crock pot, which enables
you to start dinner in the morning and leave it to simmer until
evening. When you arrive home looking for a delicious treat, all that
needs to be done is to lift the cover and serve.

Or you might want to prepare dinner-in-a-dish by using an electric
skillet or wok. Most of these appliances are attractive enough to be
placed directly on the table for serving. A delicious and colorful
example of a favorite skillet or wok meal is Stir Fried Beef, Broccoli
and Peppers (page 235). The vegetables are cooked until crisp-tender
and then combined with the beef, cashews and spices to make one of
the tastiest meals ever.

Recipes and dozens of helpful pointers in this chapter also provide
innovative ways to utilize the toaster oven, food processor, blender
and pressure cooker to your best advantage. The versatility and

adaptability of these small electrics can do much to make your life easier.

CHOOSING CONTAINERS
FOR MICROWAVE COOKING

As in all cooking methods, the right dish can make all the difference. In micro-cooking it is even more important to choose the correct size, shape and material for cooking utensils.

Size: Each microwave recipe will cook best if you use a container with the volume and depth called for in that recipe.

Shape: Food in round shapes and ring molds micro-cook more evenly, since microwaves penetrate foods to about 1 inch from top, bottom and sides. Straight-sided casseroles keep the depth of food uniform, so it will micro-cook more evenly. The corners of rectangular dishes receive more energy and may overcook.

Materials: Since the microwaves must penetrate through the cooking container to reach the food being micro-cooked, you must choose those utensils which allow the microwaves to work efficiently.

●**Heat-Resistant Glassware:** The round casseroles with lids, oblong baking dishes or casseroles, pie plates and 1-, 2- and 4-cup measures all make excellent micro-cooking utensils.

●**China, Pottery or Ceramic Tableware and Baking Dishes:** These will vary with the specific manufacturer and design of the container. Do not use if they have a metal rim or attachments.

●**Glass-Ceramic Cookware and Livingware:** Cookware such as Corning Ware® and tableware such as Corelle® can be used in both microwave and conventional ovens.

●**Microwave-Safe Utensils:** Manufacturers are now answering the needs of microwave oven owners by producing utensils in material and shape to solve various micro-cooking needs. They often have a "suitable for microwave" sticker. Some of the special items are browning grills and dishes, ring molds, high-sided cake pans, tube and fluted cake pans, bacon trees, muffin makers and roasting racks. Plastic cooking bags, shallow frozen dinner trays and the new microwave/conventional oven frozen food containers can serve as easy-to-use disposable cooking utensils for micro-cooking.

TEST FOR MICROWAVE-SAFE
CONTAINERS AND DISHES

Pour 1 cup of water into a 1-cup glass measuring cup and place the cup in or beside the container to be tested in the oven. Microwave on high for 1 minute. Test the water and, if it is hot, the dish is microwave-safe; if the dish itself is warm, it should not be used in micro-cooking. As you test each container, mark it in a micro-cooking notebook; then you'll have a record for future use.

PREPARING THE INGREDIENTS
FOR MICROWAVE COOKING

Size of Ingredients: Foods cooked together should be of a uniform size, since the timing and final results of micro-cooking depend on the size and density of all ingredients.
● Select evenly sized and shaped apples, potatoes or acorn squash for baking.
● Shape meatballs evenly.
● Chicken pieces (all breasts, drumsticks or thighs) cook more evenly than a cut-up chicken.
● Cut the meat, potatoes and vegetables for a stew into similar thicknesses.
Quantity: Smaller portions of the same recipe will cook much more quickly than one big batch. So if the family eats on the split-shift, divide the recipe into individual servings and let each person micro-cook his own meal.
Density: The denser the food, the longer it will take to micro-cook, so it is better to use potatoes in a beef stew (since both the beef and potato are dense), and rice in a fish casserole (since fish and rice are more porous foods).
Temperature: Foods taken directly from the refrigerator or freezer will take longer to micro-cook than foods which start cooking from room temperature. Casseroles and stews will cook more evenly if all the ingredients are the same temperature (refrigerator or room).
Tenderness: Ingredients should all be raw or precooked when they are combined in a micro-cook recipe. So precook raw ingredients before adding leftover or cooked foods.
Composition: The amount of bone and/or fat affects cooking time.
● The amount and distribution of bone in meat and poultry has an

effect because bone conducts heat, so follow directions for shielding bones.

• Pockets of fat will attract micro-power away from the meat; trim away excess amounts.

Moisture: Vegetables, fish, meat and other foods with a moderate to high moisture content micro-cook very well. However, foods with low moisture content, such as dried beans and peas, do not micro-cook well and should be prepared by conventional methods.

REARRANGING WHILE MICRO-COOKING

Since the micro-cooking process starts at the edges of the dish and works toward the center, it is essential to stir, turn over or rotate foods during micro-cooking to assure even results and shorter cooking times.

• **Stirring:** This is the easiest way to bring the more-cooked foods from the outer edges of the dish to the center and let the less-cooked foods in the center get the extra energy at the edges. Follow our recipe directions for stirring or stir every 5 to 10 minutes for your favorite recipes.

• **Turn Over:** Whole vegetables, such as potatoes, acorn squash or cauliflower, or large pieces of meat will cook more evenly if they are turned over halfway through the cooking period; otherwise, the top will be overcooked, while the bottom will still be underdone.

• **Rotating:** When it is difficult to stir or turn over a food, such as a cake or a meatloaf, give the cooking container a one-quarter or one-half rotation once or twice during the cooking process. This allows the food to cook more evenly.

ORIENTAL SHRIMP AND VEGETABLES

Microwave at full power for 13 minutes.
Makes 6 servings.

2   tablespoons butter or margarine
4   green onions, sliced (½ cup)
1   tablespoon cornstarch
¼   cup soy sauce
1   can (8 ounces) water chestnuts, drained and sliced
1   can (8 ounces) bamboo shoots, drained
1   can (4 ounces) mushroom pieces, drained
1   envelope instant chicken broth
¼   teaspoon ground ginger
1   pound frozen shelled and deveined shrimp (small shrimp or broken pieces can be used and are less expensive)
1   package (6 ounces) frozen snow peas

1. Combine the butter and onions in a 2-quart deep microwave-safe casserole. Microwave, uncovered, at full power for 2 to 3 minutes, or until bubbly.

2. Combine the cornstarch and soy sauce in a small 1-cup measure; stir into the casserole with the water chestnuts, bamboo shoots, mushrooms, chicken broth, ginger and shrimp. Cover with plastic wrap.

3. Microwave at full power for 8 minutes, stirring occasionally. Stir in the snow peas and again cover with plastic wrap. Microwave at full power for 3 to 4 minutes longer, or until the mixture boils and the shrimp are firm. Serve over hot cooked rice, if you wish.

SOUTH SEA CHICKEN

Sweet potatoes and pineapple make the perfect accompaniments for chicken.

Microwave at full power for 20 minutes.
Makes 4 servings.

1	broiler-fryer (3 pounds), cut up	1	teaspoon ground ginger
1	teaspoon salt	1	can (8¼ ounces) crushed pineapple in syrup
¾	teaspoon leaf rosemary, crumbled	1	can (16 ounces) sweet potatoes, drained
¼	teaspoon seasoned pepper	1	package (10 ounces) broccoli spears, thawed
2	tablespoons chopped shallots OR: ¼ cup frozen chopped onion		

1. Rub the chicken pieces with the salt, rosemary and pepper; arrange the chicken pieces in a 3-quart shallow microwave-safe casserole. (Place large pieces in corners and small ones in the center.) Sprinkle shallots over.

2. Gently stir the ginger into the pineapple; spoon over the chicken and cover with plastic wrap.

3. Microwave at full power for 10 minutes, rotating the dish several times. Arrange the sweet potatoes and broccoli around the chicken; spoon part of the sauce over; again cover with plastic wrap and microwave for 10 minutes, or until the chicken is tender. Allow to stand for 4 minutes before serving. Adjust seasonings, if desired.

CRAB MONTEREY

Spinach and artichoke hearts in a sour cream sauce—what could be more delicious?

Defrost for 10 minutes.
Microwave at full power for 5 minutes.
Makes 4 servings.

2   packages (10 ounces each) frozen chopped spinach
2   teaspoons or envelopes instant chicken broth
½   teaspoon salt
1   cup dairy sour cream
    Pinch of cayenne pepper

1   can (13¾ ounces) artichoke hearts, drained and quartered
1   can (7 ounces) crabmeat, drained and flaked
1   tablespoon butter or margarine
    Lemon slices and parsley

1. Place the frozen spinach in a 2-quart shallow microwave-safe casserole; sprinkle with the instant chicken broth and salt; cover with wax paper.
2. Defrost in the microwave for 10 minutes, or until completely thawed, rotating the dish and stirring once; drain well. Stir in the sour cream and cayenne; arrange the artichoke hearts and crab on top; dot with the butter and cover with wax paper.
3. Microwave at full power for 5 minutes, or until heated through; garnish with lemon slices and parsley. Adjust seasonings, if desired.

ZIPPY ENCHILADAS

Mexican dishes are becoming America's favorite fast food.
Microwave at full power for 12 to 16 minutes.
Makes 4 servings.

1	pound lean beef	¾	cup water
⅓	cup thinly sliced green onion	8	corn tortillas, softened
1	can (4 ounces) green		(directions below)
	jalapeño peppers, seeded	2	tablespoons chili sauce
	and chopped		Shredded Monterey Jack
2	cans (11½ ounces each)		cheese
	condensed bean with bacon		Sliced green onions
	soup		

1. Combine the ground beef, green onion and jalapeño peppers in a 2-quart microwave-safe bowl; cover with a lid or plastic wrap.

2. Microwave at full power for 3 to 5 minutes, stirring once to separate the meat. Drain off all fat from the casserole; stir in 1 can of the bean with bacon soup and ¼ cup of the water.

3. Spoon about ½ cup of the meat mixture on each tortilla; roll up; arrange seam-side down in a 2-quart microwave-safe shallow baking casserole. Combine the chili sauce, remaining can of bean with bacon soup and ½ cup water in the same bowl the ground beef was cooked in. Pour the sauce over the enchiladas and cover the casserole with plastic wrap.

4. Microwave at full power for 9 to 11 minutes, rotating the dish one-half turn after 5 minutes; sprinkle with the cheese and green onions. Let stand, covered for 2 minutes, or until ready to serve. Top with shredded iceberg lettuce, chopped tomatoes, a dollop of dairy sour cream and pitted black olives, halved, if you wish.

Cook's Tip: To soften tortillas, wrap them in damp paper towels. Microwave on high for 1 to 3 minutes, or until easy to fold.

Note: If milder heat is desired, use only ½ can of jalapeño peppers or substitute 1 can (4 ounces) green chili peppers, seeded and chopped.

RAINBOW SUPPER BAKE

Mixed vegetables add color, as well as variety, to a
simple supper casserole.

Microwave at full power for 16 to 20 minutes.
Makes 4 servings.

1   pound lean ground beef
1   can (10¾ ounces) condensed
    cream of chicken soup
½   cup milk
1   teaspoon onion powder
1   teaspoon leaf oregano,
    crumbled
1   can (16 ounces) whole
    potatoes, drained

1   package (10 ounces) frozen
    mixed vegetables, cooked
    and drained
3   tablespoons butter or
    margarine
1   cup packaged herb-seasoned
    stuffing mix
1   teaspoon paprika

1. Place the ground beef in a 2½-quart microwave-safe deep casserole.

2. Microwave at full power for 5 minutes, stirring after 3 minutes to break up the meat; drain off the fat.

3. Blend in the soup, milk, onion powder and oregano. Stir in the potatoes and mixed vegetables and cover with a lid or plastic wrap.

4. Microwave at full power for 8 to 10 minutes, stirring occasionally; let stand for 5 minutes.

5. Microwave the butter or margarine in a 4-cup glass measure at full power for 1 to 2 minutes, or until the butter melts. Stir in the stuffing mix and paprika. Sprinkle over the beef mixture and cover with a lid or plastic wrap.

6. Microwave at full power for 2 to 3 minutes, or until hot. Let stand, covered for 2 minutes before serving. Adjust seasonings, if desired.

HEARTY KNACKWURST

All the deep flavor of the slow-cooked classic, yet ready in minutes.

Microwave at full power for 19 to 23 minutes.

Makes 4 servings.

2   medium-size potatoes,
    pared and cubed
1   can (12 ounces) beer OR:
    1½ cups beef broth
½   cup frozen chopped onion
½   teaspoon caraway seeds,
    crushed

1   pound knackwurst, scored
1   jar (16 ounces) sauerkraut,
    rinsed and drained
¼   cup chopped parsley
2   tablespoons light brown
    sugar

1. Combine the potatoes, ¼ cup of the beer or broth, onion and caraway in a 3-quart microwave-safe deep casserole; cover with a lid or plastic wrap.

2. Microwave at full power for 7 to 9 minutes, or until the potatoes are tender, stirring occasionally. Stir in the remaining beer or beef broth, knackwurst, drained sauerkraut, parsley and brown sugar until well blended; cover the casserole.

3. Microwave at full power for 12 to 14 minutes, or until bubbly hot, stirring occasionally. Let stand, covered for 2 minutes before serving.

SAUSAGE 'N' PEPPERS

Italian sausages and green pepper simmer in a savory tomato sauce.

Microwave at full power for 20 to 25 minutes.

Makes 4 servings.

1   large onion, thinly sliced
    (1 cup)
1   large sweet green pepper,
    halved, seeded and cut into
    1-inch pieces
1   pound sweet or hot Italian
    sausages, cut into 2-inch
    pieces

1   can (8 ounces) stewed
    tomatoes
1   can (16 ounces) whole
    potatoes, drained
1   teaspoon leaf thyme,
    crumbled

1. Combine the sliced onion and green pepper pieces in a 2½ quart microwave-safe deep casserole; cover with a lid or plastic wrap.

2. Microwave at full power for 2 to 3 minutes. Add the sausages and cover with a lid or plastic wrap.
3. Microwave at full power for 10 to 12 minutes, stirring occasionally. Drain the fat from the dish; stir in the stewed tomatoes, whole potatoes and thyme and cover with a lid or plastic wrap.
4. Microwave at full power for 8 to 10 minutes, or until the sausages are done, stirring once. Let stand, covered, for 2 minutes before serving.

MICROWAVE DO'S AND DON'T'S

- Never operate the oven with the door open.
- Never operate the oven if it is damaged in any way.
- Avoid metal cooking containers—pots and pans; aluminum foil-lined paper bags, boxes and baking trays; skewers; aluminum foil trays. They reflect microwaves and, therefore, interfere with the cooking process.
- Only use utensils suitable for the microwave oven—ovenproof glass or glass-ceramic oven baking dishes (without metallic trim or signatures on the outside); paper cups, plates, towels and wax paper (best for defrosting or heating foods); dishwasher-safe plastics (best for reheating foods). Many companies now label containers and utensils that are "microwave-safe."
- Don't leave meat or candy thermometers in food when microwave cooking unless they are specifically designed for microwave use.
- Some foods do not microwave well. Don't microwave eggs in shells, popcorn, pancakes (except to reheat), large food loads, such as a dozen potatoes or a 25-pound turkey.
- Do not attempt to deep-fry or can foods in a microwave oven. Canning necessitates prolonged high temperatures and deep-fat frying may cause burns.
- Do not heat bottles with narrow necks—they may shatter.
- Arrange foods of equal size in a ring, leaving the center empty, so that all sides are exposed to the microwave energy.
- Arrange foods, such as chicken drumsticks, with the thicker portion to the outside of the dish, letting them cook through without overcooking the thinner areas.
- Quick-to-heat foods, such as rolls, are placed near the center of a dish; slower-cooking foods are placed near the outside of the dish.
- Prick potatoes in their skins, egg yolks and chicken livers before cooking, to prevent bursting.

SWISS BRUNCH ROLLS

Fill rolls with cooked ham, cheese and eggs, then microwave them until bubbly hot. Serve with spinach salad.

Microwave at full power for 3 minutes.
Makes 4 servings.

½	pound ground cooked ham (about 2 cups)	1	teaspoon prepared Dijon mustard
2	hard-cooked eggs, finely chopped	½	cup mayonnaise or salad dressing
2	tablespoons finely chopped onion	4	large Kaiser or hero rolls
2	tablespoons finely chopped sweet green pepper	½	cup shredded Gruyère cheese
1	tablespoon finely chopped parsley		

1. Mix the ham with the eggs, onion, green pepper, parsley, Dijon mustard and mayonnaise or salad dressing in a medium-size bowl.

2. Cut off the tops of the rolls and scoop out the crumbs, leaving a ½-inch shell. Fill with the ham mixture and sprinkle with the cheese. (Save the crumbs for another recipe.)

3. Place the filled rolls side by side in a 3-quart shallow microwave-safe casserole. Cover with paper towels.

4. Microwave at full power for 3 minutes, or until the filling is heated through and the cheese is melted.

SLOW COOKER TIPS FOR FIRST TIME USERS

Read the use and care booklet that comes with your slow cooker. To cook foods safely, the heat control setting must be at least 180°. If your cooker has a warming setting (140°-160°) for heating cooked foods, *never* use the setting for cooking.

Slow cookers come in a variety of sizes. It is best to choose recipes that will at least half fill the slow cooker, so the top surface of the food can be "basted" by the condensed steam under the slow cooker's cover.

It takes about 2 hours for the temperature to come to 160°, so do not lift the cover at this time or you'll lose valuable heat.

Some slow cookers have heat coils on the bottom. If your model does, it is best to place some of the vegetables at the bottom of the cooker and place the meat on top. The vegetables act as a grid and keep the meat from sticking after many hours of contact with the heated surface.

If you have an older model of the multi-purpose electric pots, do not try a slow cooker recipe in it for the first time unless you plan to be home while it cooks. Set the control on 200° and cook, following low (190° to 200°) cooking times. Check the pot every few hours. If the liquid seems to be boiling, or if you smell food that is about to scorch, open the pot and stir; then lower the temperature on the heat control. If your first recipe is a success use your pot as a slow cooker in the future. Do not try to use the 300° setting. The food will quickly burn and not cook the slow-simmering slow cooker way.

For a quicker start in assembling your slow cooker recipe in the morning, brown the meat or poultry and sauté the vegetables the night before. Store in a covered bowl overnight, then place in the slow cooker with the other ingredients in the morning. (Don't refrigerate browned food in the cooker unless it is one of the new removable stoneware bowls that come in some slow cookers.)

To start your slow cooker after you have left the house, use the automatic time plug on your range, following the manufacturer's directions, or use an appliance timer. Plug the slow cooker into the appliance timer that is plugged into the electrical outlet. Set the cooker's heat control to the setting in the recipe. Then set the appliance timer, following manufacturer's directions.

When cooking at altitudes above 4,000 feet, increase the cooking time 1 hour on low (190°-200°) for every 1,000 feet of altitude above 4,000 feet. Dried beans will be tender if you pre-cook them in a pressure cooker before adding them to the slow cooker.

In most cases it is not necessary to stir foods in the slow cooker, but in some recipes, we found that stirring at the halfway point in the cooking time helped to distribute the food more evenly and keep the heavier foods from sinking to the bottom. The heat loss from opening the slow cooker adds about 30 minutes to the cooking time, so if you do not stir you can expect dishes to be ready a little sooner.

Use long-handled wooden spoons when stirring foods in your slow cooker. This will protect the inside surface of the cooker and keep your hands from getting too close to the hot food and cooker.

VIENNESE PORK STEW

Hungry diners can eat this hearty pork stew at any hour of the evening, because it's cooked and kept warm in a slow cooker.

Cook on 190° to 200° for 8 hours, or on 290° to 300° for 4 hours. Makes 6 servings.

1	can (16 ounces) sauerkraut	6	medium-size potatoes, pared and cut into small cubes
1	tablespoon chicken bouillon granules		
½	cup boiling water	1½	pounds lean pork shoulder, cut into 1-inch cubes
1	medium-size onion, chopped (½ cup)	2	tablespoons cornstarch
2	tablespoons dried parsley flakes	2	tablespoons cold water
			Dairy sour cream
2	teaspoons paprika		Paprika
¼	teaspoon pepper		

1. Turn the sauerkraut into a strainer; rinse under running water and drain well; place in a medium-size bowl.

2. Dissolve the chicken bouillon in boiling water; pour over the sauerkraut. Add the onion, parsley flakes, paprika and pepper.

3. Place half of the sauerkraut mixture on the bottom of a slow cooker; add the potatoes and pork; top with the remaining sauerkraut mixture. Cover the cooker.

4. Cook on low (190° to 200°) for 8 hours or on high (290° to 300°) for 4 hours, or until the pork is tender and the potatoes are soft.

5. Blend the cornstarch and water in a small cup; stir into the pork mixture; turn the cooker to high. Cook for 15 minutes, or until the mixture comes to boiling. Serve topped with dollops of sour cream and sprinkle with paprika. If the mixture is to be held for eating later, turn the cooker to low.

BORSCHT

A Russian favorite that is classically served with a dollop of sour cream.
Cook on 190° to 200° for 8 hours, or on 290° to 300° for 4 hours.
Makes 8 servings.

2	cups shredded cabbage	2	pounds chicken wings
2	large onions, chopped (2 cups)	1	pound boneless chuck, cubed
1	cup chopped celery	10	cups water
4	large beets, pared and shredded	1	can (6 ounces) tomato paste
2	large carrots, pared and shredded	2	teaspoons salt
3	tablespoons butter or margarine	¼	teaspoon pepper
			Dairy sour cream

1. Sauté the cabbage, onions, celery, beets and carrots in butter in a large skillet or a 5-quart slow cooker with a browning unit, stirring occasionally.

2. Combine the vegetables with the chicken wings, cubed beef, water, tomato paste, salt and pepper in a 5-quart slow cooker; cover the cooker.

3. Cook on low (190° to 200°) for 8 hours, or on high (290° to 300°) for 4 hours, or until the soup is rich and flavorful. Taste and season with additional salt and pepper, if you wish.

4. Serve in heated soup bowls and top each serving with sour cream.

CLEANING CROCKERY SLOW COOKERS

Here's a kitchen formula for removing stains that may build up on the surface of a crockery slow cooker:

1 cup water
½ cup chlorine bleach
2 tablespoons baking soda

Pour mixture into slow cooker and wipe well over stained area. Cover cooker. Set heat control to high (290° to 300°) for 2 hours. Wash with sudsy hot water, rinse well and wipe with a towel.

SMOKY HAM AND LIMAS

Dried lima beans and smoked ham bake in one big flavorful supper dish.

Cook on 190° to 200° for 10 hours, or on 290° to 300° for 5 hours.
Makes 8 servings.

1	pound dried large lima beans	1	cup sliced celery
4	cups cold water	1	cup pared shredded carrots
1	large onion, chopped (1 cup)	2	teaspoons salt
1	can (16 ounces) tomatoes	1	teaspoon leaf basil, crumbled
3	cups diced cooked ham	½	teaspoon leaf thyme, crumbled

1. Pick over the beans and rinse them. Combine the beans and cold water in a large saucepan; cover. Bring to boiling; cook for 2 minutes; remove from the heat; let stand, stirring the beans once, for 1 hour. (Or cover the beans with water in the slow cooker and soak overnight at room temperature.)

2. Pour the beans and water into the slow cooker; add the onion, tomatoes, ham, celery, carrots, salt, basil and thyme; stir to blend; cover the cooker.

3. Cook on low (190° to 200°) for 10 hours, or on high (290° to 300°) for 5 hours, or until the beans are tender. Adjust the seasonings, if desired. Serve with toasted cornbread, if you wish.

ENGLISH HOT POT

British cooks have made these one-pot specialties for generations.

Cook on 190° to 200° for 8 hours, or on 290° to 300° for 4 hours.
Makes 8 servings.

2	pounds boneless lamb shoulder, cut into 1½-inch cubes	¼	teaspoon pepper
		1	large onion, sliced and separated into rings
¼	cup all-purpose flour	3	small yellow squash, cut into 2-inch pieces (¾ pound)
2	envelopes or teaspoons instant chicken broth		
2	teaspoons salt	12	small potatoes, pared and halved (1 pound)
1	teaspoon leaf oregano, crumbled	1	cup boiling water
½	teaspoon leaf rosemary, crumbled	2	tablespoons butter or margarine, melted

1. Trim all excess fat from the lamb. Shake cubes, part at a time, in the flour in a plastic bag to coat well.

2. Mix the instant chicken broth, salt, oregano, rosemary and pepper in a cup.

3. Place half of the lamb, onion and squash into a slow cooker, sprinkling each layer with the seasoning mixture. Repeat the layering.

4. Lay the potatoes, rounded sides up, on top; pour the boiling water over. Brush the potatoes with butter and cover the cooker.

5. Cook on low (190° to 200°) for 8 hours, or on high (290° to 300°) for 4 hours, or until the meat and vegetables are tender. Serve with hearts of lettuce and cold apple cider, if you wish.

SLOW COOKER DO'S AND DON'T'S

Your electric slow cooker can be one of the most useful appliances in your kitchen, but there are a few precautions that you should take for the safest use:

Choose a flat moisture-free surface in easy reach of a 120 volt AC wall outlet, and out of the reach of young children.

Turn the heat control to OFF: then insert into the slow cooker.

Fill the slow cooker with the recipe ingredients and then cover.

Plug the cord into an electric outlet, being sure that the cord does not touch the slow cooker. Turn the heat control to the setting in the recipe.

When cooking is completed, turn the heat control to OFF; then pull the plug from the electrical outlet. Do not touch the outside surface of the cooker unless the cooker is insulated.

Do not pull the heat control out of the slow cooker until it has cooled down.

Never immerse the heat control in water.

Read your use and care booklet and immerse your slow cooker in water only if the booklet advises it.

Use an extension cord with a slow cooker only if its electrical rating is equal to or greater than the electrical rating of your cooker. Most slow cookers use 70 watts on low (190° to 200°) and 140 watts on high (290° to 300°), so be sure that you use a heavy-duty extension cord. Do not let the cord drape over the counter or get entangled with other cords on the counter.

GUIDELINES FOR ADAPTING ONE-DISH RECIPES TO A SLOW COOKER

• Uncooked meat and vegetable combinations will require 8 to 10 hours on low (190° to 200°) or 4 to 5 hours on high (290° to 300°).
• One hour of simmering on the range or baking at 350° in the oven is equal to 8 to 10 hours on low (190° to 200°) or 4 to 5 hours on high (290° to 300°).
• Reduce the liquid in your recipe to about 1 cup since the slow cooker method of simmering foods saves all the food's natural juices.
• Use canned soups and broths, wine or water as the liquid in your slow cooker.
• Don't add dairy products, such as milk, sour cream or cream, until the final 30 minutes of cooking.
• Cook noodles and macaroni products, following label directions; then add to the slow cooker near the end of the cooking.
• Frozen vegetables and frozen fish should be thawed slightly, (especially if your slow cooker is made of crockery) and added only during the last hour of cooking, since they require so little cooking.
• Don't peek while your slow cooker is at work. You lose the equivalent of 30 minutes cooking time in heat each time the cover is removed.

WINE-BRAISED OXTAILS

Great when the gravy is spooned over mountains of mashed potatoes.

Cook on 290° to 300° for 2 hours and then on 190° to 200° for 8 hours.

Makes 6 servings.

3½ pounds oxtails, cut up	1 large leek, washed and sliced
⅓ cup all-purpose flour	
2 teaspoons salt	¼ cup chopped parsley
¼ teaspoon pepper	4 whole allspice
3 tablespoons vegetable oil	¼ teaspoon leaf thyme, crumbled
12 small white onions, peeled	
2 small white turnips, pared and cubed	1 can (10½ ounces) condensed beef broth
2 large carrots, pared and sliced	1 cup dry red wine
	1 bay leaf

1. Shake the oxtails, a few pieces at a time, in a mixture of flour, salt and pepper in a plastic bag to coat well.

2. Brown in the oil in a large skillet or a slow cooker with a browning unit; remove and reserve.

3. Sauté the onions, turnips, carrots, leek and parsley in the pan drippings for 5 minutes, stirring occasionally; season with the allspice and thyme.

4. Combine the oxtails and vegetables in a slow cooker; pour the beef broth and wine over; add the bay leaf and cover.

5. Cook on high (290° to 300°) for 2 hours. Turn the heat control to low (190° to 200°) and cook for 8 hours, or until the oxtails are so tender that the meat falls from the bones.

6. Unplug the slow cooker and let the mixture cool for 5 minutes so that the fat rises to the surface; skim off the fat. Serve the oxtails with a bowl of mashed potatoes and a coleslaw and apple salad, if you wish.

Cook's Tip: This recipe can be started the night before and allowed to slow cook while you sleep. In the morning, place in a refrigerator container and cover. Refrigerate until evening. Remove the fat layer from the oxtails; heat the oxtails in a large saucepan or place in an 8-cup casserole and bake in moderate oven (350°) for 1 hour and 15 minutes, or until bubbly hot.

TOASTER OVEN TIPS

The toaster oven requires less than half the amount of power needed to heat a large oven.

• Read manufacturer's directions for use. Many units are not recommended for broiling, but all top-brown foods in a few minutes.

• Check accuracy of oven temperature with a thermometer and make allowances, if necessary.

• Make sure your baking pans fit into the toaster oven without touching the sides or top of the heating element. Also, do not allow aluminum foil coverings to touch the element.

• Use the removable tray, if available, when browning.

• Heat canapés, sauced meatballs and other appetizers in disposable aluminum foil pans that are the right size for your toaster oven, for minimum effort at party time.

• Use as a second oven when one menu item requires one temperature and a second dish should bake at a different temperature. Place the smaller dish in the toaster oven.

• Use as a broiler, when oven is being used for a baking project.

• Defrost and heat casseroles, side dishes or desserts you have made ahead and frozen. Hint: When making these items, be sure to use pans that are the shape and size of your toaster oven. (Most toaster ovens can accommodate an 8-inch square pan, or an 8 x 3 x 2-inch loaf pan.) If you are preparing a casserole or a side dish, line a pan with heavy-duty aluminum foil leaving overhang on all sides; fill with prepared food; seal tightly and freeze until firm; then remove foil packet from pan. Label, date and return to the freezer. At party time, return package to dish, heat until bubbly hot then spoon into serving dish.

• Freshen rolls and bread by sprinkling with water and heating for 3 to 10 minutes in a toaster oven set at 300°. Defrost frozen rolls and sliced bread in a 325° oven for 10 minutes.

• For easy garlic bread, spread slices of French bread with butter, sprinkle with garlic salt and grated Parmesan cheese. Toast until golden.

• For a quick dessert, spread raspberry jam on pound cake slices; top-brown. Slice and bake refrigerator cookies or hors d'oeuvres on toaster-oven tray.

• Bake a glazed ham slice and canned (drained) yam slices together. Bake individual pizzas, frozen or homemade, from French bread or English muffins.

• For crisper crackers or roasted nuts, place in a single layer on the toaster-oven tray. Top-brown frankfurters in a single layer on tray and heat rolls on top of oven at same time.

HAM STEAK JAMAICA

Ham and vegetables bake together in a spicy glaze.
Bake at 375° for 40 minutes.
Makes 4 servings.

1 slice ready-to-eat ham, cut about 1 inch thick

2 cans (8 ounces each) pineapple chunks

¼ cup firmly packed light brown sugar

1 tablespoon prepared mustard

½ teaspoon ground ginger

¼ teaspoon ground allspice

1 can (16 ounces) sweet potatoes, drained

1 package (10 ounces) frozen broccoli spears, thawed and drained

1. Preheat the toaster oven to moderate (375°).

2. Score the ham steak and place in the center of a 9¼ x 6½ x 2-inch toaster oven dish or other 2-quart shallow casserole that will fit in the toaster oven.

3. Drain the syrup from the pineapple into a 2-cup glass measure. (There will be about ¾ cup.) Stir in the brown sugar, mustard, ginger and allspice and pour over the ham.

4. Bake in the preheated moderate toaster oven (375°) for 30 minutes; arrange the pineapple chunks, sweet potatoes and broccoli in piles around the ham; baste with the syrup in the dish. Bake 10 minutes longer, or until the top is glazed and the broccoli is cooked. Serve with a tall glass of limeade made with part quinine water, if you wish.

SAUSAGE HERO

Crusty hero rolls make edible containers for this meal-in-a-sandwich. You may need a knife and fork for these super heroes.

Bake at 350° for 10 minutes.
Makes 4 servings.

1	pound sweet Italian sausages	1	teaspoon garlic salt
1	large onion, sliced (1 cup)	1	teaspoon Italian seasoning
1	large sweet green pepper, halved seeded and cubed	¼	teaspoon seasoned pepper
¼	pound mushrooms, sliced OR: 1 can (4 ounces) sliced mushrooms, drained	2	large hero rolls
		1	medium-size tomato, thinly sliced
1	can (4 ounces) pimiento, drained and cut into cubes	4	slices Swiss cheese, cut into triangles

1. Prick the sausages with a fork; cook slowly, turning often, in a large skillet; remove and drain on paper toweling.

2. Pour off all but 2 tablespoons of fat; sauté the onion, green pepper, mushrooms and pimiento in the skillet for 5 minutes; season with garlic salt, Italian seasonings and seasoned pepper.

3. Preheat toaster oven to moderate (350°).

4. Cut a thin slice from the tops of the hero rolls; hollow out the rolls with a dinner fork. (Save the tops and crumbs for a casserole topping.)

5. Spoon about ½ cup of the vegetable mixture into each roll; layer the sliced tomatoes over; then top with the remaining vegetable mixture. Arrange the sausages on the rolls and top with the cheese triangles.

6. Bake, one hero at a time, in the preheated moderate oven (350°) for 10 minutes, or until the cheese melts. Cut the first hero into 4 portions and serve while the second sandwich heats.

MUSHROOM SLICING

To slice mushrooms neatly and quickly, use an egg slicer.

TUNA DINNER ITALIANO

A quick and easy one-dish dinner to make after a long day.

Bake at 350° for 35 minutes.
Makes 4 servings.

2   cans (6½ ounces each) tuna in vegetable oil
½   teaspoon salt
¼   teaspoon leaf basil, crumbled
¼   teaspoon pepper
2   teaspoons lemon juice

1   small eggplant, sliced ¼ inch thick (about ¾ to 1 pound)
1   large onion, sliced
1   can (16 ounces) tomatoes
    Grated Parmesan cheese

1. Preheat the toaster oven to moderate (350°).
2. Mix the tuna, salt, basil, pepper and lemon juice in a large bowl. Layer the eggplant slices on the bottom of an 8x8x2-inch baking casserole. Top with the tuna mixture, onion and tomatoes with liquid.
3. Bake in the preheated moderate toaster oven (350°) for 35 minutes, or until the eggplant is tender. Sprinkle with the Parmesan cheese just before serving. Adjust the seasonings, if desired.

CURRIED TURKEY BAKE

Dinner's ready in minutes when you keep a few convenience foods on hand.

Bake at 350° for 15 minutes.
Makes 2 servings.

1   package (9 ounces) frozen small onions in cream sauce
1   cup frozen cut green beans (from a 1-pound bag)
¾   cup water
1   tablespoon butter or margarine
½   teaspoon curry powder

1   cup cubed cooked turkey or ham (about ½ pound) OR:
1   can (6½ ounces) tuna, drained and flaked
1   can (5 ounces) refrigerated buttermilk flaky biscuits
    Sesame seeds

1. Preheat the toaster oven to moderate (350°).
2. Combine the frozen onions and green beans, water, butter and

curry powder in a medium-size saucepan. Bring to boiling; stir with a wooden spoon; cover the saucepan and simmer for 5 minutes.

3. Add the turkey, ham or tuna and spoon into an 8 x 5 x 1-inch aluminum foil pan. Separate the refrigerated biscuits into 10 pieces; overlap on top of the curry mixture and sprinkle with sesame seeds.

4. Bake in the preheated moderate toaster oven (350°) for 15 minutes, or until biscuits are golden and mixture is bubbly.

Note: This dish may also be baked in a 9-inch round pie plate.

PORK HOT POT

Frozen vegetables are often the most economical form of vegetables in the winter.

Makes 4 servings.

4 loin or shoulder pork chops, cut 1 inch thick	Pinch of ground allspice
2 tablespoons vegetable oil	1 package (9 ounces) frozen cut green beans
1 large onion, sliced (1 cup)	1 package (10 ounces) frozen French fried potatoes
1 teaspoon seasoned salt	1 tablespoon all-purpose flour
¼ teaspoon pepper	2 tablespoons cold water
2 envelopes or teaspoons instant chicken broth	Chopped parsley
1¼ cups water	

1. Remove the excess fat from the edges of the chops. Heat the oil in an electric frypan set at 375°; brown the chops on both sides; remove and reserve.

2. Sauté the onion in the pan drippings until soft. Return the chops to the pan and sprinkle with seasoned salt and pepper. Add the instant chicken broth, water and allspice. Lower the heat to 200°; cover the pan. Cook for 30 minutes, or until the chops are tender when pierced with a two-tined fork.

3. Pile the chops to one side of the frypan; add the green beans and potatoes to the other side; cover. Cook for 5 minutes.

4. Stir the flour into the cold water in a cup; stir into the liquid in the pan; cook, stirring constantly, until the sauce bubbles for 1 minute. Pile the chops onto a heated serving platter; arrange the vegetables around and spoon the sauce on top. Sprinkle with chopped parsley.

FRANKFURTER SUKIYAKI

This easy skillet frank-and-vegetable dish can be prepared at the table if you have an electric skillet.

Makes 4 servings.

1	package (1 pound) frankfurters	1	can (16 ounces) bean sprouts
2	cups fresh spinach, packed	4	tablespoons vegetable oil
4	carrots	½	cup soy sauce
2	medium-size onions	4	tablespoons sugar
¼	pound mushrooms	½	cup sake or dry sherry

1. *Prepare in advance:* Cut the frankfurters diagonally into ¼-inch slices.

2. Wash and drain the spinach well; remove the stems and break the leaves into small pieces; pare the carrots; cut into 2½-inch chunks and then into matchlike pieces; cut the onions into ½-inch slices; cut the mushrooms into ¼-inch slices; rinse the bean sprouts in a strainer under cold running water; drain thoroughly.

3. Arrange the frankfurters and vegetables attractively on a large platter; cover the platter with plastic wrap and refrigerate until serving time.

4. *At the table for each serving:* Heat a skillet or an electric skillet to hot or 400° to 425°. Place 1 tablespoon of oil in the skillet.

5. Put a quarter of the frankfurters in the skillet; pour in 2 tablespoons of the soy sauce and sprinkle the meat with 1 tablespoon of the sugar. Cook until the mixture begins to coat the frankfurters, for about 1 minute, stirring and turning; then push to one side.

6. Add a quarter of the vegetables; sprinkle with 2 tablespoons of the sake or dry sherry. Cook, stirring often, for about 3 minutes, or until the vegetables are crisp-tender. Remove to individual serving plates. Repeat three more times. Serve with rice, if you wish.

OTHER SMALL ELECTRICAL HELPERS

Electric Wok—Prepare Chinese or Japanese dishes at the table, and also use it to make entertaining easier.

• Reheat rice or pasta by adding water to the depth of 1 inch in the wok; add cooked rice or pasta and set dial to 250°; cover wok and heat for 5 minutes; stir once; lower the heat to simmer, and keep warm until serving time; drain.

Electric Skillet—This particular appliance is versatile; it can do the work of a burner *or* an oven.

• Use the skillet to heat rolls or wedges of garlic bread.

• Insert a wire rack in the bottom and use it to bake potatoes, roast a chicken or roast up to 4 Rock Cornish game hens.

• Pour in water to the depth of 1 inch and place a small trivet on the bottom; then bake custards, corn pudding or other delicate dishes.

• Use in place of a wok to stir-fry Oriental entrées.

• Use as a steamer to cook a whole cauliflower, extra-long asparagus or a large quantity of vegetables. Place a wire rack or trivet in the bottom and add water to the depth of the wire rack or trivet. Arrange the vegetables on the rack or trivet. Set the dial to 400° until steam starts; then lower the heat to simmer; close the vent and steam the vegetables just until you begin to smell them—they will be crisp-tender.

• Bake upside-down cakes. Use an 8- or 9-inch square metal pan. Place a wire rack in the skillet; place the cake pan on top. Cover and close the vent. Set the dial to 375° and bake for 30 mintues, or until a wooden pick inserted near the center of the cake comes out clean.

• Use to melt butter or chocolate. Place the butter or chocolate in a metal measuring cup and set the cup in the skillet; set the dial to simmer and butter or chocolate should be melted in 5 minutes.

• A skillet can become an extra burner; place a saucepan on the surface of the electric skillet and set the dial to 425° until the liquid in the saucepan boils; lower the dial to 225° to maintain heat.

STIR-FRIED BEEF, BROCCOLI AND PEPPERS

Makes 4 servings.

½	bunch broccoli (1 pound)	4	tablespoons vegetable oil
1	medium-size sweet red pepper	1	teaspoon finely shredded gingerroot
3	green onions	2	cups cooked beef strips (3 x ¼ inches)
2	teaspoons cornstarch		
¼	cup soy sauce	1½	teaspoons sugar
2	tablespoons dry sherry	2	tablespoons cashews
⅓	cup cold water		Hot cooked rice

1. Pare the tough outer layer of the broccoli stalks; cut the stalks in half crosswise; separate the top half into flowerets; cut the lower half into ⅛-inch slices. Halve, seed and cut the pepper into strips. Cut the green onions into 1-inch lengths. Combine the cornstarch, soy sauce and sherry in a small bowl; stir in the water.
2. Heat a large deep skillet or wok over high heat. Add 3 tablespoons of the oil; swirl to coat the bottom and side. Add the broccoli; toss to coat; stir-fry for 2 minutes. Add the red pepper, green onion and ginger; stir-fry for 2 minutes, or until crisp-tender. Remove to a large bowl; keep warm.
3. Reheat the skillet; add the remaining oil and the beef strips; sprinkle on the sugar; stir-fry until the sugar begins to glaze the beef.
4. Return the vegetables to the skillet. Restir the cornstarch mixture; slowly mix into the skillet and cook just until the mixture thickens and the beef and vegetables are coated. Spoon the mixture onto a heated serving platter and sprinkle with the cashews. Serve with hot cooked rice.

SWEET AND SOUR CABBAGE WITH PORK

This classic combination goes together faster in a wok.

Makes 4 servings.

¾	pound boneless lean pork	3	carrots, thinly sliced (1 cup)
¼	pound brown-and-serve sausage	2	tablespoons sugar
1	tablespoon butter or margarine	1	small savoy or green cabbage, shredded (8 cups)
1	teaspoon salt	3	tablespoons cider vinegar
¼	teaspoon pepper	¾	teaspoon anise seeds, crushed

1. Slice the pork ¼-inch thick; cut into 1-inch wide strips; cut the sausages in half.

2. Swirl the butter in the hot wok or a large skillet to coat the bottom. Add the pork; stir-fry over medium to high heat, for 3 to 4 minutes. Remove to a plate. Sprinkle the pork with ½ teaspoon of the salt and the pepper.

3. Add the sausage and carrots to the wok and stir-fry for 2 minutes. Sprinkle with the sugar. Cook until the sugar melts. Stir in the cabbage and cook until coated, for 2 to 3 minutes.

4. Sprinkle with the vinegar, anise seeds and the remaining salt. Cook, stirring and tossing the cabbage occasionally, for 5 minutes. Return the pork to the wok; cook and stir for 1 minute. Serve with dark pumpernickel bread, if you wish.

SWEET AND SOUR PORK

Makes 4 servings.

1	can (20 ounces) pineapple chunks in pineapple juice	3	tablespoons vegetable oil
4	teaspoons cornstarch	1	pound boneless lean pork loin, cut into 2 x ¼-inch strips
¼	cup cold water		
½	cup firmly packed light brown sugar	3	cloves garlic
1	teaspoon ground ginger	1	large sweet green pepper, halved, seeded and cut into ¼-inch strips
¼	cup soy sauce		
3	tablespoons red wine vinegar	2	cups matchstick-cut carrot strips
1	tablespoon dry sherry	4	cups hot cooked rice

1. Drain the pineapple; reserve the fruit and juice separately.

2. Blend the cornstarch and water in a small saucepan. Stir in the reserved pineapple juice, brown sugar, ginger, soy sauce, vinegar and sherry. Bring to boiling; lower the heat and simmer, stirring constantly until thickened and bubbly. Remove from the heat; reserve the sweet-sour sauce.

3. Heat 2 tablespoons of the oil in a large skillet or wok. Stir-fry the pork for 10 minutes. Add remaining 1 tablespoon oil, garlic, green pepper and carrots; stir-fry for 4 minutes longer.

4. Add the pineapple and the sweet-sour sauce. Simmer for 2 minutes. Serve over hot rice.

RATATOUILLE PROVENÇAL

Electric woks are great for stir-frying dishes in various international flavors. This dish captures the taste of Southern France in little time.

Makes 4 servings.

4 chicken breast fillets, cut into 1-inch pieces (about 1½ pounds total weight)
3 tablespoons vegetable oil
1 clove garlic, finely chopped
1 large onion, sliced (1 cup)
1 small zucchini, trimmed and cut into sticks
1 small yellow squash, trimmed and cut into sticks
1 small eggplant, cut into 1-inch pieces
1 large sweet green pepper, halved, seeded and cut into squares
1 large red pepper, halved, seeded and cut into squares
½ pound mushrooms, sliced
1 can (16 ounces) tomato wedges, drained
2 teaspoons salt
1 teaspoon Italian seasoning, crumbled
¼ teaspoon seasoned pepper

1. Heat the electric wok to 375°. Brown chicken and garlic in the oil; remove with a slotted spoon and reserve.

2. Stir-fry the onion rings in the wok for 2 minutes; add the zucchini, yellow squash, eggplant, peppers and mushrooms and stir-fry for 3 minutes, or until the vegetables are shiny and bright.

3. Return the chicken to the wok; add the tomato wedges, salt, Italian seasoning and pepper; stir-fry, just to blend; cover the wok and lower the temperature to 225°.

4. Steam for 5 minutes, or just until the vegetables are crisp-tender. Serve with hot French bread, if you wish.

HOW TO KEEP THE MUSH OUT OF A MUSHROOM

Don't soak mushrooms in water, as they absorb it. Just wipe the mushrooms with a damp cloth. Cook them rapidly over high heat.

SHRIMP AND SCALLOPS IN MUSTARD-DILL SAUCE

Makes 4 servings.

1 tablespoon vegetable oil	½ pound sea scallops, split or sliced crosswise
1 small cucumber, pared, halved, seeded and sliced ½ inch thick	3 tablespoons white wine vinegar
½ pound thin asparagus or green beans, cut into 1-inch lengths	4 teaspoons Dijon-style mustard
1 tablespoon butter or margarine	¾ cup heavy cream, heated
½ pound shelled and deveined shrimp	¼ cup snipped fresh dill

1. Heat the oil in a wok or large skillet. Sauté the cucumber and asparagus for 3 to 5 minutes. Remove to bowl.

2. Add the butter, shrimp and scallops to the wok. Stir-fry until the shrimp turn pink and the scallops firm up, for 4 minutes. Remove to the same bowl.

3. Swirl the vinegar in the wok over high heat until reduced by half. Stir in the mustard and cream; cook and stir until slightly thickened, for 2 to 3 minutes. Add the dill and shrimp-vegetable mixture. Heat through over high heat. Serve with new potatoes or brown rice and garnish with sprigs of dill, if you wish.

SPICY LAMB WITH GREEN PEPPERS

Makes 4 servings.

1 pound lean boneless lamb	3 small onions
½ teaspoon sugar	½ pint cherry tomatoes
1 tablespoon cornstarch	¼ cup vegetable oil
1 tablespoon dry sherry	1 clove garlic, finely chopped
2 tablespoons soy sauce	½ teaspoon crushed red pepper flakes
2 medium-size sweet green peppers, seeded	

1. Cut the lamb into 1-inch cubes. Place in a bowl; add the sugar, cornstarch, sherry and soy sauce; toss to mix. Cut the green peppers into ¼-inch slivers; cut the onions into wedges; put in the bowl. Cut the tomatoes into halves.

2. Heat a large deep skillet, Dutch oven or wok over high heat. Add 2 tablespoons of the oil; swirl to coat the bottom and side. Add the peppers and onions; stir-fry with slotted spoon until crisp-tender; remove to a bowl.

3. Heat the remaining oil in the pan. Add the garlic, red pepper flakes and lamb. Stir-fry until the lamb is browned. Return the peppers and onions; add the tomatoes. Stir-fry just until heated through. Serve with hot fluffy rice, if you wish.

HOW TO GET THE MOST FROM YOUR FOOD PROCESSOR

• To make sure you use your processor often, keep it in a convenient spot on the counter.

• Think through favorite recipes carefully and find how your processor can be used in the preparation.

• Learn to control your processor by turning it on and off quickly. Think "off" as quickly as you think "on." Timing can make the difference between a chopped and puréed vegetable.

• Practice with an onion. Peel and quarter it. Cut each quarter in half crosswise. Insert the steel blade in the container of the processor and add the onion; cover. Turn on the processor, then off immediately. Check the texture of the onion; process on/off again. Then try with a potato or a carrot as you get them ready for a recipe. Soon your sense of timing will become automatic.

• Keep wash-ups to a minimum by organizing your ingredient-preparation work-steps. First process dry, bland foods, such as bread or nuts, then such foods as carrots, celery or chocolate pieces; finally chop onions or garlic or beat batters.

• Chop cranberries or candied fruits with ½ cup flour (from recipe); use pulse switch. Check degree of fineness.

• Combine last bits of cheeses with dairy sour cream or cottage cheese and process until smooth for party dip, or add a little lemon juice and use as a dressing for salads.

• Freeze raw meat for 30 minutes, or until firm, but not frozen solid before slicing or chopping in processor.

• Chop parsley in processor, then store in plastic container with tight-fitting lid and refrigerate or freeze.

• Grate firm cheese, such as Parmesan, at room temperature; shred medium-firm cheese, such as Cheddar cold from the refrigerator.

• Use leftover vegetables by puréeing in processor and adding to soup or as a base for a sauce; process very ripe fruits and fold into whipped cream as a topping for cake.

CRAB AND SPINACH QUICHE

Bake crust at 425° for 5 minutes.
Bake quiche at 425° for 15 minutes and then at 350° for 30 minutes.
Makes 6 servings.

½ package piecrust mix
1 package (10 ounces) frozen chopped spinach
2 eggs, lightly beaten
1 container (8 ounces) plain yogurt
1 tablespoon all-purpose flour
1 teaspoon salt
¼ teaspoon pepper

1 can (6½ ounces) crabmeat, well drained and flaked
1 can (4½ ounces) sliced mushrooms, drained
1 cup shredded mild Cheddar cheese (4 ounces)
1 small onion, chopped (¼ cup)

1. Preheat the oven to hot (425°).
2. Place the plastic mixing blade into the mixing container of an electric food processor. Place mix in the container and add the water a little at a time through the feed tube, processing until the dough is moist enough to form a ball. Stop the machine, unplug and remove dough. Follow package directions for rolling a 9-inch single shell.
3. Bake in the preheated hot oven (425°) for 5 minutes, or until set. Place on a wire rack.
4. Cook the spinach following label directions. Drain. Squeeze out excess water.
5. Place the steel blade into the mixing container. Place the eggs, yogurt, flour, salt and pepper in the mixing container. Process until smooth. Carefully stir in the spinach and crabmeat.
6. Sprinkle the mushrooms, cheese and onion over the crust. Pour in the spinach mixture.
7. Bake in the preheated hot oven (425°) for 15 minutes. Lower the oven temperature to moderate (350°). Bake for 30 minutes, or until a knife inserted in the center comes out clean.

Note: If the crust begins to brown too quickly, cover it with aluminum foil.

CORN QUICHE

Great as a luncheon dish.

Bake crust at 425° for 5 minutes.
Bake quiche at 425° for 30 minutes.
Makes 8 servings.

½ package piecrust mix
4 eggs
1 cup heavy cream
1¼ teaspoons salt
¼ teaspoon pepper
1 small onion, finely chopped
  (¼ cup)

1 can (8 ounces) whole corn
  niblets, drained
¾ cup shredded Swiss cheese
  (3 ounces)

1. Preheat the oven to hot (425°).
2. Place the plastic mixing blade into the mixing container of an electric food processor. Place the mix in the container and add the water a little at a time through the feed tube, processing until the dough is moist enough to form a ball. Stop the machine, unplug and remove the dough. Follow the package directions for rolling a 9-inch single shell.
3. Bake in the preheated hot oven (425°) for 5 minutes.
4. Place the steel blade into the mixing container. Place the eggs, heavy cream, salt and pepper in the mixing container. Process until smooth. Carefully stir in the onion, corn and cheese. Turn into the partially baked shell.
5. Bake in the preheated hot oven (425°) for 10 minutes. Lower the oven temperature to moderate (350°).
6. Continue baking for 30 minutes, or until the custard mixture is almost set in the center. (Do not overbake.) Sprinkle with chopped chives, parsley or crumbled bacon, if you wish.

PRESSURE COOKER POINTERS

• Do not attempt to remove the control or cover from the pressure cooker until the pressure is reduced—either by allowing the pressure to drop slowly after the pressure cooker is removed from the heat (5 to 15 minutes, depending on amount of food in cooker) or with quick-cooling by setting closed cooker under faucet of cold running water (just a few minutes).

• After reducing the pressure, nudge the control with the tines of a fork. If you hear hisses, the pressure is not reduced, so continue cooling. When there are no more "hisses," remove the control with the tines of a fork; then remove the cover.

• Do not attempt to remove the cover if you have to tug or use force to pry the handles apart. Continue to cool under cold running water. (Note: Some pressure cookers have an automatic air-vent valve which rises when pressure is up and goes down when pressure is reduced.)

• Before using cooker, be sure that the vent pipe is open. Clean with a wooden pick or pipe cleaner. Check by looking through the hole while you hold the cover up against the light.

• Be sure to add enough liquid to the cooker so steam forms and builds up pressure. Check the recipe or instruction book for the amount.

• Do not fill cooker more than two-thirds full.

• Do not cook cranberries, barley, applesauce, split pea soup, rhubarb, cereals, noodles, macaroni or spaghetti in a pressure cooker. These foods get frothy and may block the vent pipe.

• Lower the heat after pressure is reached and control starts to rock; begin timing from this point.

• Store pressure cooker with cover inverted on top of the cooker and a paper towel between.

• Each pressure cooker has slight design differences, so follow your manufacturer's instructions. If you have lost your instruction book, write to the manufacturer.

BOSTON BEEF DINNER

You don't need hours to prepare corned beef and cabbage if you have a pressure cooker.

Makes 6 servings.

1	corned beef brisket (about 4 pounds)	2	sprigs parsley
1	bay leaf	1	cup apple cider
6	whole black peppercorns	6	carrots, pared and halved crosswise
1	onion, stuck with 2 whole cloves	6	new potatoes, scrubbed
1	carrot, sliced	1	small cabbage, cut into 6 wedges
1	celery stalk, sliced		

1. Wash the corned beef under cold running water. Place in a 6-quart pressure cooker; add the bay leaf, peppercorns, onion with cloves, sliced carrot, celery, parsley and apple cider. Add enough water to just cover the meat. (Do not fill cooker more than two-thirds full.)

2. Close cover securely; put the pressure control on the vent (15 pounds, if your control has multi-pressure selections.) Turn the heat on high until the pressure rises and control starts to rock, about 5 minutes. Lower the heat slowly to medium-low so control rocks gently; cook for 30 minutes.

3. Remove pressure cooker from heat; let cool for about 5 minutes. Then place closed cooker under cool running water until pressure is reduced and no steam hisses; carefully remove control and cover.

4. Remove the corned beef to a platter and keep warm. Bring the liquid in the pressure cooker to boiling. Add the carrots and potatoes to cooker; cover and cook in open cooker for 15 minutes. Add the cabbage; cover; cook in open cooker for 10 minutes longer, or until the vegetables are tender.

5. Slice the corned beef and arrange on a platter with the vegetables. Serve with Dijon mustard and gherkin pickles, if you wish.

ITALIAN CHICKEN STEW

Pungent oregano adds the classic flavor to chicken and vegetables.

Makes 4 servings.

1	broiler-fryer (3 pounds), cut up	1	can (8 ounces) whole tomatoes
3	tablespoons olive or vegetable oil	1	teaspoon leaf oregano, crumbled
2	medium-size onions, sliced	3	tablespoons chopped parsley
2	teaspoons salt		
½	teaspoon pepper	1	cup water
1	cup sliced celery	1	package (10 ounces) frozen peas
2	cups diced potatoes (about ¾ pound)		

1. Brown the chicken pieces, part at a time, in the oil in an open 6-quart pressure cooker; remove the pieces as they brown. Add the onions to pan and sauté for 5 minutes. Return the chicken; add the salt, pepper, celery, potatoes, tomatoes, oregano, parsley and water; bring to boiling.

2. Close the cover securely; put the pressure control on the vent (15 pounds, if your control has multi-pressure selections). Turn the heat on high until the pressure rises and control starts to rock, about 5 minutes.

3. Lower the heat slowly to medium-low so the control rocks gently; cook for 10 minutes.

4. Remove the pressure cooker from the heat; let cool for about 5 minutes. Then place the closed cooker under cool running water until the pressure is reduced and no steam hisses; carefully remove the control and cover.

5. Add the peas; cook in the open cooker for 5 minutes, or until the peas are tender. Serve hot with linguine, if you wish.

GAZPACHO WITH HAM AND RICE

Makes 6 servings.

2	cloves garlic, crushed and peeled	1	cup water
2	pounds medium-size tomatoes (about 6), peeled and chopped	¼	cup olive or vegetable oil
		2	cups ground cooked ham (about ½ pound)
1	medium-size cucumber, pared and cut in chunks	1	cup *cooked* rice
		¼	teaspoon salt
1	large sweet green pepper, seeded and chopped (1 cup)	¼	teaspoon pepper
			Cucumber slices
2	slices white bread, trimmed and crumbled	½	cup chopped green onion
		½	cup chopped sweet green pepper
¼	cup red wine vinegar		
2	cups tomato juice	½	cup packaged garlic croutons

1. Combine the garlic, tomatoes, cucumber, green pepper, bread and vinegar in the container of an electric blender; cover and whirl until smooth.

2. Press the mixture through a sieve or food mill, discarding the solids. Add the tomato juice, water, oil, ham, rice, salt and pepper to the tomato liquid; chill well.

3. Serve in chilled bowls; garnish with the cucumber slices, green onion, green pepper and croutons.

CURRIED SPINACH SOUP

Serve with homemade drop biscuits for a light, delicious supper.

Makes 6 servings.

1	large onion, chopped (1 cup)	1	to 3 teaspoons curry powder
1	clove garlic, finely chopped		
2	tablespoons butter or margarine	¼	teaspoon salt
		¼	teaspoon pepper
4	cups chicken broth	2	cups *cooked* rice
2	packages (10 ounces each) frozen chopped spinach	1	cup diced cooked ham (about ⅓ pound)
½	cup light cream or evaporated milk	1	lemon, thinly sliced

1. Sauté the onion and garlic in the butter until tender in a large saucepan. Add the chicken broth; cover and bring to boiling. Stir in the spinach, cover, and simmer for 10 minutes. Pour the mixture into a large bowl and cool about 20 minutes.

2. Pour the mixture, about 2 cups at a time, into the container of an electric blender; cover. Whirl until smooth. Return to the saucepan.

3. Add the milk, curry powder, salt, pepper, rice and ham; heat slowly. Serve with a slice of lemon. Adjust the seasonings, if desired.

13

Meals for Company

Planning a get-together for friends or relatives is a party in itself. Whether you're cooking for a crowd or for a small group, this chapter will give you the recipes and know-how to make your gathering a success.

If large feasts are your forte, why not try our Giant Brunswick Stew (page 271)! A classic dish made with chicken drumsticks, corn, peas and dried beans, it yields enough servings for 25 hearty eaters. Another of our favorites is Chili for a Crowd (page 270), which would be a fantastic addition to a "Super Bowl Sunday" party with the neighbors. A real plus is that it can be made well in advance.

One-dish salads and vegetable casseroles can also be important accompaniments to buffet settings. Several dishes, such as our cheesy Eggplant Pastitsio (page 260), can be prepared and frozen in advance of the party and then thawed and reheated.

Like barbecues? For whatever reason, food cooked outside sometimes tastes better, and our Lamb Kabobs with Vegetables (page 276) are no exception. A sour cream-cucumber salad and crusty hard rolls warmed on the grill round out this colorful creation. Barbecuing tips from A to Z are included in this chapter to instill confidence in the most fledgling outdoor chef.

• A ready supply of the prettiest and freshest garnishes you can find can cover a multitude of sins or not-quite-perfect dishes. Fresh parsley, sliced mushrooms, and thinly cut lemon slices work wonders on the fish that didn't quite make it to the platter intact or the roast that is a bit rough around the edges.

• That ubiquitious container of heavy cream teamed with a bit of vanilla and just a trace of sugar can be whipped up in what may seem like hours, but is actually minutes, to cover any imperfections in any dessert.

• Unexpected guests call for an emergency larder trhat handles the situation with the aplomb that leaves visitors dazzled, if slightly bewildered. For some, a wedge of cheese, a canned ham, pasta and the makings for a quick fresh sauce are the answer. Others look to their freezers. However you store provisions, what's important is to work with dishes that are quick, easy and aren't new to your cooking repertoire. The second important rule is to remember to restock your larder each time you deplete your basic stores.

• It may be a weighty subject to deal with when planning a party, but make sure that any tall glasses you buy are weighted at the bottom. It counterbalances the liquid and keeps glasses from tipping.

• Every little bit helps. Giving your wood furniture an extra-heavy waxing the day before a party may give it that added edge of protection against spills and stains.

• With coasters, napkins and ash trays in hand do a slow walk through your party room(s) before a party begins. Stop every place guests might just stand and leave some of each item. It's a lot simpler than making sure guests get a napkin with each drink or hors d'oeuvre, and guests won't be tempted to use the floor as an ash tray.

• Everybody needs a really good friend or two. When planning a formal dinner party, it's nice to know there's a couple or a single person you can call on if someone suddenly drops off the guest list due to an emergency.

• It really isn't tactful to try to remove a wine stain during a dinner party even though the urge is there. However, there is a way to handle this problem even weeks after the stain first occured. Place the cloth in a basin of warm water and add ½ cup water softener. Let stand overnight or longer if necessary.

• Wax doesn't belong on tablecloths. To remove it, place a white paper towel (never use a colored one, the dye will rub off onto the cloth) over the set wax and iron the towel with a warm iron. The wax will transfrer to the paper towel.

• Foods sometimes aren't finished on time, no matter how much advance planning you provide. To cope, reschedule your menu and serve the salad, along with some interesting crackers or breads, and some aperitifs, in the living room.

BEST FOODS TO SERVE

• Finger and non-dripping fork foods are easiest to serve and eat—especially when there are many guests and little elbow room for maneuvering forks and knives.
• To avoid last-minute cooking, or if your facilities are limited, plan one hot dish that will keep warm in a large kettle or casserole until serving time. For example, chili served with cornbread and salad is a tasty, inexpensive buffet.
• Other all-in-one casseroles—such as stews and creamed dishes with vegetables over rice, noodles or frozen patty shells—are also simple to make, eat *and* clean up (there's only one pot to wash!).
• Salads that don't wilt (slaws, for instance), or green salads with dressing served separately, are also good buffet choices. To cut costs, increase the number of salad offerings and place them on the table first.
• For a party with spice—serve prepared-ahead Tex-Mex: enchiladas, tamales, tacos, burritos and refried beans, rice and guacamole. This mix is probably the cheapest buffet you can put together!
• Think twice about using perishable foods or sauces and gravies that separate—they can give a bad appearance.
• Keep seasons and temperature in mind when deciding on a menu (serve some cool dishes in warm weather; some hot dishes in cold weather).
• Vary the types of dishes served—but *do* make them compatible. It's likely that guests will sample almost everything.
• To make sure hot foods stay hot, use warming trays and crock pots. Or, to keep cold foods chilled, set in bowls of ice. Also, replenish dishes often rather than put out large quantities at the beginning of the party.

CREOLE BOUILLABAISSE

This Creole version of the French classic makes good use of the bounty of the rivers, bays and Gulf waters. This spectacular creation will really stand out presented in a pristine white soup tureen and served in matching deep plates or bowls.

Makes 8 servings.

3 tablespoons vegetable oil
2 tablespoons all-purpose flour
1 large onion, chopped (1 cup)
2 cloves garlic, chopped
1 can (28 ounces) tomatoes
1½ teaspoons salt
1 bay leaf
1 teaspoon leaf thyme, crumbled
½ teaspoon ground allspice
¼ teaspoon crumbled saffron threads

¼ teaspoon cayenne pepper
½ cup water
1 cup dry white wine
2 to 2½ pounds fish fillets (red snapper and/or bass*), cut into 1½-inch pieces
½ pound scallops
2 lobster tails, cut into chunks OR: ½ pound, shelled and deveined fresh or frozen shrimp
½ cup sliced green onion
Toasted sliced French bread
French parsley (optional)

1. Heat the oil in a large Dutch oven or deep skillet; stir in the flour. Cook, stirring constantly, over low-to-medium heat, until the flour turns a rich brown, for about 3 minutes. Stir in the onion and garlic. Cook, stirring until soft, for about 5 minutes. Add the tomatoes, salt, bay leaf, thyme, allspice, saffron, cayenne pepper and water. Bring to boiling, crushing the tomatoes. Cover.
2. Simmer for 15 minutes; stir in the wine. Add the fish fillets, scallops, lobster and green onion; cover. Cook for 5 to 10 minutes longer, or just until the fish is tender and flakes easily.
3. Serve in deep plates or bowls over toasted French bread. Sprinkle with chopped parsley, if you wish.

*Substitute any firm white fish (halibut, cod or haddock) or substitute frozen fish cut into chunks and allow 5 to 10 minutes longer cooking time.

BLANQUETTE OF VEAL

A light flavorful stew that freezes perfectly for a delicious meal
when you need it.

Makes 12 servings.

1	boneless shoulder of veal (3½ pounds), cut into 1½-inch cubes Water to cover	2	teaspoons salt
		½	teaspoon pepper
		½	teaspoon leaf thyme, crumbled
6	cups water	¼	cup (½ stick) butter or margarine, softened
6	carrots, pared and cut into 1-inch pieces	¼	cup all-purpose flour
24	small white onions, peeled	2	cups heavy cream
6	parsley sprigs	4	egg yolks
2	celery stalks, sliced	1	pound mushrooms
2	leeks, washed well and sliced	2	tablespoons butter or margarine
2	bay leaves		
2	cloves garlic, crushed and peeled		

1. Parboil the meat in enough water to cover in a kettle or Dutch oven for 5 minutes. Drain and return the meat to the pan. Add the 6 cups water, carrots, onions, parsley, celery, leeks, bay leaves, garlic, salt, pepper and thyme. Bring to boiling; lower the heat; cover and simmer for about 1 hour and 30 minutes, or until the meat is tender.

2. Remove the meat and vegetables to a serving platter; place in a low oven to keep warm.

3. Bring the remaining broth to boiling; reduce to one-third the volume. Cream the softened butter with the flour in a small bowl. Add a small amount at a time to the reduced broth, stirring until well blended. Boil for 1 minute, stirring constantly.

4. Combine the cream and egg yolks in a small bowl; add to the broth, stirring constantly, over medium heat until thoroughly heated. Serve over the meat and vegetables, with hot cooked noodles, if you wish.

Note: Serve 6 portions; freeze remaining 6 portions in boilable plastic bags.

PASTA SALAD WITH SUMMER VEGETABLES

Your guests will be even more impressed when you show off this rainbow of colors in a crystal-clear glass salad bowl.

Makes 10 servings.

1 cup mayonnaise	1 yellow summer squash, cut into ¼-inch slices, then into ¼-inch strips
½ cup plain yogurt	
1 tablespoon lemon juice	½ pound mushrooms, sliced
1 package (1 pound) macaroni shells or elbow macaroni	½ cup chopped green onion
	1 clove garlic, minced
1 sweet green pepper, halved, seeded and cut into thin strips	1 teaspoon salt
	½ teaspoon pepper
	1 bunch parsley, chopped
1 sweet red pepper, halved, seeded and cut into thin strips	3 ripe tomatoes, cored and cut into wedges
1 medium-size zucchini, cut into ¼-inch slices, then into ¼-inch strips	2 hard-cooked eggs, cut into wedges

1. Combine the mayonnaise, yogurt and lemon juice in a large bowl. Stir until smooth.

2. Cook the pasta following label directions just until tender; drain. Place in the large bowl containing the mayonnaise mixture.

3. Add the green and red peppers, zucchini and squash, mushrooms, green onion, garlic, salt, pepper and parsley; toss lightly.

4. Refrigerate until ready to serve. (The salad may need a bit more mayonnaise and yogurt at serving time.) Garnish with the tomato wedges and hard-cooked eggs.

FRANKFURTER AND FOUR-BEAN SALAD

A take-off on the favorite three-bean salad in a tangy sour cream-mustard dressing.

Makes 12 servings.

⅓ cup vegetable oil
3 tablespoons vinegar
1 clove garlic, finely chopped
1 tablespoon salt
½ to 1 teaspoon crushed red pepper flakes
1 package (1 pound) frankfurters, sliced ¼ inch thick
1 can (19 ounces) chick-peas, drained
1 can (15 ounces) red kidney beans, drained

1 can (16 ounces) green lima beans, drained
1 can (16 ounces) cut green beans, drained
1 cup chopped celery
1 medium-size onion, chopped (½ cup)
¾ cup dairy sour cream
1½ tablespoons prepared mustard
Leaf lettuce for garnish
2 tomatoes, cut into wedges for garnish

1. Combine the oil, vinegar, garlic, salt and red pepper flakes in a large bowl; stir to mix.

2. Add the frankfurters, chick-peas, kidney beans, lima beans, green beans, celery and onion to the oil mixture; toss gently to coat. Cover and chill for 2 to 3 hours.

3. Just before serving, combine the sour cream and mustard in a small cup; fold into the frankfurter-and-bean mixture. Line a large salad bowl with lettuce; spoon the salad into the bowl; ring with the tomato wedges.

MEXICAN HAMBURGER STEW

This stew, served over corn chips, resembles the popular Mexican tacos. A pitcher of tangy fruit-filled sangria, ready-to-eat salsa and extra corn chips will really add pizazz to this stew.

Makes 10 servings.

2½	pounds lean ground chuck	1	can (10¾ ounces) condensed tomato soup
1	medium-size onion, chopped (½ cup)	1	can (10¾ ounces) condensed vegetable-beef soup
2	teaspoons salt	1	can (15 ounces) red kidney beans, drained
1	teaspoon chili powder		
¼	teaspoon pepper		
	Pinch of garlic salt		

1. Brown the chuck in a large skillet; push to one side. Sauté the onion in the same pan until soft; season with salt, chili powder, pepper and garlic salt.

2. Combine the tomato soup, vegetable-beef soup and kidney beans in a large kettle or Dutch oven. Bring to boiling; lower the heat and simmer for 10 minutes; stir in the ground meat mixture.

3. Simmer several minutes to blend the flavors. Serve over corn chips and with a mixed green salad.

PARTY TIP

To make everyone feel as if they really are on an adventure south-of-the-border, purchase a few colorful piñatas to decorate the dining room.

ROMAN LAMB STEW

Made with an inexpensive cut of lamb, this stew is perfect for family and company dinners.

Makes 6 servings.

3 pounds shoulder of lamb, cut into 1½-inch pieces
3 tablespoons all-purpose flour
2 teaspoons salt
¼ teaspoon ground pepper
2 teaspoons ground sage
4 tablespoons olive or vegetable oil
2 garlic cloves
1 cup chicken or beef bouillon or broth
½ cup red or white wine vinegar
1 teaspoon leaf rosemary, crumbled
3 carrots, cut into 1-inch chunks
12 small onions, peeled
1 tablespoon lemon juice
1 cup frozen green peas

1. Trim the excess fat from the meat. Combine the flour, salt, pepper and sage; sprinkle over the meat; toss to coat completely with the flour mixture.
2. Heat the oil and garlic in a large skillet until the garlic is browned; remove and discard garlic.
3. Brown the meat in the oil, part at a time. Remove the meat to a flameproof casserole as it browns. Pour the oil from the skillet; add the broth, vinegar and rosemary to the skillet; bring to boiling, scraping the browned bits from the bottom; pour over the meat. Add the carrots and onions.
4. Cover and simmer over low heat for 45 minutes, or until the meat is tender. Skim off the excess fat. Stir in the lemon juice; add the peas; cover and simmer for 10 minutes longer. Sprinkle with parsley, if you wish.

BEEF SUKIYAKI

Makes 4 servings.

1 pound boneless sirloin steak

1 package (about 7¾ ounces) cellophane noodles or bean threads

3 to 4 tablespoons vegetable oil

2 teaspoons sesame oil

2 medium-size onions, sliced

3 celery stalks, sliced diagonally ½ inch thick

½ pound mushrooms, sliced ¼ inch thick

¾ pound fresh spinach, washed and trimmed (6 cups)

1 small eggplant (½ to ¾ pound), sliced ¼ inch thick

½ cup soy sauce

2 to 3 tablespoons sugar

1 can (8 ounces) sliced water chestnuts, drained

⅓ cup chicken broth

⅓ cup dry sherry

Sliced radishes for garnish

1. Place the meat in the freezer for 30 minutes for easier slicing; slice ⅛ inch thick.

2. Soak the cellophane noodles in boiling water for 10 minutes, or until they are transparent; drain.*

3. Combine the vegetable and sesame oils in a cup.

4. Heat a wok or large skillet and add 1 tablespoon of the oil mixture. Stir-fry the onions and celery for 2 to 3 minutes; remove to a plate. Stir-fry the mushrooms for 2 to 3 minutes; remove to a plate. Stir-fry the spinach quickly, just until barely wilted; remove to a strainer. Stir-fry the eggplant for 3 to 4 minutes; remove to a plate. Add oil as needed.

5. Add about one third of meat to the wok in one layer; sprinkle with 2 to 3 tablespoons of the soy sauce and 1 to 2 teaspoons of the sugar; cook for 1 minute; turn the meat over and push it to one side or remove to a plate. Repeat with the remaining meat.

6. Arrange the meat, vegetables, water chestnuts and noodles in the wok in separate mounds. Combine the remaining soy sauce, sugar, broth and sherry; pour over all. Cover and cook on high heat for 2 minutes, or until heated. Garnish with radishes.

7. Let each diner serve himself right from the wok. Serve with rice and additional soy sauce, if you wish.

*Or substitute 6 ounces cooked vermicelli.

OLIVE-ARTICHOKE-SAUSAGE QUICHE

Bake at 425° for 10 minutes and then at 375° for 30 minutes.
Makes 6 servings.

Wrapper
½ package piecrust mix

Olive-Artichoke-Sausage Filling*
½ pound sweet Italian sausage
1 package (9 ounces) frozen artichoke hearts

2 eggs
½ cup chopped pimiento-stuffed olives
2 cups ricotta cheese
2 tablespoons grated Parmesan cheese

1. Prepare the piecrust mix following label directions for a 9-inch pastry shell with a high-fluted edge.
2. Place the sausage in a medium-size skillet and cover with water. Bring to boiling; lower the heat and simmer for 5 minutes; drain. Cut the sausage into thin crosswise slices; reserve.
3. Cook the artichoke hearts in a small amount of boiling water in the same skillet for 5 minutes; drain. Reserve 5 or 6 halves for garnish; chop the remainder.
4. Preheat the oven to hot (425°).
5. Combine the eggs, olives, ricotta and Parmesan cheese in the container of an electric blender; cover and whirl until smooth.
6. Spoon the sliced sausage and chopped artichoke hearts over the bottom of the pastry shell. Pour in the cheese mixture. Arrange the reserved artichoke hearts on top.
7. Bake in the preheated hot oven (425°) for 10 minutes. Lower the oven temperature to moderate (375°). Bake for 30 minutes longer, or until a knife, when inserted 1 inch from the edge, comes out clean. Cool on a wire rack for 10 minutes before serving.

*To stuff canneloni, crêpes or lasagne, chop the sausage and artichokes finely; combine with the cheese mixture.

STUFFED HEAD OF CABBAGE

An easy way to make this Old World favorite.

Makes 6 servings.

1	large head green cabbage (about 3 pounds)	1	bay leaf
¼	cup (½ stick) butter or margarine	½	teaspoon leaf basil, crumbled
1	can (13¾ ounces) beef broth	1	pound ground lean round or chuck
1	can (8 ounces) tomato sauce	½	cup packaged bread crumbs
4	carrots, finely chopped (2 cups)	½	cup chopped parsley
		1	egg
		1	teaspoon salt

1. Cut off a 1-inch thick slice from the core end of the cabbage. Cut out and remove the core of the cabbage with a small knife; hollow out the cabbage, leaving a shell about ¾ inch thick. Chop the scooped out cabbage.

2. Melt the butter in a large kettle; sauté the chopped cabbage until soft; remove 1 cup of the cabbage and place it in a large bowl. Add the broth, tomato sauce, carrots, bay leaf and basil to the cabbage remaining in the kettle; cover; bring to boiling.

3. Combine the beef, crumbs, parsley, egg and salt with the reserved cabbage. Toss until well mixed; spoon into the shell; fit the cut slice back into place; tie a string, criss-cross fashion, securely around the head of cabbage.

4. Place the stuffed cabbage, stem end down, in the sauce. Cover and simmer over low heat for 1 hour and 30 minutes, or until the cabbage is tender. Lift it from the sauce with two large spoons onto a heated serving dish. Remove the string; spoon the sauce over the cabbage. Cut the cabbage into wedges to serve. Serve with hot cooked rice, if you wish.

SPINACH-LASAGNE ROLL-UPS

Bake at 350° for 35 minutes.
Makes 8 servings.

16 lasagne noodles
(about ¾ pound)
2 packages (10 ounces each)
frozen chopped spinach,
thawed and drained
1 container (16 ounces)
cream-style cottage cheese
(2 cups)
2 cups shredded Cheddar
cheese (8 ounces)
1 egg

2 teaspoons salt
¼ teaspoon pepper
1 teaspoon Italian seasoning
¼ cup (½ stick) butter or
margarine
3 tablespoons all-purpose
flour
2 cups water
10 tablespoons instant nonfat
dry milk powder

1. Preheat the oven to moderate (350°).

2. Cook the noodles following label directions for the minimum amount of cooking time; drain well.

3. Place the spinach in a colander; press out the excess liquid by pressing against the side of the colander with a wooden spoon (or squeeze spinach between your hands). Turn into a large bowl; add the cottage cheese, ½ cup of the Cheddar, egg, 1½ teaspoons of the salt, the pepper and Italian seasoning; mix with a fork until well blended. Place 2 tablespoons of the spinach-cheese filling along the length of the lasagne noodles; roll up, jelly-roll style.

4. Melt the butter in a medium-size saucepan. Blend in the flour and remaining ½ teaspoon salt; cook, stirring constantly, just until bubbly. Combine the water and dry milk in the same pan used to cook the noodles. Stir the mixture into the saucepan. Continue cooking and stirring until the mixture thickens and bubbles. Add the remaining Cheddar, stirring until the cheese is melted.

5. Spread ½ cup of the cheese sauce in the bottom of an 11¾ x 7-inch baking dish; arrange the lasagne roll-ups in the casserole; pour the remaining sauce over the roll-ups, covering completely.

6. Bake in the preheated moderate oven (350°) for 35 minutes, or until bubbly and brown.

*The prepared dish can be made ahead and refrigerated. Increase the baking time to 1 hour.

EGGPLANT PASTITSIO

Eggplant and macaroni baked in a wonderful custardy cheese sauce.

Bake at 350° for 30 minutes.
Makes enough for two meals (6 servings each).

2	eggplants (1 pound each)	½	teaspoon ground allspice
6	to 8 tablespoons vegetable oil	1	teaspoon leaf oregano, crumbled
1	large onion, chopped (1 cup)	1	pound elbow macaroni
2	tablespoons butter or margarine		Cheese Sauce (recipe follows)
1	can (6 ounces) tomato paste	3	eggs
1	cup dry white wine	½	cup grated Parmesan cheese
1	teaspoon salt	1	container (12 ounces)
½	teaspoon ground cinnamon		cream-style cottage cheese

1. Wash the eggplants; cut into ½-inch slices; then cut the slices into cubes. Heat 6 tablespoons of the oil in a large skillet; sauté the eggplant over high heat, stirring often, for about 10 minutes, adding more oil if necessary. Remove the eggplant to a bowl.

2. In the same skillet sauté the onion in the butter until soft. Stir in the tomato paste, wine, salt, cinnamon, allspice and oregano. Bring to boiling. Return the eggplant to the skillet. Lower the heat and simmer, covered, for 15 minutes.

3. Preheat the oven to moderate (350°).

4. Cook the macaroni following label directions; drain.

5. Make the Cheese Sauce. Reserve 2 cups of the sauce for tops; add the remaining to the macaroni. Stir in the eggs and ¼ cup of the Parmesan cheese.

6. Spread one fourth of the macaroni mixture over the bottom of each of two 8x8x2-inch baking dishes. Divide the cottage cheese over each layer. Spoon the eggplant mixture in an even layer over the cottage cheese. Top with the remaining macaroni. Spoon the reserved sauce over and sprinkle with the remaining ¼ cup Parmesan cheese.

7. Bake one dish in the preheated moderate oven (350°) for 30 minutes, or until the top is browned and bubbly. Cool on a wire rack for 10 minutes before cutting into squares to serve.

8. Wrap, label and freeze the unbaked second dish.

9. To heat, remove from the freezer to the refrigerator in the morning. Bake, uncovered, in a preheated moderate oven (350°) for 1 hour and 20 minutes, or until the top is browned and bubbly.

Cheese Sauce: Melt 5 tablespoons butter or margarine in the same pan used to cook the macaroni; stir in 5 tablespoons flour; cook for 1 minute. Gradually stir in 4 cups milk until smooth. Cook, stirring constantly, until the sauce thickens and bubbles; cook for 2 minutes. Stir in ½ cup grated Parmesan cheese, 1 teaspoon salt and ⅛ teaspoon cayenne pepper.

GREEN CHILI AND CHEESE CASSEROLE

You'll shout olé! for this super-easy peppy casserole.

Bake at 400° for 35 minutes.
Makes 4 servings for dinner plus 4 servings to freeze.

1	pound lean ground chuck	1	pound Monterey Jack
1	cup sliced green onions		cheese, shredded (4 cups)
2	cans (4 ounces each) green	2	teaspoons salt
	chillies, drained and	½	teaspoon pepper
	chopped	2½	cups milk
2	cans (12 ounces each)	6	eggs
	whole-kernel corn with red	1½	cups buttermilk baking mix
	and green peppers, drained		

1. Preheat the oven to hot (400°).
2. Brown the meat slowly in a large skillet. Remove with a slotted spoon to a large bowl; cool slightly.
3. Add the green onions, chilies, corn, cheese, salt and pepper; mix thoroughly.
4. Beat the milk, eggs and biscuit mix in a medium-size bowl with a wire whisk or rotary beater until smooth.
5. Divide the meat mixture into each of two lightly greased 8 x 8 x 2-inch baking dishes. Pour half the milk and egg mixture over each (about 4 cups).
6. Bake one of the casseroles in the preheated hot oven (400°) for 35 minutes, or until lightly browned and bubbly.
7. Wrap, label and freeze the unbaked second dish.
8. To heat, remove from the freezer to the refrigerator in the morning. Bake, uncovered, in a preheated hot oven (400°) for 1 hour and 15 minutes, or until lightly browned and bubbly.

PORK AND EGGPLANT FRICASSÉE

A colorful addition to any party. This dish has a Middle Eastern accent.

Make 8 servings.

¼	cup all-purpose flour	¼	teaspoon leaf sage, crumbled
3	pounds boneless pork, cut into 1½-inch cubes	¼	teaspoon pepper
3	tablespoons peanut or vegetable oil	2	medium-size eggplants, cubed (about 3 pounds)
1	cup chicken broth	2	sweet green peppers, cut into chunks
2	teaspoons salt	2	jars (4 ounces each) pimiento, drained and cut into strips
1	teaspoon leaf oregano, crumbled		
1	teaspoon leaf thyme, crumbled		

1. Place the flour and pork in a plastic bag; shake to coat thoroughly.

2. Heat the oil in a heavy kettle or Dutch oven. Brown the pork, part at a time, removing the pieces to a bowl with a slotted spoon as they brown. Pour off the remaining oil.

3. Add the broth, salt, oregano, thyme, sage and pepper; return the pork to the kettle. Bring to boiling; lower the heat and simmer, covered, for 2 hours.

4. Add the eggplant and green peppers. Cook for 15 minutes, or until the eggplant is done. Add the pimiento for the last 5 minutes. Serve with hot cooked noodles, if you wish.

SPINACH SOUFFLÉ HAM ROLLS

Bake at 375° for 30 minutes.
Makes 4 servings.

2	packages (11 ounces each) frozen rice pilaf with mushrooms and onions	8	thin slices cooked ham (6 to 8 ounces)
1	package (12 ounces) frozen spinach soufflé in foil pan	2	tablespoons slivered almonds
		⅓	cup dairy sour cream

1. Preheat the oven to moderate (375°).

2. Cook the rice following label directions, but cook for only half the time, or just until the rice is easily separated.

3. Meanwhile, remove the frozen soufflé from the pan and cut crosswise into 8 strips. Wrap a ham slice around each strip. Pour the rice into a shallow baking dish and toss with a fork to mix. Arrange the ham rolls on top and cover the dish with aluminum foil.

4. Bake in the preheated moderate oven (375°) for 30 minutes. Meanwhile, place the almonds in a small baking pan or on aluminum foil. Place in the oven for 10 minutes, or until toasted.

5. To serve, uncover the dish; top the rolls with sour cream and then toasted almonds.

SAVORY SAUSAGE LOAF

Bake at 350° for 1 hour and 15 minutes.
Makes 8 servings.

2 pounds bulk pork sausage	**1½** teaspoons salt
4 medium-size carrots, finely chopped (1 cup)	**½** teaspoon pepper
1 sweet green pepper, finely chopped (1 cup)	**1** medium-size onion, finely chopped (½ cup)
1 can (8 ounces) tomato sauce	**1** tablespoon butter or margarine
1 egg	**2** cups packaged seasoned stuffing mix
1 cup packaged bread crumbs	
3 tablespoons finely chopped parsley	

1. Preheat the oven to moderate (350°).

2. Combine the sausage, carrots, green pepper, tomato sauce, egg, bread crumbs, parsley, salt and pepper in a large bowl; mix well.

3. Sauté the onion in the butter in a large skillet until soft. Add the stuffing and blend well.

4. Press half of the sausage mixture into a lightly greased 8-cup ring mold or a 9x5x3-inch loaf pan. Spread the stuffing mixture evenly over the sausage. Spoon in the remaining sausage mixture, pressing down firmly.

5. Bake in the preheated moderate oven (350°) for 1 hour and 15 minutes, or until the loaf shrinks from side of mold. Remove from the oven; pour off any juices. Unmold onto a serving platter. Serve with buttered cooked carrots and marinated cherry tomatoes, if you wish.

HAM MOUSSE WITH FRUIT SALAD PLATTER

This is a delicate, smooth and rich ham salad, surrounded with fresh fruit in season. Ideal for special luncheons.

Makes 6 servings.

2½ cups finely ground cooked ham
1   package (8 ounces) cream cheese
⅓   cup mayonnaise
1   tablespoon finely chopped green onion
1½ teaspoons dry mustard
¼   teaspoon white pepper
    Salt
½   cup heavy cream

2   tablespoons milk
2   tablespoons lemon juice
1   tablespoon honey
2   teaspoons prepared mustard
3   papayas or large avocados, peeled, halved and seeded
    Lettuce leaves
    Any other fruit in season (grapes, pineapple spears, pear or apple slices)

1. Beat the ham, half of the cream cheese, mayonnaise, onion, dry mustard and pepper in a large bowl with an electric mixer until fluffy. Taste; season with salt if needed. Whip the cream in a small bowl until stiff and fold into the ham mixture. Cover and chill for at least 1 hour, or overnight.

2. For the mustard dressing, beat the remaining cream cheese and milk in the same bowl used to whip the cream, if only chilling for 1 hour, until fluffy. Stir in the lemon juice, honey, mustard and a dash of salt until creamy. Chill until serving time.

3. Before serving, spoon the ham into the cavities of papaya or avocado halves and arrange on a lettuce-lined platter. Place other fruit around and garnish with lime wedges, if you wish. Serve with the mustard dressing.

DARKENING CUT FRUIT?

Sprinkle freshly cut peaches, bananas, pears and apples with lemon juice or pineapple juice to prevent darkening.

RANCH-STYLE EGGS
(Huevos Rancheros)

The colorful and flavorful combinations in this dish make it a real knockout to serve at your next brunch.

Makes 6 servings.

¼	cup vegetable oil	1	can (4 ounces) green
6	canned or frozen tortillas		chilies, seeded and chopped
1	large onion, diced (1 cup)	¾	teaspoon liquid hot pepper
1	medium-size sweet green		seasoning
	pepper, seeded and diced	1	teaspoon salt
	(½ cup)	6	eggs
1	clove garlic, finely chopped	2	cups shredded romaine
3	medium-size tomatoes,		lettuce
	peeled, seeded and diced	½	cup shredded sharp
	(3 cups)		Cheddar cheese (optional)

1. Heat 2 tablespoons of the oil in a medium-size skillet. Heat the tortillas just until limp on each side. Drain on paper toweling; keep warm.

2. In same skillet, cook the onion, green pepper and garlic until tender, for about 5 minutes. (Add more oil, if necessary.) Stir in the tomatoes, green chilies, hot pepper seasoning and salt. Cook, uncovered, for 10 minutes, stirring occasionally.

3. Heat the remaining 2 tablespoons of oil in a large skillet. Break and slip the eggs into the skillet. Lower the heat and cook slowly to desired doneness.

4. Line a large serving plate with the shredded lettuce. Arrange the tortillas on the lettuce. Slip the eggs onto each tortilla and spoon the sauce around the eggs. Sprinkle with cheese. Serve with pinto beans, if you wish.

PERFECT PARTY GUIDE

HOW MUCH TO BUY

Food and Beverages needed for:	12 people	24 people	36 people
Soda	two 64-ounce bottles	three 64-ounce bottles	four 64-ounce bottles
Vegetable or fruit juice	two 46-ounce cans	three 46-ounce cans	four 46-ounce cans
Ground coffee	¾ pound	1 pound	1¼ pounds
Instant coffee	2½ ounces	14-ounce jar	1 jar + 4 tbls.
Tea bags	1 dozen	2 dozen	3 dozen
Coffee cream	2 cups	1 quart	1½ quarts
Sugar	¼ pound	½ pound	1 pound
Boneless beef, lamb, pork	4 pounds	7 pounds	13 pounds
Bone-in beef, lamb, pork	9 pounds	18 pounds	35 pounds
Broiler-fryer chickens	12 pounds	24 pounds	36 pounds
Ham (boneless)	5 pounds	10 pounds	15 pounds
Ham (bone-in)	9 pounds	14 pounds	24 pounds
Rice	1¼ pounds	2½ pounds	4 pounds
Potatoes	4 pounds	7 pounds	13 pounds
Noodles	3 pounds	6 pounds	8 pounds
Fresh vegetables (allow ½ cup cooked per serving)	3 to 5 pounds	6 to 8 pounds	8 to 10 pounds
Frozen or canned vegetables	3 pounds	6 pounds	10 pounds

RENTING PARTY EQUIPMENT

Planning a barbecue, party or home wedding? There's no need to buy all the necessary equipment, especially if you only use it once in a while. It's more economical to rent.

First, decide on the menu and from that make a list of the equipment you will need to prepare and serve the food. Then visit a rental center, where you'll find everything you need—grills, rotisseries, tables, chairs, china, even beverage fountains! Your rental center will also have table linens, skirting, and other accessories for a successful party.

Reserve early to assure the quantity and types of equipment you need. Read the rental contract thoroughly so you are familiar with any damage charges. Return the rental equipment clean to avoid additional cleaning charges.

CHILI CON CARNE

Makes about 3 quarts (12 cups).

1	pound dried pinto beans (2½ cups)	1	can (6 ounces) tomato paste
2	quarts water	1	can (10½ ounces) condensed beef broth
1½	pounds lean ground chuck	3	tablespoons chili powder
1	large onion, chopped (1 cup)		OR: 2 tablespoons ground chili pepper
2	cloves garlic, finely chopped		
1	medium-size sweet green pepper, seeded and chopped (½ cup)	2	tablespoons leaf oregano, crumbled
1	can (28 ounces) whole tomatoes	1	tablespoon ground cumin
		1	tablespoon salt

1. Wash and sort the beans. Soak overnight in the water in a large saucepan. Next morning, bring to boiling and simmer, covered, for 1 hour, stirring occasionally.

2. Brown the meat slowly in its own fat in a large kettle or Dutch oven. Add the onion, garlic and green pepper. Drain the fat from the kettle and add the tomatoes with their liquid, tomato paste, broth, chili powder, oregano, cumin and salt. Stir, breaking up the tomatoes with a wooden spoon; bring to boiling. Cover and simmer, stirring occasionally, for 1 hour.

3. Add beans and 2½ cups of the cooking liquid to the meat mixture; stir. Cover and simmer, stirring occasionally for another 2 to 3 hours or until the flavors are fully developed, the sauce is thickened and the beans are tender but not mushy.

Note: If you like very hot and spicy chili, add 1 to 2 jalapeño peppers at the end of the cooking time. To quick-soak the beans, boil them in the water for 2 minutes and let stand for 1 hour before simmering for 1 hour.

FEEDING FIFTY

Cooking for a crowd? Here's a handy chart to help you buy just the right amount. To save money, buy foods in largest available sizes.

ITEM	WEIGHT OR MEASURE	SERVING PORTION	AMOUNT TO BUY
Meats and Fish			
Bacon, sliced	pound	2 slices	5 pounds
Chicken, roast	2-pound bird	½ chicken	25 2-pound birds
Frankfurters	pound	2 frankfurters	12 pounds
Ham, baked	5-pound ham	4½ ounces	3 5-pound hams
Meatloaf,			
hamburger	pound	4½ ounces	15 pounds
Turkey, roast	18-pound bird	4½ ounces	3 18-pound birds
Fish fillets, fresh			
or frozen	pound	4 ounces, cooked	16 pounds
Vegetables			
Canned	1-pound can	½ cup	12 1-pound cans
Frozen	2-pound bag	½ cup	6 2-pound bags
Fresh			
Beans, carrots	pound	½ cup	10 pounds
Cabbage	pound	½ cup	12 pounds
Lettuce (salad)	large head	⅛ head	7 large heads
Potatoes			
baked, broiled	pound	1 medium	25 pounds
French fried	pound	4 ounces	15 pounds
mashed	pound	½ cup	15 pounds
Tomatoes	pound	3 slices	10 pounds

Pasta and Rice

Macaroni	pound	1 cup	3 pounds
Noodles, spaghetti	pound	1 cup	6 pounds
Rice, long-grain	3-pound bag	⅔ cup	1 3-pound bag

Bread, Crackers

Bread	2-pound loaf	2 slices	4 2-pound loaves
Crackers	8-pound package	4 crackers	4 8-ounce packages
Rolls	dozen	2 rolls	8½ dozen

Desserts

Fruit cocktail	29-ounce can	½ cup	8 29-ounce cans
Fruit cup, fresh	quart	½ cup	6½ quarts
Ice cream	gallon	½ cup	2 gallons
Pie	9-inch pie	⅙ of pie	9 pies

Beverages

Coffee			
ground	pound	1½ cups	2 pounds
instant	10-ounce jar	1½ cups	1 10-ounce jar
Juices	46-ounce can	½ cup	5 46-ounce cans
Tea, bags	dozen	1½ cups	8 dozen

Extras

Butter	pound	2 pats	2½ pounds
Cream (for coffee)	pint	2 tablespoons	4 pints
Lemons (for tea)	dozen	1 slice	½ dozen
Salad dressing	16-ounce bottle	2 tablespoons	3 16-ounce bottles

CHILI FOR A CROWD

Serve with baskets of saltines or breadsticks and frosted mugs of cold beer.

Makes 24 servings.

2 pounds flank steak, cut into ½-inch pieces
2 pounds coarsely ground flank steak
¼ cup vegetable oil
2 pounds boneless pork shoulder, coarsely chopped
1 teaspoon ground cumin
1 teaspoon chopped fresh oregano OR: ½ teaspoon leaf oregano, crumbled
3 medium-size onions, finely chopped (1½ cups)
½ cup chopped celery (1 stalk)
4 medium-size tomatoes, skinned and chopped OR: 1 can (16 ounces) whole tomatoes, drained

4 cans (7 ounces each) chili salsa OR: 4 cans (8 ounces each) hot taco sauce
1 tablespoon *each* mild, medium and hot New Mexico chili powders OR: 1 to 3 tablespoons chili powder
4 Anaheim chilies, roasted, peeled and chopped OR: 1 can (4 ounces) chopped green chilies
2 cloves garlic, finely chopped
Salt

1. Brown the cut up and ground flank steak in 2 tablespoons of the oil in a kettle or Dutch oven. Lower the heat; cover and simmer, stirring occasionally, for 45 minutes.

2. Brown the chopped pork in the remaining 2 tablespoons of oil in a large saucepan. Lower the heat; cover and simmer, stirring occasionally, for 45 minutes. Remove the pork with a slotted spoon; add to the beef. Pour the pan juices into a 2-cup measure; let the fat rise to the top. Skim off 4 tablespoons of the fat and return it to the large saucepan. Add the remainder of the pan liquid in the glass measure to the meat mixture; add the cumin and oregano and simmer for 30 minutes.

3. Sauté the onion and celery in the 4 tablespoons of fat in the saucepan for about 5 minutes; add the tomatoes and chili salsa. Lower the heat; cover and simmer for 30 minutes. Add the chili powders, chilies and garlic; cover and simmer 30 minutes.

4. Add the salsa mixture to the meats; cook over medium heat for 1 hour to 1 hour and 30 minutes, stirring frequently. Lower the heat and simmer the last half hour of cooking, stirring every 10 minutes to prevent sticking. Taste; add salt, if needed.

GIANT BRUNSWICK STEW

Chicken, corn, peas and dried beans make a classic dish that will feed a crowd. Good for a fund-raising party.

Bake at 350° for 2 hours.
Makes 25 servings.

2½ pounds dried large lima beans

3 large onions, chopped (3 cups)

2 large yellow turnips, pared and cut into 1-inch cubes

2 tablespoons salt

½ teaspoon pepper

1 tablespoon leaf basil, crumbled

3 quarts water

25 chicken drumsticks (about 6 pounds)

1¼ cups all-purpose flour

1½ pounds vegetable shortening (3 cups)

1 dozen ears corn, shucked and cut into 2-inch pieces

1 pound frozen peas

3 sweet red peppers, halved, seeded and cubed

Hot cooked rice

1. The day before, pick over the dried beans and rinse under cold running water; combine the beans and water to cover in a large kettle. Bring to boiling; cover the kettle; turn off the heat and allow to stand at room temperature overnight.

2. Early in the day, drain the lima beans; return the beans to the kettle; add the chopped onions, turnip cubes, 1 tablespoon of the salt, ¼ teaspoon of the pepper and basil to the kettle; add 1½ quarts (6 cups) of the water to the kettle. Bring to boiling; lower the heat; cover and simmer for 1 hour and 30 minutes, or until the lima skins burst when blown on; turn off the heat and let stand.

3. While the lima beans simmer, shake the chicken drumsticks in a mixture of flour, remaining salt and pepper in a large plastic bag; let dry on sheets of wax paper.

4. Preheat the oven to moderate (350°).

5. Add shortening to depth of ½ inch in a very large skillet; heat the shortening until a cube of bread turns brown in 30 seconds. Brown the chicken for 5 minutes on each side; remove with tongs to paper toweling to drain. Continue cooking the chicken, adding more shortening as needed, until all the chicken legs are browned.

6. Ladle the lima mixture into the bottom of a 16x12-inch baking pan. Arrange the chicken pieces over, pushing them into the lima bean mixture. Cover the pan with heavy-duty aluminum foil.

7. Bake in the preheated moderate oven (350°) for 1 hour and 30 minutes; remove the cover and top with the corn, peas and red pepper; cover the pan.

8. Bake for 30 minutes longer, or until chicken and vegetables are tender. Serve with hot cooked rice.

9. To serve later: If you won't be serving Giant Brunswick Stew soon, let cool on a wire rack, then cover with heavy-duty aluminum foil and refrigerate. To reheat, let stand at room temperature for 1 hour. Bake in a preheated slow oven (300°) for 1 hour, or until hot.

GRILLING TIPS

• Bring the meat, poultry and fish to room temperature before grilling. For each serving, allow ¾ to 1 pound of bone-in meat or chicken (⅓ to ½ pound of boneless) meat or chicken and 1 pound of whole fish.

• Trim the excess fat from the meat to prevent fire flare-ups.

• Light your fire well in advance to make sure coals are just right for barbecuing.

• Using tongs, rearrange hot coals and flick off ash.

• Rub grill with oil or bacon drippings to prevent food from sticking. Makes clean-up easier, too.

• Less tender cuts of meat can be sprinkled with unseasoned meat tenderizer, following label directions, just before grilling.

• Cook meat at the distance from the heat (about 4 to 6 inches) and for the length of time specified in each recipe.

• Place a drip pan under fatty foods. Arrange an equal number of coals on each side of the pan. The pan catches juices that drip while the food cooks, preventing flare-ups and charring. Use it when grilling large roasts, whole chickens or any long-cooking meat. To construct a drip pan: Tear off a sheet of heavy-duty aluminum foil twice the length of the meat plus 6 inches; fold in half, and then again lengthwise. Make a 1-inch rim by turning up all four sides, then reinforce corners.

• Control the heat. If a vigorous flame flares up, use water in a sprinkler bottle to extinguish the flames without diminishing the intensity of the heat.

• Cook food on the grill, turning with long-handled tongs. Food wrapped in a double thickness of heavy-duty aluminum foil, shiny side down, cooks faster and more evenly; turn often to prevent burning.

• Baste throughout cooking unless the sauce is made with honey or sugar; it will retain flavor and color if brushed on meat or poultry just before cooking time is completed.

BEEF AND VEGETABLE KABOBS

Grill meat for 12 to 15 minutes.
Grill vegetables for 5 to 8 minutes.
Makes 4 servings.

1	chuck steak 1½ inches thick (about 2 pounds)	¼	cup honey
½	pint basket cherry tomatoes	2	tablespoons vinegar
½	pound mushrooms	2	tablespoons soy sauce
2	sweet green peppers	1	large clove garlic, finely chopped
1	jar (16 ounces) whole onions in liquid	2	tablespoons finely chopped parsley
1	jar (6 ounces) marinated artichoke hearts	1	teaspoon ground ginger
½	cup vegetable oil	1	teaspoon coarse salt
		½	teaspoon cracked pepper

1. Cut the steak into 1½-inch cubes. Prepare the vegetables, leaving the tomatoes and mushroom caps whole if small; seed the peppers and cut them into squares; drain the onions and artichoke hearts, reserving the liquids.

2. Combine the oil, honey, vinegar, soy sauce, garlic, parsley, ginger, salt and pepper with the reserved liquids. Pour the marinade mixture into a large, shallow non-metal dish. Add the meat cubes.

3. Let marinate for 1 to 24 hours, turning occasionally.

4. Thread the vegetables, except the peppers, on skewers and brush generously with the marinade. Remove the meat from the marinade. Pat with paper toweling to remove excess marinade. Thread the meat and peppers alternately on skewers.

5. Grill the meat 5 inches from hot coals for 12 to 15 minutes for rare, turning the skewers several times and basting with the marinade. Grill the vegetables for about 5 to 8 minutes, brushing with the marinade and turning several times until tender.

PUTTING THE FIRE OUT

• Remove the coals one by one with long-handled tongs to a bucket of water to extinguish the fire. You can also wait until the fire is out and the coals are completely consumed before discarding them.
• Coals are reusable! Simply extinguish the coals in a bucket of sand and later pick them out. Store them in a tightly closed bag in a cool, dry place.

THE ART OF BARBECUING

How Much Charcoal to Buy?

You may wish to buy a small bag if you're an occasional barbecuer or have limited storage space. However, it's economical to buy charcoal in volume and have it on hand, especially if you cook out frequently.
Note: Once the bag has been opened, close it tightly and store in a cool, dry place so the charcoal won't absorb the moisture in the air, making it difficult to light.

BAG SIZES	NUMBER OF BRIQUETTES
1 pound	15-18
5 pounds	70-80
10 pounds	150-180
20 pounds	300-360

BASIC EQUIPMENT

Grill
Long matches
Apron
Tongs*
Long-handled fork
Spatula
Basting brush
Mitts
Water spray bottle
Grill scraper

*Two pairs, one for adjusting the coals, the other for turning the food.

How to Build a Good Bed of Coals

Start the fire for the barbecue about 45 minutes to 1 hour prior to cooking. For easy cleanup, first line the firebox with heavy-duty aluminum foil.

Whether you use charcoal briquettes or loose charcoal, a good starter is needed. Use a combustible liquid product, newspaper and kindling wood or one of the new electric starters.

If you use liquid starter (which we do not recommend), pile the coals in a pyramid; saturate with starter; then let stand for a few minutes before carefully igniting. Again, never add starter to an already burning fire.

For paper and kindling, wad pieces of newspaper into small balls and add thin pieces of wood. Make a pyramid in the center of the firebox. When it's briskly burning, add the carcoal bit by bit.

When the coals are ignited and burning, spread them out just over the area you will be using.

The fire is ready when the coals are covered with a gray ash.

WHEN IS FOOD DONE?

Food		Internal temperature:
Pork		170°-175°
Fish, whole		135°-140°
Poultry		155°-180°
Beef	rare:	130°-135°
	medium:	145°-155°
	well done:	155°-180°

• Learn to be the judge of when the food is "done to your family's taste."

LAMB KABOBS WITH VEGETABLES

Grill meat for 12 to 15 minutes.
Grill vegetables for 12 to 15 minutes.
Makes 6 servings.

½   cup vegetable oil
½   cup lemon juice
1   small onion, finely chopped
    (¼ cup)
¼   cup finely chopped parsley
1   clove garlic, finely chopped
2   teaspoons leaf marjoram,
    crumbled
1   teaspoon leaf oregano,
    crumbled
2   pounds boneless lamb
    (leg or shoulder) cut into
    1½-inch cubes

1   pint basket cherry tomatoes
2   medium-size sweet green
    peppers, cut in squares
2   medium-size sweet red
    peppers, cut in squares
1   pound large mushrooms,
    stems removed
2   summer squash, cut in
    chunks
1   small eggplant, cubed, or
    6 baby eggplants, left whole

1. Combine the oil, lemon juice, onion, parsley, garlic, marjoram and oregano in a large plastic bag or non-metal bowl. Add the meat and cover.
2. Let marinate overnight in the refrigerator, turning occasionally.
3. Thread the vegetables on skewers and brush generously with the marinade. Remove the meat from the marinade. Pat with paper toweling to remove excess marinade. Thread the meat on skewers.
4. Grill the meat 5 inches from hot coals for 12 to 15 minutes for rare, turning the skewers several times and basting with the marinade. Grill the vegetables for about 12 to 15 minutes, or until the meat is done as you like and the vegetables are tender; brush with the marinade and turn several times while grilling.

ITALIAN FIESTA SAUSAGES

Grill for 20 to 30 minutes.
Makes 4 servings (2 sausages each).

1½ pounds sweet or hot
    Italian-style sausages
    (8 to 10 sausages)
2   medium-size zucchini,
    split lengthwise and then
    cut in half

2   small sweet red peppers,
    quartered and seeded
2   small onions, peeled and
    halved
½   cup Italian or oil and
    vinegar salad dressing

1. Alternate the sausages, zucchini and peppers on skewers; thread ½ onion on the end of each skewer; brush generously with the salad dressing.

2. Grill about 5 inches from the heat over grayed coals, turning the skewers often and brushing with the dressing, for 20 minutes, or until the sausages are cooked through.

3. Serve with a mixed green salad and corn-on-the-cob, if you wish.

MARINATING TIPS

• Marinate foods the easy way by placing food and marinade in a plastic bag with no holes, tying securely. Place in a pan, to avoid leaks, and turn the bag often.

• Foods that are marinating should be refrigerated, especially if they're marinated for more than 2 hours.

• Marinating meat overnight reduces cooking time by almost half. You will not only save time and energy but have a more flavorful dish.

• Marinated meat will brown better if it's wiped dry with paper toweling before cooking.

• Glamorize a small amount of meat by cubing it and broiling it on skewers along with cubes of green pepper, cherry tomatoes, zucchini slices and whole parboiled onions. Serve the shish kabobs on a bed of well-seasoned rice.

14

Plan-Ahead Meals

Any meal you want to serve with pride, whether it be a simple family dinner, a coordinated meal for planned guests, or a pot luck supper for unexpected friends, takes a certain amount of planning. Many casseroles and other one-dish combinations freeze magnificently and taste as fresh when they are reheated as they do when prepared the same day. In this chapter, we share over a dozen of these recipes with you.

A good idea is to plan a few meals in advance. Include some for the family and others for special occasions. Set aside a block of time (perhaps on a weekend when you're less frazzled) to prepare the dishes for storage in the refrigerator or freezer. What a relief it is to get home from a long weary day, open the refrigerator or freezer and remove your evening meal in one container.

Planning to roast beef, pork, chicken or turkey for Sunday dinner? Make it large enough so two or three extra meals can be made from leftovers in the week ahead. If it's a roast turkey or chicken, freeze the carcass and you'll have the necessary beginnings for a rich and flavorful soup.

FROZEN ITALIAN BEEF-VEGETABLE SOUP

You can make this flavorful soup concentrate in 40 minutes. Freeze all of it in individual servings, or freeze half for later and serve one for dinner.

Makes 10 cups soup concentrate, about 14 servings.

1	pound lean ground chuck	1	tablespoon dried parsley
1	large onion, diced (1 cup)		flakes
1	cup sliced celery	1	teaspoon salt
1	cup sliced carrots	½	teaspoon leaf oregano,
2	cloves garlic, finely chopped		crumbled
1	can (16 ounces) tomatoes	½	teaspoon leaf basil,
	(with liquid)		crumbled
1	can (15 ounces) tomato	¼	teaspoon pepper
	sauce	2	cups shredded cabbage
1	can (15 ounces) red kidney	1	cup frozen green beans
	beans (with liquid)		(from an 18-ounce bag)
1	cup water	½	cup small elbow macaroni
5	teaspoons beef bouillon		
	granules		

1. Brown the beef in a 5-quart Dutch oven or kettle, breaking it up with a spoon as it cooks; drain off any excess fat.

2. Add the onion, celery, carrots, garlic, tomatoes with liquid, tomato sauce, kidney beans with liquid, water, beef bouillon granules, parsley flakes, salt, oregano, basil and pepper. Bring slowly to boiling; lower the heat; cover and simmer for 20 minutes.

3. Add the cabbage, green beans and macaroni. Bring to boiling; lower the heat; cover and simmer for 10 minutes. Vegetables and macaroni should not be completely tender. Cool slightly.

4. To freeze: Ladle ¾ cup soup concentrate into 1-cup freezer containers; cover. (Plastic tubs that originally contained margarine are good for short-term freezer storage.) Label, date and freeze.

5. To reheat: Place the container in a pan of warm water to loosen the soup. Turn the soup concentrate out into a small saucepan and add ½ cup water. Bring to boiling; lower the heat; cover and simmer for 10 minutes or until hot. Sprinkle with Parmesan cheese, if you wish.

6. To serve part of soup immediately and freeze remainder: Ladle ¾ cup soup concentrate in each of eight 1-cup freezer containers; cover, label and date. To remaining soup concentrate add 3 cups water. Bring to boiling; lower the heat; cover and simmer for 10 minutes, or until hot and vegetables are tender. Sprinkle with

Parmesan cheese, if you wish. Makes about 8 cups soup. Serve with a mixed green salad, crusty bread and ice cream for dessert, if you wish.

PLAN-AHEAD SUGGESTIONS

• Start a file of one-dish meat and vegetable combinations and main-dish stews. They're easy to reheat, and all you need is the addition of a beverage and a salad or fruit for a nutritious meal.

• Stir-frying is a great do-it-yourself idea. Chop, slice, and cut the meat or poultry and vegetables in small pieces, place in bowls, cover with plastic wrap, and store in the refrigerator. Each person can take out his share and cook a dinner in just a few minutes.

• Make up a batch of small pizza crusts and freeze. Leave directions and makings for toppings for late-comers to help themselves.

• Keep salad greens on hand to bring texture, flavor, vitamins and minerals to a meal. Wash the greens, toss together in a large bowl, then place in individual bowls and cover each with plastic wrap and store in the refrigerator. Also have croutons, shredded cheese, cherry tomatoes, and thin carrot slices available for variety. When ready, each family member can toss his own salad with bottled dressing. Have a selection in the refrigerator.

• For a change, try molded salads or refrigerator salads, such as three-bean or carrot and apple, which are nutritious.

COOKING TIPS FOR PLANNING AHEAD

• If you're cooking a dish to freeze and use later, undercook it slightly so it won't get overcooked when reheated.

• When you hold foods for an hour or two, keep hot foods hot (140° and above) and cold foods cold (below 40°) to prevent rapid bacterial growth.

• Make use of small appliances. The electric skillet is efficient both in cooking food and keeping it warm. To reheat a small amount of food, use a toaster oven. A slow cooker also performs well both in cooking and keeping foods warm.

• You can put hot food directly in the refrigerator if it doesn't raise the refrigerator's temperature to 45°. Cool large quantities of hot food in a bowl or basin of ice water.

• An easy way to keep soups and stews hot is in a vacuum bottle.

NEW ENGLAND FISH CHOWDER

Hearty and satisfying—a meal in itself.

Makes 4 servings.

3	slices bacon, diced	1	bay leaf
1	large onion, chopped (1 cup)	1	package (12 ounces) frozen cod or haddock fillets, cut up
1	potato, pared and diced (1 cup)	1	package (10 ounces) frozen mixed vegetables
1	cup water		
1½	teaspoons salt	1½	cups milk
⅛	teaspoon cayenne pepper	½	cup light or heavy cream

1. Cook the bacon until crisp in a large saucepan; remove with a slotted spoon and reserve. Add the onion to the drippings and sauté until tender but not brown. Add the potato, water, salt, cayenne and bay leaf. Simmer covered for 10 minutes.

2. Add the fish and vegetables to the saucepan; cook for 10 minutes longer, or just until fish flakes easily with a fork and the vegetables are tender.

3. Heat the milk and cream and add to the saucepan; heat through. Top with the cooked bacon.

4. To serve another time, pour the chowder into individual freezer containers. Add bacon to each; cover; label, date and freeze (3 weeks maximum). To reheat: Turn the frozen chowder into the top of a double boiler. Heat over simmering water for about 15 minutes, or until piping hot.

GREEK BOW TIES WITH FETA CHEESE
AND GARLIC-ANCHOVY DRESSING

Makes 6 servings.

½ cup vegetable oil
½ cup olive oil
2 cans (2 ounces each) anchovy fillets
6 tablespoons lemon juice
6 large cloves garlic, chopped
1 teaspoon leaf oregano, crumbled
¼ teaspoon pepper
1 pound large bow tie macaroni

1 pint basket cherry tomatoes, halved
10 ounces feta cheese, cubed
1 cup oil-cured black olives, halved, pitted and sliced
1 cup chopped green onions
1 medium-size cucumber, halved lengthwise and sliced crosswise

1. Combine the vegetable oil, olive oil, anchovy, lemon juice, garlic, oregano and pepper in the container of an electric blender; cover. Whirl on low speed until smooth, stopping 2 or 3 times to scrape down the sides.

2. Cook the bow ties following label directions. Drain, but do not rinse. Transfer to a large bowl. Pour the dressing over the hot pasta; toss to coat. Cool. Cover; refrigerate overnight, stirring once.

3. Remove the bow ties from the refrigerator; let stand for 15 minutes. Before serving, stir in the tomatoes, feta, olives, green onions and cucumber.

COOKING IN BATCHES

- Plan your time so that you will have at least 3 hours for cooking.
- Check supermarket ads for specials on ground meat, large packages of pasta, rice, beans, canned and frozen vegetables, and dairy items.
- Sharpen knives and get out a large chopping board.
- Use large kettles and pans for quantity cooking.
- Clear off counters to make more work space.
- Find safe jobs for the children, such as stirring mixtures or measuring ingredients.
- Chop all vegetables such as onions, for all recipes at once; then pack vegetables individually into plastic bags to be measured as needed.
- Use a food processor, If you have one, to crumble bread crumbs, shred or grate cheese, chop vegetables, make pastry crust. Begin with mild foods and then go on to stronger ones.

MOLDED ORZO SALAD WITH SAUSAGE AND SWEET PEPPERS

Makes 6 servings.

1	pound orzo macaroni	1	medium-size onion,
2	cups mayonnaise		chopped (½ cup)
1	large clove garlic, chopped	2	teaspoons lemon juice
¼	cup chopped parsley		Leaf lettuce
½	teaspoon leaf thyme,		Slices of cooked hot and
	crumbled		sweet Italian sausage
½	teaspoon leaf basil,		(about 1 pound)
	crumbled, OR: 2 teaspoons		Sautéed strips of sweet red
	chopped fresh basil		and green peppers (about 4
⅛	teaspoon salt		medium-size sweet peppers)
	Pinch of cayenne pepper		
1	package (10 ounces) frozen		
	peas, thawed		

1. Grease an 8-cup soufflé dish or mold.

2. Cook the orzo following label directions. Drain; rinse under cold water; drain; cool.

3. Combine the mayonnaise, garlic, parsley, thyme, basil, salt and cayenne in large bowl; mix until well blended and smooth. Stir in the peas, onion and lemon juice. Gently stir in the orzo.

4. Spoon the mixture into the prepared dish; pack well. Cover and refrigerate overnight.

5. Run a long thin knife around the inside of the mold. Unmold onto bed of lettuce on a platter. Arrange the cooked sausage and sautéed peppers around the base of the salad.

ZITI AND HAM SALAD WITH BASIL VINAIGRETTE

Refrigerate the cooked ziti with the vinaigrette overnight to intensify the flavors.

Makes 6 servings.

1½ cups olive oil
⅓ cup red wine vinegar
¼ cup lemon juice
¼ cup chopped fresh basil
1½ teaspoons salt
1 teaspoon pepper
1 pound ziti macaroni

1½ pounds zucchini, cut into 1½ x ¼-inch sticks (6 cups)
1 pound carrots, pared and cut into 1½ x ¼-inch sticks (4 cups)
¾ pound cooked ham, cut into ½-inch cubes

1. Combine the olive oil, vinegar, lemon juice, basil, salt and pepper in a large bowl.
2. Cook the ziti following label directions. Drain, but do not rinse. Transfer to the bowl containing the oil mixture. Toss gently to coat. Cool to room temperature. Cover and refrigerate overnight, stirring once.
3. Cook the zucchini and carrots in a large kettle or Dutch oven in boiling salted water until the vegetables brighten in color and are crisp-tender, for about 2 minutes. Drain and rinse under cold water. Drain again and cool.
4. To serve, remove the pasta from the refrigerator; let stand for 15 minutes. Add the zucchini, carrots and ham; toss gently to mix.

CURRIED MACARONI AND BOLOGNA SALAD

A slightly sweet and sour combination heightened by a mild curry dressing.

Makes 4 servings.

½ pound *farfalle* (bow ties)
½ cup finely chopped dill pickle
2 tablespoons dill pickle juice
½ pound bologna, sliced ¼ inch thick

1 cup diced celery
1 tart apple, quartered, cored and coarsely chopped
¾ cup dairy sour cream
½ cup mayonnaise
¾ teaspoon curry powder

1. Cook the *farfalle* following label directions just until *al dente*; drain. Put in a large bowl. Add the dill pickle and juice; toss to mix and cool.

2. Cut the bologna into ¼-inch cubes. Add to the pasta along with the celery and apple.

3. Combine the sour cream, mayonnaise and curry powder in a small bowl, blending well. Add two thirds of the dressing to the salad; toss until the ingredients are well coated. Cover and refrigerate for at least 4 hours. Just before serving, add the remaining dressing and toss again. The salad can be covered and refrigerated for up to 2 days.

WINTER LAMB STEW

A delicious lamb stew with an abundance of vegetables.

Bake at 350° for 1 hour and 30 minutes.

Makes 4 servings for dinner plus 4 servings to freeze.

½	cup diced slab bacon (about 4 ounces)	½	teaspoon leaf thyme, crumbled
¼	cup all-purpose flour	2	tablespoons butter or margarine
1	tablespoon sugar		
1	teaspoon salt	12	small white onions (about ¾ pound)
¼	teaspoon pepper		
3	pounds boneless lamb, cut into 1-inch cubes	4	medium-size turnips, pared and quartered (about 1 pound)
¼	cup chopped shallots or green onion		
2	cloves garlic, finely chopped	3	medium-size sweet potatoes, pared, halved lengthwise and then cut into 1-inch slices (about 1 pound)
1	can (28 ounces) whole tomatoes		
2	cans (10½ ounces each) condensed beef broth	4	large carrots, halved and cut into 2-inch pieces
1	teaspoon leaf rosemary, crumbled	1	package (10 ounces) frozen peas

1. Cook the bacon slowly in a 4-quart saucepan until the fat is rendered and the pieces are brown. Remove with a slotted spoon to paper toweling; drain.

2. Preheat the oven to moderate (350°).

3. Combine the flour, sugar, salt and pepper in a plastic bag; shake the lamb in the flour mixture to coat thoroughly. Brown the lamb, part at a time, in the bacon drippings. (Add a small amount of vegetable oil if needed.)

4. Pour off all but 1 tablespoon of the drippings from the saucepan; add the shallots and garlic. Sauté, stirring often, until tender, for about 2 minutes. Stir in the tomatoes, beef broth, rosemary and thyme; bring to boiling, stirring constantly to loosen the browned bits in the saucepan. Add to the lamb along with the browned bacon. Cover.

5. Bake in the preheated moderate oven (350°) for 1 hour.

6. While the lamb bakes, melt the butter in the same saucepan; add the onions, turnips and sweet potatoes. Sauté, stirring, for 10 minutes, or until the vegetables are lightly browned and glazed.

7. Add the glazed vegetables and carrots to the lamb, pushing them down under the liquid; cover. Bake for an additional 30 minutes, or until the lamb is tender and the vegetables are soft, but not mushy. Stir in the peas.

8. Dinner Portion: Place half of the stew mixture in a serving casserole. Garnish with chopped parsley, if you wish.

9. To Freeze: Divide the remaining mixture into 4 individual boilable bags, making sure you have enough meat and vegetable assortment; heat-seal. Label, date and freeze. Recommended freezer storage: 2 months.

10. *To serve freezer portion:* Bring water to boiling in a medium-size saucepan. Place boilable bag into water; bring back to boiling; boil for 30 minutes, or until thoroughly heated. Remove bag from water; cut off top of bag with scissors; slide mixture into serving casserole or individual soup bowls. Garnish with chopped parsley, if you wish.

NEW MEXICAN CHILI POT ROAST

Makes 8 servings.

3 to 3½ pounds chuck or round, rolled for pot roast
2 tablespoons all-purpose flour
2 tablespoons vegetable oil
4 cloves garlic, finely chopped
2 to 4 tablespoons chili powder
1 can (10½ ounces) condensed beef broth
1 cup beer
2 teaspoons leaf oregano, crumbled

1 teaspoon ground cumin
1½ teaspoons salt
1 package (10 ounces) frozen whole-kernel corn
1 can (15 ounces) red kidney beans, drained
Tortillas, about 16 (2 frozen or refrigerated packages or 1 large can)
Avocado slices
Tomato slices
Shredded lettuce
Shredded Cheddar cheese

1. Roll the beef in the flour to coat thoroughly; brown on all sides in the hot oil in a Dutch oven or large kettle. Stir the garlic and chili powder into the drippings in the pan; cook, stirring constantly, for 1 minute.

2. Add the beef broth, beer, oregano, cumin and salt. Bring to boiling, stirring often. Cover; lower the heat and simmer for 2 hours, or until the meat is tender. Remove the meat to a cutting board.

3. Add the corn and beans to the chili sauce in the pan; cover and simmer for 10 minutes.

4. Slice the meat into about ¼-inch-thick slices. Arrange the slices in a shallow serving bowl or baking dish; spoon sauce over.*

Party suggestion: Arrange a basket of hot tortillas, and another with sliced avocado, sliced tomato, shredded lettuce and cheese to spoon over each serving. Serve ice cream and coffee for dessert.

*The recipe can be prepared ahead up to this point. Cool completely; cover and refrigerate overnight. Reheat in a preheated moderate oven (350°) for about 30 minutes.

HONEY-MUSTARD GLAZED CORNED BEEF

The vegetables are cooked in the broth for this satisfying one-pot-meal.

Makes 4 servings plus enough for 2 bonus meals.

1	corned beef brisket (about 5 pounds)	½	head cabbage (about ¾ pound), cut into 4 wedges and cored
1	medium-size onion, quartered	¼	cup honey
2	celery tops	1	tablespoon spicy brown mustard
4	carrots, pared and halved crosswise		Horseradish Cream (recipe follows)
12	small new potatoes (about 1 pound)		

1. Place the corned beef in a large kettle. Add enough water to cover. Heat slowly to boiling; skim the fat. Add the onion and celery; lower the heat; cover and simmer for 3 hours.

2. Add the carrots, potatoes and cabbage wedges to the kettle; cover and simmer for 30 minutes longer, or until the meat and vegetables are tender.

3. Preheat the broiler.

4. Remove the vegetables with a slotted spoon to a large heated serving platter; cover and keep warm. Lift the corned beef, draining over kettle, onto a shallow roasting pan. Combine the honey and mustard in a small bowl; brush over the meat.

5. Broil the meat 6 inches from the heat for about 5 minutes, or just until the honey mixture bubbles and begins to brown.

6. Slice the corned beef thinly against the grain. Transfer to the serving platter with the vegetables. Garnish with chopped parsley, if you wish. Serve with Horseradish Cream.

Horseradish Cream: Whip ½ cup heavy cream with 1 to 2 tablespoons prepared horseradish until soft peaks form.

For Bonus Meals: Wrap the remaining meat in plastic wrap or aluminum foil; refrigerate. When ready to use, slice the remaining meat into thin slices. Trim all fat. Use part for sandwiches and part for a main-dish salad. Combine with spinach, cauliflower flowerets, sliced mushrooms and hard-cooked eggs and dress with your favorite vinaigrette.

STRAW AND HAY CASSEROLE

This do-ahead pasta dish is based on the classic Italian Paglia e Fieno.

Bake at 375° for 30 minutes.

Makes 12 servings.

1	pound sweet Italian sausage or lean ground round	½	cup (1 stick) butter or margarine
5	medium-size onions, chopped (2½ cups)	½	cup all-purpose flour
½	pound fresh mushrooms, thinly sliced	3	cups milk
		2	cups water
2	packages (10 ounces each) frozen chopped spinach, thawed and drained	3	chicken-flavored bouillon cubes
		1	cup dry white wine
1	package (12 ounces) fettuccine noodles	¼	teaspoon ground nutmeg
		¼	teaspoon pepper
1	package (8 ounces) spinach noodles	2	cups shredded sharp Cheddar cheese (8 ounces)
		1	cup grated Parmesan cheese

1. Remove the sausage casings and crumble the sausage into a large skillet. Cook, breaking up with a spoon for 5 minutes. If beef is used, melt 1 tablespoon of butter in the skillet before adding the meat.

2. Add 2 cups of the onion to the skillet; sauté for 5 minutes, or until the onions are tender and meat loses its pink color. Add the mushrooms and spinach and cook for 5 minutes longer, stirring often, until the mushrooms are lightly browned.

3. Heat a kettle or Dutch oven filled with salted water to boiling. Add the fettuccine noodles to the pot first and cook for 2 minutes. Add the spinach noodles and cook for 3 minutes longer. Drain the noodles and rinse with cold water until cold; spoon into a large bowl; reserve.

4. Preheat the oven to moderate (375°).

5. Rinse out the kettle; dry. Add the butter; melt. Stir in the remaining onions and sauté for 2 minutes. Sprinkle with flour and stir for 1 minute. Stir in the milk, water, bouillon cubes and wine and bring to boiling; lower the heat. Cook, stirring constantly until the sauce is thickened and bubbly, for about 5 minutes; turn off the heat. Stir in the nutmeg, pepper and 1 cup combined of the Cheddar and Parmesan cheeses.

6. Stir 1 cup of the sauce into the sausage or meat mixture.

7. Butter an 11 x 15 x 2-inch baking dish. Spoon a thin layer of sauce in the bottom. Top with half the noodles. Spoon over the sausage or meat mixture. Top with one third of the remaining sauce and sprinkle with 1 cup of the cheese mixture. Finish with the remaining noodles, sauce and cheese; cover with aluminum foil.

8. Bake in the preheated moderate oven (375°) on the center shelf for 30 minutes, or until bubbly hot. Turn on the broiler and place the baking dish 6 inches from the heat to brown the top lightly.

Note: The casserole can be assembled ahead of time, covered and refrigerated until the final baking. Increase the baking time for a cold casserole to 50 or 60 minutes.

REHEATING WHEN YOU HAVE PLANNED AHEAD

• For maximum flavor and nutritive value, bring foods just to serving temperature. Overcooking will only dry them out.

• To reheat food in the oven, place in a covered container, or wrap in aluminum foil and heat at 325°; *don't* cover foods that should be crisp, such as fried chicken or fried fish.

• Reheat small amounts of creamed dishes, stews, chowders and other foods with sauces in the top of a double boiler over boiling water. If you don't have a double boiler, put a heatproof bowl in a pan of boiling water; cover the bowl with aluminum foil.

Mashed potatoes. Heat in the top of a double boiler or wrap in aluminum foil and bake in a slow oven (300°).

Rice and pasta. Heat in the top of a double boiler or in a strainer over boiling water. Cover top of strainer with paper toweling. Stir once during cooking.

Pot roast. Slice and reheat in gravy in the top of a double boiler or in a covered casserole in the oven. If you don't have gravy, use a canned or made-from-mix gravy or a little beef broth.

Roast poultry, pork, veal, well-done beef and lamb. Reheat, covered, in a very slow oven (275°).

Rare or medium roast beef or lamb. Heat, uncovered, in a very slow oven (200°). Meat will not change color within 1 hour.

Cooked vegetables. Reheat briefly in a small amount of cooking liquid or broth in the top of a double boiler or in a small saucepan.

CHICKEN CASSEROLE

Bake at 325° for 1 hour.
Makes 6 servings.

8   slices or heels of bread
2   cups diced cooked chicken
1   small onion, chopped
    (¼ cup)
½   cup chopped celery
½   cup mayonnaise
½   teaspoon salt
⅛   teaspoon pepper

2   eggs
1½ cups milk (may use liquified
    dry milk)
1   can (10¾ ounces) condensed
    cream of chicken soup
¼   pound pasteurized process
    American cheese, shredded
    (1 cup)

1. Cube 2 slices of bread and place in a greased 11 x 7-inch baking dish.
2. Combine the chicken, onion, celery, mayonnaise, salt and pepper in a medium-size bowl; spoon over the cubed bread. Top with the remaining bread slices.
3. Beat the eggs lightly with the milk in the same bowl; pour over the chicken and bread. Cover and refrigerate for 4 hours or overnight. Preheat the oven to slow (325°). Spoon the soup evenly over the bread; sprinkle with the cheese; cover.
4. Bake in the preheated slow oven (325°) for 1 hour. Let stand, covered, for 5 minutes before serving.

SHRIMP CURRY

A light and elegant curry with a sauce you prepare beforehand and store in the freezer.
Makes 8 servings.

4   tablespoons butter or
    margarine
1   large onion, chopped
    (1 cup)
1   apple, quartered, cored and
    chopped
2   to 3 teaspoons curry powder
4   tablespoons all-purpose
    flour

2   teaspoons salt
1   cup tomato juice
1   cup water
1½ pounds cooked, shelled and
    deveined shrimp
2   cucumbers, pared, halved,
    seeded and sliced ¼ inch
    thick (2 cups)
½   cup plain yogurt

1. Heat the butter in a large skillet; add the onion and apple and sauté until soft, for about 5 minutes. Stir in the curry powder; cook, stirring constantly, for 1 minute. Blend in the flour, salt, tomato juice and water. Bring to boiling and simmer, covered, for 5 minutes. Cool. Spoon into a freezer container; freeze up to one week.

2. To serve, remove the sauce from the freezer; defrost for several hours; heat slowly in large saucepan. Add the shrimp and cucumber; heat, stirring often, until the curry is piping hot and the cucumbers are just tender. Stir in the yogurt. Serve with parslied rice and bowls of any of the following condiments: kumquats, chopped radishes, shredded coconut, salted peanuts or green pepper.

ITALIAN SAUSAGE STRATA

A super-savory dish, rich with the flavors of sausage and tomato.

Bake at 325° for 1 hour.
Makes 4 servings.

½ pound Italian sausage (sweet, hot or a combination)	½ loaf of Italian bread
	3 eggs
½ cup chopped sweet green pepper	2½ cups milk
	1 teaspoon salt
1 medium-size onion, chopped (½ cup)	1 tablespoon grated Parmesan cheese
1 can (16 ounces) tomatoes, drained	

1. Remove the casing from the sausage. Brown the sausage in a large skillet for about 10 minutes, breaking it up with a wooden spoon as it browns. Stir in the green pepper and onion. Cook for another 5 minutes; add the tomatoes, breaking up the pieces. Cook for 15 minutes to remove most of the liquid.

2. Slice the bread and place half of the slices in the bottom of a buttered 8 x 8 x 2-inch baking pan; spread with the meat mixture. Top with the remaining bread.

3. Beat the eggs in a medium-size bowl. Stir in the milk and salt. Pour over the bread. Sprinkle with the cheese. Cover and refrigerate for at least 1 hour or overnight.

4. Preheat the oven to slow (325°).

5. Bake in the preheated slow oven (325°) for 1 hour, or until puffed and golden. Remove to a wire rack. Let stand for 10 minutes before serving.

CURRIED EGG STRATA

For a pleasant flavor combination, serve with chutney or
pickled melon rind.

Bake at 375° for 45 minutes.

Makes 4 servings.

¼ cup mayonnaise
1 teaspoon curry powder
4 slices firm whole-wheat
 bread, lightly toasted
4 slices firm white bread,
 lightly toasted
3 hard cooked eggs

¼ cup chopped green onion
2 ounces Swiss cheese,
 shredded (½ cup)
3 eggs
2½ cups milk
1 teaspoon salt

1. Combine the mayonnaise and curry powder in a medium-size
bowl. Spread on two slices of the whole-wheat and two slices of the
white bread. Cut the slices into quarters. Place in the bottom of a
buttered 6-cup shallow baking pan.

2. Slice the hard-cooked eggs and place on top of the bread. Sprinkle
with the green onion and the cheese.

3. Cut the remaining 4 slices of bread into quarters. Arrange in a
checkerboard design over the cheese.

4. Beat the eggs slightly in the same bowl; stir in the milk and salt.
Pour over the bread.

5. Cover and chill for at least 1 hour or overnight.

6. Preheat the oven to moderate (375°).

7. Bake, uncovered, in the preheated moderate oven (375°) for 45
minutes, or until puffed and golden. Remove to a wire rack. Let stand
for 10 minutes before serving.

STUFFED TOMATOES

For those hot summer days, here is an easy make-ahead meal. With 4 ripe red tomatoes and a little cooked rice as a start you can make any one of three different fillings that improve in flavor as they chill.

Makes 4 servings.

4   **large ripe tomatoes**
½   **cup long-grain white rice**
    Tuna and Rice Filling
    (recipe follows)

Ham and Rice Filling
(recipe follows)
Lettuce

1. Cut the tomatoes into 6 or 8 petals with a sharp knife, cutting about halfway down. With a spoon, scoop out the seeds and pulp. Carefully turn upside down on paper toweling to drain while preparing the filling.

2. Cook the rice following label directions; cool.

3. Prepare the filling of your choice. Stuff the tomatoes gently; cover loosely with plastic wrap; refrigerate until serving time.

Tuna and Rice Filling: Combine the cooked rice with one 6½-ounce can drained tuna, ½ cup diced sweet green pepper and ¼ cup diced pimiento in a medium-size bowl. Blend ½ cup mayonnaise, ⅓ cup catsup, 1 tablespoon milk, ¼ teaspoon salt, ½ teaspoon paprika and ⅛ teaspoon pepper in a small bowl until smooth. Add ⅔ cup of the dressing to the rice mixture; toss until the ingredients are coated. Serve the tomatoes on lettuce. Pass the remaining dressing to spoon over. Garnish with parsley, if you wish. Makes 4 servings.

Ham and Rice Filling: Combine the cooked rice with 4 ounces diced cooked ham, 1 small chopped carrot, ¼ cup cooked peas and 1 tablespoon finely chopped parsley in a medium-size bowl. Combine ⅓ cup white wine vinegar, ⅔ cup vegetable oil, ¼ teaspoon salt and ⅛ teaspoon pepper in a screw-top jar; shake well. Pour ⅔ cup of the dressing over the rice mixture; toss until ingredients are coated. Serve on lettuce. Pass the remaining dressing to spoon over. Garnish with shredded carrot, if you wish. Makes 4 servings.

LITTLE ITALY

Broil for 20 minutes.
Bake at 400° for 10 minutes.
Broil for 3 to 4 minutes.
Makes 2 servings.

2 sweet red peppers, halved, seeded and cut into strips Olive or vegetable oil	**½** cup tomato sauce with onions
1 large Italian hero roll, split Butter or margarine, softened	**½** teaspoon leaf oregano, crumbled
¼ pound pepperoni, sliced	**½** cup shredded mozzarella cheese

1. Preheat the oven to broil.

2. Brush the pepper strips with oil and arrange in a single layer on a large cookie sheet. Broil, 4 inches from the heat, for 10 minutes; turn; brush with additional oil; broil for 10 minutes longer. Lower the oven temperature to hot (400°).

3. Spread the bread with the butter; bake in the preheated hot oven (400°) for 10 minutes, or until golden.

4. Place the roasted peppers on the bread; top with the pepperoni slices. Spoon the tomato sauce over; sprinkle with oregano and then with shredded cheese.

5. Broil 3 to 4 inches from the heat for 3 minutes, or until the cheese melts.

Make-ahead Note: Prepare the peppers and bread. Slice the pepperoni and shred the cheese; cover and refrigerate.

APPIAN WAY

Bake at 400° for 10 minutes.
Broil 3 to 5 minutes.
Makes 4 servings.

1	large Italian hero roll, split Garlic Butter (recipe follows)	4	slices (from an 8-ounce package) Provolone cheese, quartered
1	jar (6 ounces) marinated artichoke hearts, drained		Black olives, sliced Whole pimiento, cut into strips
½	pound thinly sliced prosciutto or country-cured ham		

1. Preheat the oven to hot (400°).
2. Spread the bread with Garlic Butter. Bake in the preheated hot oven (400°) for 10 minutes, or until golden brown.
3. Top the bread with the artichoke hearts, prosciutto and cheese.
4. Broil 3 to 4 inches from the heat for 3 to 5 minutes, or until the cheese is melted and bubbly. Top with the olive slices and pimiento strips.

Garlic Butter: Combine ½ cup (1 stick) butter or margarine, softened, with 1 large clove garlic, finely chopped, in a small bowl; cover and refrigerate. Makes ½ cup.

Make-ahead Note: Prepare the bread up to 3 days ahead. Assemble the sandwich, cover and refrigerate. Add 3 minutes to the broiling time.

THE DRUGSTORE WRAP

This is the only way to wrap and seal packets of food for the barbecue or meats for the freezer. In either case, it is essential that the seal be tight, so that the cooking food juices won't spill over into the fire and the air won't get into the meat and cause freezer-burn. Start by placing the item to be wrapped in the center of a piece of heavy-duty aluminum foil that is large enough to go around the food and allow for folding at the top and sides. Bring the two long sides up and over the food and fold them over about 1-inch. Make a crease the entire length; make one more tight fold to bring the wrapping down to the level of the food surface. Press out the air toward the ends. Fold the ends up and over, pressing out the air and shaping to the contours of the food.

HOW TO MAKE YOUR FREEZER WORK FOR YOU

- Buy a thermometer and be sure your freezer, when set at coldest, reaches 0° F. before planning to freeze recipes.
- Turn freezer to lowest setting 1 day before preparing dishes for freezing.
- Never freeze more than one 4-serving casserole for each cubic foot of freezer space at one time.
- Mix and shape meatloaf mixtures, then package and freeze. They will be more moist when baked from a frozen state.
- Cool hot foods to room temperature before placing in freezer to prevent the freezer from warming up.
- Package foods carefully for the freezer. Use plastic containers with tight-fitting lids and allow about ½ inch of headroom for food to expand. Use freezer-to-oven dishes with an overwrapping of aluminum foil, or better still, line the freezer-to-oven casserole with aluminum foil, allowing enough for an overlapping. When food is frozen, lift out frozen packet and have dish for other cooking. When ready to bake frozen casserole, remove foil and return food to the same dish.
- Fast-freeze casseroles by placing them on the coldest part of the freezer.
- Freeze liquids, such as soup, in coffee cans lined with plastic bags. When the liquid is frozen, remove the bag from the can and the liquid will store easily. The can may then be reused.
- Package cooked foods in serving-size portions so they will reheat faster.
- Stack packages of frozen foods after making a record of the food, servings and date for future menu planning.
- Place the foods to be frozen on a shelf of the freezer, not on already frozen foods.
- Plan to use home-frozen dishes within 2 to 3 months when held at 0°F.
- Keep frozen casseroles moving, store the newest to the back and push the older ones to the front.
- Never thaw a frozen casserole at room temperature. This is a perfect way to encourage the growth of those bacteria that cause food poisoning. Either place the frozen casserole in the oven and bake or thaw in the refrigerator overnight and then bake.
- To remove aluminum foil or wax paper stuck to frozen foods, simply place the package in a 300° oven for 5 minutes.

QUICK AND CRUNCHY PIZZA

Make a fast pizza with already baked bread and a thick
Italian cooking sauce.

Bake at 350° for 15 minutes.
Makes 4 servings.

1	medium-size onion, chopped (½ cup)	½	teaspoon leaf oregano, crumbled
2	tablespoons vegetable oil	1	loaf Italian or French bread
1	pound lean ground round	1	cup shredded mozzarella cheese (4 ounces)
1	teaspoon salt		
1	jar (15½ ounces) thick Italian-style cooking sauce		

1. Preheat the oven to moderate (350°).

2. Sauté the onion in the oil in a large skillet until soft. Stir in the beef and salt and cook, stirring constantly, until the pink color is gone. Stir in the sauce and oregano; cook for 1 minute.

3. Cut the loaf in half; slice each half horizontally in half. Spread the cut surfaces with the tomato-meat sauce.* Sprinkle with the cheese. Place on a cookie sheet.

4. Bake in the preheated moderate oven (350°) for 15 minutes, or until the cheese is melted. To freeze, wrap unbaked pizzas in aluminum foil; label. Reheat in a preheated moderate oven (350°) for about 40 minutes.

*If there is extra sauce, serve it on top of the pizza.

RECOMMENDED FREEZER-STORAGE TIMES

FOOD	MAXIMUM STORAGE TIME
APPETIZERS (Canapés, hors d'oeuvres)	½ to 1 month
BREADS	
Quick	
Baked muffins, biscuits, and simple quick breads	2 to 3 months
Rich, fruit, nut, or spicy quick breads	1 to 2 months
Unbaked dough	Up to 1 month
Yeast	
Baked bread and rolls	3 months
Danish pastry	3 months
Doughnuts, cake or yeast	3 months
Half-baked ("brown 'n' serve")	2 to 3 months
Unbaked	Up to 1 month
CAKES	
Any type butter cake, frosted or unfrosted	4 to 6 months
Angel or chiffon	2 months
Fruit	12 months
CANDIES	12 months
COOKIES	
Baked	6 to 8 months
Unbaked refrigerator	6 months
DAIRY PRODUCTS	
Butter	6 months
Margarine	12 months
Cheese	
Cottage, uncreamed	2 to 3 months
Natural Cheddar (all forms) and natural Swiss	1½ months
Cream cheese, for use as an ingredient	2 months
Process cheese products (identified on the label.	
If not so designated, the cheese is natural.)	4 months
Cream	
Heavy cream and half and half	2 months
Whipped cream	1 month
DESSERTS	
Cream puffs or éclairs	1 to 2 months
Fruit	2 to 4 months
Steamed Puddings	6 months
EGGS	
Whole, yolks or whites separated	12 months
FISH AND SHELLFISH	
Cooked	3 months
Raw	
Lean (bass, cod, perch, pike, sunfish etc.)	6 to 8 months
Oily (Catfish, herring, salmon, mackerel)	2 to 3 months
Shrimp	9 to 12 months

FOOD	MAXIMUM STORAGE TIME
MEATS (RAW)	
Beef	
Steaks, roasts	8 to 12 months
Ground	2 to 4 months
Stew meats	2 to 4 months
Lamb	
Roasts	6 to 9 months
Chops	3 to 4 months
Pork	
Cured (bacon, ham)	Up to 2 months
Roasts	4 to 8 months
Chops	3 to 4 months
Sausage	1 to 3 months
MEAT (COOKED)	
Casseroles, pies, prepared dinners	2 to 3 months
Gravy, broth, sauces, and steaks	2 to 3 months
Loaves	2 to 3 months
MEAT (PROCESSED)	
Frankfurters	Up to 3 months
Bologna and luncheon meats	Not recommended
POULTRY (RAW)	
Chicken	
Cut up	9 months
Whole	12 months
Livers	1 month
Duck (Whole)	6 months
Turkey	
Cut up	6 to 9 months
Whole	12 months
POULTRY (COOKED)	
Casseroles, pies, prepared dinners	6 months
Without gravy or broth	1 month
Fried	4 months
Stuffing	1 month
Whole, unstuffed*	6 months
PASTRIES	
Pastry dough	
Unbaked	1½ to 2 months
Baked	6 to 8 months
Pies	
Unbaked	2 to 4 months
Baked	6 to 8 months
Chiffon	Up to 2 months
SANDWICHES	
Meat, poultry, cheese, jelly, or jam	1 to 2 months
SOUPS	
Including concentrated and stock	1 to 3 months
VEGETABLES (Most)	8 to 12 months depending on original quality

*Do not freeze home-stuffed poultry, because of the danger of bacterial contamination.

INDEX